IRISH UNIVERSITY REVIEW

A JOURNAL OF IRISH STUDIES

EDITOR
Emilie Pine

ASSISTANT EDITOR
Lucy Collins

BOOKS EDITOR
Paul Delaney

T0322516

Volume 47 Number 1   Spring/Summer 2017

Subscription rates for 2017

Two issues per year, published in May and November

		Tier	UK	EUR	RoW	N. America
Institutions	Print & Online	1	£56.00	£63.30	£67.90	$115.50
		2	£71.00	£78.30	£82.90	$141.00
		3	£87.50	£94.80	£99.40	$169.00
		4	£106.00	£113.30	£117.90	$200.50
		5	£120.00	£127.30	£131.90	$224.00
	Online	1	£47.50	£47.50	£47.50	$81.00
		2	£59.50	£59.50	£59.50	$101.00
		3	£74.50	£74.50	£74.50	$126.50
		4	£90.00	£90.00	£90.00	$153.00
		5	£102.00	£102.00	£102.00	$173.50
	Additional print volumes		£49.50	£57.00	£61.50	$104.50
	Single issues		£39.00	£43.00	£45.50	$77.50
Individuals	Print		£31.50	£39.00	£43.50	$74.00
	Online		£31.50	£31.50	£31.50	$53.50
	Print & Online		£39.50	£47.00	£51.50	$87.50
	Back issues/single copies		£17.50	£21.00	£23.50	$40.00

How to order

Subscriptions can be accepted for complete volumes only. Print prices include packing and airmail for subscribers outside the UK. Volumes back to the year 2000 are included in online prices. Print back volumes will be charged at the current volume subscription rate.

All orders must be accompanied by the correct payment. You can pay by cheque in Pounds Sterling or US Dollars, bank transfer, Direct Debit or Credit/Debit Card. The individual rate applies only when a subscription is paid for with a personal cheque or credit card. Please make your cheques payable to Edinburgh University Press Ltd. Sterling cheques must be drawn on a UK bank account.

Orders for subscriptions and back issues can be placed by telephone, on +44(0)131 650 4196, by fax on +44(0)131 662 3286, using your Visa or Mastercard credit cards, or by email on journals@eup.ed.ac.uk. Don't forget to include the expiry date of your card, and the address that the card is registered to. Alternatively, you can use the online order form at www.euppublishing.com/iur/page/subscribe.

Requests for sample copies, subscription enquiries, and changes of address should be sent to Journals Department, Edinburgh University Press Ltd, The Tun – Holyrood Road, 12(2f) Jackson's Entry, Edinburgh EH8 8PJ, UK; email: journals@eup.ed.ac.uk

IASIL MEMBERSHIP

Subscription to the journal comes with membership of the International Association for the Study of Irish Literatures (IASIL). Details of IASIL membership can be found at www.iasil.org

Advertising Advertisements are welcomed and rates are available on request. Advertisers should send their enquiries to Ruth Campbell, the Journals Marketing Manager (email: Ruth.Campbell@eup.ed.ac.uk).

Contents

Abstracts

Marguérite Corporaal, Moving towards Multidirectionality: Famine Memory, Migration and the Slavery Past in Fiction, 1860–1890

What happens to memories when migrants carry their pasts with them to their receiving countries? How do these migrated memories of a past originally connected to the native country develop when they intersect with the cultural legacies of other communities? Fiction which remembers Ireland's Great Famine and which was written between 1854 and 1890 provides an interesting case study to explore these questions: many novels and short stories which recollected the bleak years of mass starvation were written and published in North-America, the continent where the largest percentage of emigrants of the Famine generation settled. As this article will demonstrate, these early works of Famine fiction frequently testify to the 'multidirectional' (Rothberg 2009) nature of memory in cultural transfer, in that reconfigurations of the Famine past interact with memories of the Middle Passage and current as well as past debates on slavery in the American South.

Graham Dawson, The meaning of 'moving on': From Trauma to the History and Memory of Emotions in 'Post-Conflict' Northern Ireland

'Trauma' has become a pervasive trope in discourse and practice concerned with the affective legacies of the Northern Ireland Troubles. This article argues that its productivity may now be exhausted. Whether homogenised as the trace of an unspeakable wound or medicalised as PTSD, orthodox concepts of trauma offer limited understandings of subjectivities shaped by violent conflict and the possibilities of their transformation. These constraints are identified in three areas: academic studies of the history and memory of the Troubles, victims' support, and storytelling conceived as an aspect of

Irish University Review 47.1 (2017): v–viii
DOI: 10.3366/iur.2017.0249
© Edinburgh University Press
www.euppublishing.com/iur

peacebuilding. The article advocates shifting the frame of investigation towards conceptions of the internal world of embodied feelings and the meanings ascribed to emotions, that are capable of recognizing the complex temporalities of emotional experience and exploring the shifting modes of its management, containment, expression and performance within social and political relations and practices. In object-relations psychoanalysis, Raymond Williams' 'structures of feeling', and the emerging field of emotional history, the article locates critical resources with potential to inform new thinking about the affective legacies of the Irish conflict and the meaning of 'moving on'.

Fionnuala Dillane, Breaking Memory Modes: Anne Enright's and Tana French's Silent Interruptions

Anne Enright's trauma novel, *The Gathering* (2007), and Tana French's crime novel, *The Secret Place* (2014), can be seen to operate purposefully within the familiar codes of their respective genres to a degree that draws attention to the processes of emotional and cognitive recognition that give such codified works their emotional power: repetitive, affective, recognisable framing patterns. Both authors, however, also deploy what I call, following Marianne Hirsch, an aesthetics of interruption: this is an affective, political resistance to the gratifying dispensations that characterise most memory modes and that feature in closure-driven detective fictions in particular. Both novelists exceed genre parameters to make us think about genre frames and what exceeds both the frame and its contained, comprehensible narrative. The aesthetic interruptions in both texts force us to think about the silences that obtain around community collusion in criminal actions and unrelenting structural oppression, and that produce, facilitate and sustain asymmetrical relations of power.

Oona Frawley, Edmund Spenser and Transhistorical Memory in Ireland

Edmund Spenser has been beleaguered by some critics who deem him to be a willing and active representative of the worst of English colonial aspirations, and defended by others who see him as a humanist poet caught in the closing jaws of an imperial mission. This vacillation of opinion is seen in the rewriting of Spenser by Irish writers over time. Spenser has also haunted Irish critical work, moving through the contemporary academy in a swift transmission beginning in the 1980s, when 'Spenser and Ireland' became a subject of some significance. Yet now, only thirty years later, that attention has been diverted, leaving Spenser, in an Irish context at least, as a placeholder of memory. This essay considers key moments or changes in the rewriting of Spenser's cultural memory in Ireland, considering the long duration of his figuring in Irish literature and culture as a case study of transhistorical memory.

Stefanie Lehner, 'Parallel Games' and Queer Memories: Performing LGBT Testimonies in Northern Ireland

This essay explores how the notion of 'parallel games' works to queer memory in two productions of Northern Ireland's first publicly funded gay theatre company, TheatreofplucK, led by artistic director Niall Rea: the testimonial monologue *D.R.A.G. (Divided, Radical and Gorgeous)* (2012), written by Rea, and the performed archive installation, *Tr < uble* (2015), written by Shannon Yee. As post-conflict memory works, both productions trouble a progressivist understanding of 'moving on' from the conflict: instead of memories being harnessed to the ethno-nationalist template established by the Belfast Agreement, the plays 'move' memory work in different directions at the same time, giving rise to a diverse set of emotions.

Joseph Lennon, 'Dreams that hunger makes': Memories of Hunger in Yeats, Mangan, Speranza, and Irish Folklore

This essay explores Irish social memories of fasting and hunger by reading works by James Clarence Mangan, Speranza (Lady Wilde), W.B. Yeats, and three folk stories recorded in the Schools Collection of the National Folklore Archive. In Famine lyric poetry about hunger and dreams, listeners appear indicted by hungry voices that become increasingly close to the reader. Folk stories both remember the Famine and recall the dynamics of hospitality and fasting in medieval Irish texts, where the Middle Irish word *troscud* suggests fasting against something or someone, unlike spiritual fasting, *óine*, which implies an emptying. Focussing on dreams of the hungry, these works indicate how hospitality and fasting entwine in Ireland's social memory of hunger.

Claire Lynch, 'Everything not saved will be lost': Videogames, Violence, and Memory in Contemporary Irish Fiction

In Paul Murray's *Skippy Dies* (2010), Eimear McBride's *A Girl is a Half-Formed Thing* (2013) and Rob Doyle's *Here Are the Young Men* (2014), fictional characters are depicted playing both real and imagined videogames featuring a number of avatar perspectives. Unlike the fragile human body, an avatar can survive multiple virtual deaths; kicks, punches, bullet wounds, even decapitations, can all be undone, the virtual body resurrected and the game re-played. The blurring of player and avatar which takes place during gameplay raises several questions about how memory is experienced, articulated, and mediated. Do an avatar's actions subsequently become a player's memories? Does playing videogames alter memory or shape the way a player interacts with the past? And perhaps most crucially, when an avatar stabs, punches, or shoots an opponent, does the player remember that act of violence as a witness or a collaborator?

Naomi McAreavey, Portadown, 1641: Memory and the 1641 Depositions

The mass drowning of Protestants in Portadown is the defining cultural memory of the 1641 rebellion, yet it is a little known and highly contested incident. In this essay I return to the earliest recorded memories of the massacre found among the 1641 depositions to show how the Portadown drownings were represented by eyewitnesses as well as through rumour and hearsay; by survivors and by the bereaved; by refugees speaking within weeks and months of the event, to those recalling the event over a decade later. Identifying different 'stories' of the atrocity, and considering how they were shaped by time and circumstance, I discuss how a range of deponents diversely remembered the Portadown atrocity, and illuminate the tensions, inconsistencies and contradictions in their memories. By recovering part of the history of 1641 memories, I suggest that the 1641 depositions are a rich resource for memories of the rebellion but not its 'facts'.

Notes on Contributors

MARGUÉRITE CORPORAAL is Associate Professor in English Literature at Radboud University Nijmegen, the Netherlands. She was the principal investigator of the research project *Relocated Remembrance: The Great Famine in Irish (Diaspora) Fiction, 1847–1921*, for which she obtained a Starting Grant from the European Research Council (2010–15). She is the author of *Relocated Memories: The Great Famine in Irish and Diaspora Fiction, 1846–1870* (2017). She is co-editor of *Recollecting Hunger: An Anthology. Cultural Memories of the Great Famine in Irish Fiction, 1847–1920* (2012), *Global Legacies of the Great Irish Famine* (2014), and *Irish Studies and the Dynamics of Memory* (2016).

STEF CRAPS is an Associate Professor of English literature at Ghent University, where he directs the Cultural Memory Studies Initiative. He is the author of *Postcolonial Witnessing: Trauma Out of Bounds* (Palgrave Macmillan, 2013) and *Trauma and Ethics in the Novels of Graham Swift: No Short-Cuts to Salvation* (Sussex Academic Press, 2005). He has also co-edited *Memory Unbound: Tracing the Dynamics of Memory Studies* (Berghahn, 2017) and special issues of *Criticism* (2011) and *Studies in the Novel* (2008) on the topics of transcultural negotiations of Holocaust memory and postcolonial trauma novels.

GRAHAM DAWSON is Professor of Historical Cultural Studies and Director of the Centre for Research in Memory, Narrative and Histories at the University of Brighton, England. He is author of *Soldier Heroes: British Adventure, Empire and the Imagining of Masculinities* (1994), and *Making Peace with the Past? Memory, Trauma and the Irish Troubles* (2007); and co-editor of *Trauma and Life Stories* (1999), *The Politics of War Memory and Commemoration* (2000), *Contested Spaces: Sites, Representations and Histories of Conflict* (2007), and *The Northern Ireland Troubles in Britain: Impacts, Engagements, Legacies and Memories* (2017).

FIONNUALA DILLANE, lecturer in Victorian literature and culture, School of English Drama and Film, University College Dublin, has research interests in the fields of nineteenth-century print cultures, memory studies, and gender studies. Recent work includes

Irish University Review 47.1 (2017): ix–xiv
DOI: 10.3366/iur.2017.0250
© Edinburgh University Press
www.euppublishing.com/iur

Before George Eliot: Marian Evans and the Periodical Press (Cambridge University Press, paperback edition, 2016), joint winner of the Robert and Vineta Colby Prize, 2014; *Ireland, Slavery, Anti-Slavery and Empire*, a special edition of *Slavery & Abolition; a Journal of Slave and Post-Slave Studies*, 37.3 (2016), co-edited with Maria Stuart and Fionnghuala Sweeney; and *The Body in Pain in Irish Literature and Culture*, co-edited with Naomi McAreavey and Emilie Pine (Palgrave Macmillan, 2016).

ASTRID ERLL is Professor of Anglophone Literatures and Cultures at Goethe-University Frankfurt am Main and the initiator of the Frankfurt Memory Studies Platform (www.memorystudies-frankfurt. com). She holds degrees in English, German and psychology from the University of Gießen (Germany). Publications include monographs on memories of the First World War (*Gedächtnisromane*, 2003) and the 'Indian Mutiny' (2007), and an introduction to memory studies (*Memory in Culture*, Palgrave 2011). With A. Nuenning she is general editor of the series *Media and Cultural Memory* (de Gruyter, since 2004) and co-editor of *A Companion to Cultural Memory Studies* (2010). With A. Rigney she edited *Mediation, Remediation and the Dynamics of Cultural Memory* (2009).

OONA FRAWLEY is a native New Yorker, received her PhD from the Graduate School and University Center, and held post-doctoral fellowships at Queen's University Belfast and Trinity College Dublin. She has lectured in English at Maynooth University since 2008. Oona is the author of *Irish Pastoral: Nature and Nostalgia in 20th Century Irish Literature*, and edited the 4-volume *Memory Ireland* project (Syracuse University Press, 2010–2014), among other books. Her debut novel *Flight* (Tramp Press, 2014) was nominated for an Irish Book Award, and led to her being named one of 'the stars of post-crash Irish fiction' by the *Guardian*.

ÚNA KAVANAGH is a figurative artist whose work crosses the boundaries of many art forms including sculpture, performance, text, painting, film, installation, and animation. Una holds a BA and MA from The National College Of Art & Design in Craft Design and Sculpture. For over twenty-five years she has exhibited in solo and group exhibitions throughout Ireland including The Royal Hibernian Academy Annual Exhibition, Sculpture In Context, and RDS Craft Exhibition, where she received The Royal Dublin Society Decorative and Architectural Ceramics Certificate Of Merit. Most recently she has created the performance artwork 'Fata Morgana' in Liwa and 'Mirari' a collection of paintings and film exhibiting in the Art Hub, Abu Dhabi, UAE. Foremost of Una's artistic collaborations is her work as an artist, original company member, and collaborator with ANU. She has just completed the ANU Triptych *Sunder, On Corporation Street* and *These Rooms* (2016).

KATHRYN KIRKPATRICK is Professor of English at Appalachian State University where she also serves as editor of the eco-journal *Cold Mountain Review*. She is the author of six collections of poetry, most recently two recipients of the North Carolina Poetry Society's Brockman-Campbell award, *Our Held Animal Breath* (2012), and *Her Small Hands Were Not Beautiful* (2014). As a literary scholar in Irish studies and the environmental humanities, she has published essays on class trauma, eco-feminist poetics, and animal studies. She is the editor of *Border Crossings: Irish Women Writers and National Identities* (2000), and with Borbála Faragó, *Animals in Irish Literature and Culture* (2015).

STEFANIE LEHNER is Lecturer in Irish Literature at Queen's University, Belfast, and Fellow at the Senator George J. Mitchell Institute for Global Peace, Security and Justice. Her current research explores the role of the arts, specifically performance, in conflict transformation processes, with a focus on the Northern Irish context. She also researches and teaches on representations of trauma and memory in (Northern) Irish drama, fiction, film, and photography. She is author of *Subaltern Ethics in Contemporary Scottish and Irish Literature* (2011) and her work has been published in *Contemporary Theatre Review*, *Irish Review*, *Irish Studies Review*, and *Nordic Irish Studies*.

JOSEPH LENNON is the Emily C. Riley Director of the Center for Irish Studies and Associate Dean of International and Interdisciplinary Initiatives at Villanova University. His book, *Irish Orientalism: A Literary and Intellectual History* (Syracuse UP, 2004), won the Donald Murphy Prize from the American Conference for Irish Studies. He has published articles on literature and cultural history in journals such as *New Hibernia Review, Women's Studies, The European Legacy,* and *The Times Literary Supplement*, as well as chapters in books on British, Irish, and Indian literature and culture. Salmon Poetry published his volume of poems, *Fell Hunger,* in 2011, and his current book project focuses on the beginnings of the modern hunger strike in the early twentieth century in England, Ireland, and India.

LOUISE LOWE is a theatre maker, creating site-specific and immersive art works within communities of space, place, and interest. Since founding ANU in 2009, Louise has directed all of the company's productions to date, including the multi-award nominated and winning: *These Rooms* (Art:2016), *Sunder, On Corporation Street* (Home Manchester / Culture Ireland), *Pals* (National Museum of Ireland), *Reflecting the Rising* (RTÉ), *Rebel Rebel, Beautiful Dreamers* (Limerick City of Culture), *Angel Meadow* (Home Manchester), *Thirteen, Dublin Tenement Experience, Vardo, The Boys of Foley Street* (Public Art Commission), *Laundry, World's End Lane, Fingal Ronan* (New York), *Memory Deleted* and *Basin*. Other directing credits include: *Test Dummy* (Theatre Upstairs), *Deep* (Cork Opera House), *The End of the Road* (Fishamble), *Across the Lough* (Performance Corporation), *Secret City, Right Here Right Now, The Baths, Demeter Project:* Cultural Olympiad Production (Prime Cut Productions), *The Bell Room, Come Forward to Meet You,* and *Evensong* (Upstate). Louise teaches devising at the LIR Academy (Trinity College Dublin). She was awarded the Captain Cathal Ryan Scholarship Award and the International Artist Residency at the Robert Wilson Centre, New York.

CLAIRE LYNCH is a Reader in English Literature at Brunel University London and Secretary of the British Association of Irish Studies. She is the author of two monographs, *Irish Autobiography* (Peter Lang, 2009) and *Cyber Ireland: Text, Image, Culture* (Palgrave Macmillan, 2014) and several articles on twentieth and twenty-first century Irish Writing.

NAOMI McAREAVEY is Lecturer in Renaissance Literature in UCD School of English, Drama and Film, and has published widely on the literary cultures of the 1641 rebellion, and especially women's writing. With Fionnuala Dillane and Emilie Pine she has co-edited *The Body in Pain in Irish Literature and Culture* (Palgrave, 2016), and is co-editor, with Julie Eckerle, of *Women's Life Writing and Early Modern Ireland* (University of Nebraska Press, 2017). She is author of *The Letters of the First Duchess of Ormonde* (forthcoming with the Renaissance English Text Society), and is currently developing a book project on the memory cultures of the 1641 rebellion in Ulster.

PAULA McFETRIDGE has been Artistic Director of Belfast-based Kabosh since August 2006. The company is committed to challenging the notion of what theatre is, where it takes place and who it is for (www.kabosh.net). She was the recipient of the Belfast Ambassador Award 2014 for her work in using the arts to tackle difficult social issues and the NITB NI Hero Award 2012 for her work in cultural tourism. She is a fellow of Salzburg Global Seminar Session 532 'Conflict Transformation through Culture: Peace-building and the Arts'.

CHARLOTTE McIVOR is a Lecturer in Drama and Theatre Studies at the National University of Ireland, Galway. She is the author of *Migration and Performance in Contemporary Ireland: Towards A New Interculturalism*, and the co-editor of *Staging Intercultural Ireland: Plays and Practitioner Perspectives* (with Matthew Spangler), and *Devised Performance in Irish Theatre: Histories and Contemporary Practice* (with Siobhán O'Gorman). She has published in *Modern Drama, Irish University Review, Irish Studies Review*, and multiple edited volumes on contemporary theatre and performance.

PAULA MEEHAN was born in Dublin where she still lives. A playwright and poet, she has received many awards for her work. She was Ireland Professor of Poetry, 2013–2016. A volume of her public lectures from the Professorship – *Imaginary Bonnets with Real Bees in Them* – was published in 2016 by UCD Press. *Geomantic*, her latest collection of poems, was published by Dedalus Press, Dublin in November 2016.

VUKASIN NEDELJKOVIC is a PhD candidate at Dublin Institute of Technology. He initiated the multidisciplinary project *Asylum Archive*. *Asylum Archive* is a platform open for dialogue and discussion inclusive to individuals who have experienced a sense of sociological/geographical 'displacement', social trauma, and violence. It is an act of solidarity to bring a different perspective on the life of people who came to Ireland to seek protection. *Asylum Archive*'s objective is to collaborate with asylum seekers, artists, academics, civil society activists, and immigration lawyers, amongst others, with a view to creating an interactive documentary cross-platform online resource, critically foregrounding accounts of exile, displacement, trauma and memory. www.asylumarchive.com

ANN RIGNEY is Professor of Comparative Literature at Utrecht University and founder of the Utrecht Forum for Memory Studies (www.utrechtmemorystudies.nl). She has published widely in the field of nineteenth and twentieth century memory cultures, including most recently *The Afterlives of Walter Scott: Memory on the Move* (Oxford UP, 2012). She is co-editor of *Mediation, Remediation, and the Dynamics of Cultural Memory* (De Gruyter 2009; with A. Erll), *Commemorating Writers in Nineteenth-Century Europe* (Palgrave, 2014; with J. Leerssen) and *Transnational Memory: Circulation, Articulation, and Scales* (De Gruyter, 2014; with C. De Cesari). She has recently started a new project on cultural memory and protest movements.

DOMINIC THORPE is an Irish visual artist working primarily through the body in performance, drawing, video and photography. His work often involves contextual and relational processes. In 2014/15 he was the first artist in residence at the College of Arts and Celtic Studies of University College Dublin where he researched relationships between memory, trauma and processes of performance art. He has shown and performed work widely internationally and in Ireland, including at the Irish Museum of Modern Art, Bangkok Cultural Centre, Xiamen University China, SASA Gallery Adelaide, Temple Bar Gallery and Galway Arts Centre. He currently works at the Creative Well, Riverbank Arts Centre Newbridge and KCAT Arts Centre Kilkenny.

Emilie Pine

Introduction: Moving Memory

2016 was a year for memory. The Irish commemorative calendar was packed, as both nationally and internationally the 1916 Rising was remembered. Though in many ways this functioned as a conservative assertion of the primacy of the nation as a container for identity, the year also illustrated a welcome range of narratives that suggested a new inclusivity and openness to multiple experiences, both of the past and of ways of remembering that past. This shift in the narrative, however, was not without conflict or controversy. In October 2015, the Abbey Theatre launched its 'Waking the Nation' programme, with a year-long series of shows that aimed to 'interrogate rather than celebrate the past' and to use this platform to 'hold a mirror up to our society' and thereby to 'reflect on our past, the Ireland of today and of the future'.[1] The programme included highlights from the canon, with Sean O'Casey's *The Plough and the Stars* alongside Frank McGuinness's *Observe the Sons of Ulster Marching Towards the Somme*, showcasing the imaginative reaching out of the Abbey to the different 'sides' and affiliations that mark Ireland's history. These monumental plays stood alongside new works by playwrights David Ireland and Philip McMahon, who had been 'challenged to reflect on the legacy of the 1916 Rising and write plays about Ireland today'. Unfortunately within this reflective and challenging programme, the mirror was angled to display the words and images of men, thereby consistently and pointedly side-lining women, both past and present.

The fall-out of the 'Waking the Nation' launch is now well-known, as this centenary programme provoked widespread complaints of gender bias, leading Lian Bell, with others, to establish the Waking the Feminists grass roots campaign in response.[2] This year-long campaign, comprised of women and men who volunteered their time, spoke out on behalf of the marginalised women in the theatre community in Ireland, calling for equality across the theatre sector. The volunteers organised meetings to give space to people working within the sector to voice their discontent, with the first mass meeting held in November 2015 in the Abbey Theatre itself

Irish University Review 47.1 (2017): 1–6
DOI: 10.3366/iur.2017.0251
© Edinburgh University Press
www.euppublishing.com/iur

(as was the closing event in November 2016). Additionally, volunteers worked with the Abbey, the Arts Council, and every major theatre and theatre company in Ireland, to develop comprehensive policies on gender, and to issue clear objectives and recommendations.[3] This initiative ran parallel to the archive work the campaign undertook to examine the levels of gender representation in different areas of Irish theatre-making from playwriting to production, which starkly revealed the chronic problem of lack of gender balance and equality in the industry as a whole.[4]

The Waking the Nation / Waking the Feminists moment showed up three significant aspects of commemorative performance. Firstly, the intensity of the response to the Abbey's programme vividly illustrates that the past and how it is remembered is of crucial importance. Though theatre in Ireland had been an unequal and un-level playing field for decades, it took the centenary programme to provoke such a groundswell of protest, underlining the point that commemoration is as much about the present as it is about the past. Secondly, it illustrates a lesson learned from history – there is no point rebelling if change does not follow. The consultation process with theatre companies and funding agencies, the drafting of policies, and the institution of those policies actively redefined the commemorative moment as not backward but forward looking. Finally, the Waking the Feminists organisation enabled voices from outside the dominant establishments of the memory marketplace to be heard and to change the structure of that marketplace. Rather than the further segmentation of the cultural memory marketplace, with the inclusion of some 'token' female-authored plays while the male-dominated mainstream remains fundamentally unchallenged, the gender-balance policies that have now been implemented suggest that the WTF movement goal of 50/50 representation in five years may be achievable. And it is not too much of a stretch, I think, to read the WTF campaign as a reaction in the present to the remembrance of a past rebellion, and thus as evidence of the ways in which memory moves people in powerful ways.

*

This issue is called *Moving Memory* with the ambition that the title suggests some of the diversity of memory, in its ability to move, both metaphorically and literally, across physical and disciplinary boundaries. The title, of course, also suggests memory's affective power. This makes memory, as a transforming and transformational practice, both inherently fluid and transdisciplinary. This issue seeks to bring these understandings of memory to bear as contributors consider the relationship between memory and the tradition of Irish writing about the past, and how that is always informed by, and informs, the present. The issue thus reads memory as always both backwards and forwards looking, a space of narratives and myths constructed by and for individuals and communities. As artist Dominic Thorpe puts it in the issue's closing Roundtable, 'In many ways, I can't think of a more potent place.'

Movement is key to many of the essays herein, beginning with the diaspora famine fiction considered by Marguérite Corporaal that not only speaks to the memories that travelled with migrants from Ireland, but the ways in which those memories were reshaped in their new contexts, in particular by the interaction with America's history of slavery. Movement is, metaphorically, also possible across time, as Oona Frawley discusses in relation to the re-imagined and re-written figure of Edmund Spenser, who shifts meaning for different writers at different times, illustrating the plastic nature of durational memory. Likewise, Joseph Lennon in his essay on tropes of hunger considers how across forms – poetry and oral storytelling – and across time, from the nineteenth to the twentieth century, remembrance of hunger is mediated and re-mediated. And Naomi McAreavey considers how memories of the 1641 Rebellion in Portadown are currently shaped by dominant Orange forms of remembrance, yet McAreavey returns to the original seventeenth-century depositions to explore the initial process of constructions of a written narrative of that event. These four essays cumulatively suggest the roles of both emotions and politics, and the needs of particular communities at different points in time, in shaping how memories are narrativised, and how those memories are subject to change depending on the point – geographical and temporal – from which the past is being remembered.

What happens when the narrative of the past is deliberately challenged? Stefanie Lehner looks at the impact of queer memory in her essay on Northern Irish drama, exploring how non-canonical memory not only tests particular narratives, but also form, resulting in a double disorientation of the audience for whom the past is being performed, and re-performed. The further dimension of queering memory here is how it makes possible while also challenging notions of 'moving on'. The idea of performance is also central to Claire Lynch's discussion of the representation of digital memory, via video game, in contemporary Irish fiction. The identities of these novels' central figures are played out onscreen via digital avatars, in a format that constantly re-inscribes present performance over past, yet that also remembers each past iteration of the game self. The resulting insecurity of identity is threatening to the character, though it equally results, as Lehner also highlights in drama, in new possibilities for narrative direction.

How we feel about the past is, obviously, crucial in determining how each of us as individuals, and as communities, configures the multidirectional relationships between past, present, and self. Graham Dawson explores this subject, critically reflecting on the dominance of the trauma narrative as a way of framing the past, particularly in relation to Northern Ireland. In questioning the trauma model and the narrative of healing that accompanies it, Dawson suggests reading memories in relation to the afterlives of emotion, thereby consolidating a new theoretical framework for thinking about painful pasts. Fionnuala Dillane considers how emotional afterlives can be represented by contemporary fiction in her analysis of Anne Enright and Tana French's aesthetic of interruption. Dillane argues that it is what remains outside the frame of representation and explication that is most troubling to readers and to the tendency of generic modes of memory, such as trauma and crime narratives, towards explanatory closure. Further opening up questions of trauma, affect, and ethics, in the closing Roundtable (convened by Charlotte McIvor and Emilie Pine) participants Stef Craps, Astrid Erll, Paula McFetridge, Ann Rigney, and Dominic Thorpe discuss the critical and creative possibilities of memory. The Roundtable participants probe at the recent history of memory studies and what interdisciplinarity might actually look like; consider the burden of cultural commemoration, with its emphasis on trauma and its engagement (or lack of engagement) with contested and contesting voices; and look to where memory might move next.

In asking a combination of academics and artist practitioners to respond to questions of moving memory, this issue aims to position memory studies as more than simply a theoretical field, by considering it in moving practice. In the opening section of the issue, we present three poems by Paula Meehan, introduced by Kathryn Kirkpatrick as a writer of witness and memory. And in a profoundly reflective piece on their artistic mission, Louise Lowe and Una Kavanagh discuss the processes and ambitions of creating ground-breaking immersive memory performances for Anu Productions.

Painful presents are, of course, also necessary for us to consider, as informed by, and forming, memory. As the title of one of Meehan's poems puts it, the worry is that 'Commemorations Take Our Minds Off the Now'. This special issue cannot tender the idea of moving memory without consideration of what current migration patterns mean for memory today. Recent years have seen the forced-migration of millions, bringing into sharp relief myths of home and hospitality, and marking the resurgence of constructions of Otherness. In Ireland, it now seems evident that the cultural memory of an experience of forced migration has not created a widespread openness to understanding others' experience of hunger, conflict, and displacement. This all too real context pushes us as scholars and global citizens to recognise both the urgent humanitarian needs of refugees, as well as the cultural impact of these movements on individual and collective memory. How do theories of memory as transcultural, transnational, and multidirectional stand up in the current contexts of migration crises and the policies of fortress Europe? And how does the historical duty to remember inform how those present policies are drafted, promoted, and, indeed, voted for?

It is particularly fitting to conclude this introduction with an image that constitutes one small part of the *Asylum Archive*, a body of aural, found object, and photographic work by the artist Vukasin Nedeljkovic, that responds to the ways that asylum seekers have been rehoused, but not re-homed, in Ireland since 1999. Nedeljkovic's body of work illuminates some of the memories that are being formed

Vukasin Nedeljkovic, *Clock, found object in Gardiner House* (2012). This photograph is part of the *Asylum Archive* body of work by Nedeljkovic, available at www.asylumarchive.com.

in Ireland now, and this photograph of a found object, *Clock* (2012), gives us a telling insight into the temporal and spatial dislocations, and the difficulty of re-locating oneself, in the context of migration. *Clock* further suggests the traumatic disruptions caused by the scandal of the system of Direct Provision, which works to undermine the nation as an inclusive space and instead actively others asylum seekers through practices of curfew, over-crowding, the banning of cooking, the refusal of asylum seekers' right to work or to study at third level, and, of course, deportation. If memory is one of the strategies by which each of us orients ourselves in time, and in relation to our own self, and other selves, then *Asylum Archive*'s work suggests the insecurity of that current experience, in addition to these other disempowerments.

What is our duty to remember and how can we best remember? How can a supra-national community of people make and witness memories, coming together as equal stakeholders in both recent and distant pasts, in order to imagine and create an equal future? These are questions that go beyond literary study and to the heart of social responsibility itself. Attending to these questions, both in relation to the biases and systems of structural callousness that we witness today, and in relation to other painful pasts, may give us the tools for considering memory not as a closed narrative, but as a provocation of movement and change, so that we act now to shape an Ireland, and a new story of Irishness, for which we would like to be remembered.

NOTES

1. Waking the Nation launch Press Release: https:// www.abbeytheatre.ie/waking-the-nation-2016-at-the-abbey-theatre/
2. See http://www.wakingthefeminists.org/about-wtf/how-it-started/
3. See http://www.wakingthefeminists.org/objectives-recommendations/
4. See http://www.wakingthefeminists.org/research/

Paula Meehan

Three Poems from *Geomantic* (2016)

THE CLOUDS

Some mornings the room is full of clouds,
clouds where the students' heads ought to be,
little weather systems of their own.

They put all their work up on the cloud:
dream song and secret and story.
Consciousness seeds the digital zone

with cold fronts, sunny spells, cirrus clouds.
Every weather of the room I grieve
the cloud children of the new machines.

Irish University Review 47.1 (2017): 7–9
DOI: 10.3366/iur.2017.0252
© Edinburgh University Press
www.euppublishing.com/iur

THE COMMEMORATIONS TAKE OUR MINDS OFF THE NOW
A boon to the Government; they rule
      in the knowledge that none can keep track
of just how much of the country has
been flogged like an old nag to within
an inch of its life. The karmic wheel
      goes round and round. I commemorate
the poor going round and round the bend.
      How mad do you have to be to make
sense of the state of the State we're in?

THE HANDFUL OF EARTH
Under scrutiny it tells us all
we need to know about our futures,
it being composted of our past lives,
the nine years in this house by the sea.
Under the paths stars make, wild birds call.

I fancy I could read it like leaves
of tea, yarrow stalks, thrown down, tarot,
its minutest narratives of grief,
its aboriginal patternings.

Kathryn Kirkpatrick

Memory in Paula Meehan's *Geomantic* (2016)

Writing in the wake of the calamitous 2016 US election, I find the ongoing project of witness and memory in Paula Meehan's poems profoundly orienting. Meehan's work has never acquiesced to neoliberalism's trickle-down con. From 'The Statute of the Virgin at Granard Speaks' (1991) to 'Death of a Field' her poems have served as correctives to official narratives by remembering not only people and places forgotten by religious institutions and urban development but also by recalling forgotten ways of knowing and being. As I face the dangerous nostalgia of my own country, now manifested in a white supremacy movement and the denial of climate crisis, I find in Meehan's seventh and newest collection of poems, *Geomantic*, not only spirited interventions in global capitalism's failed narratives but also positive alternatives.

Meehan has said that the poems in *Geomantic* are inspired by the memorial quilts 'made by family networks who support each other through loss of loved ones' from drug use in Ireland. An outgrowth of the memorial quilts honoring the memories of those lost to AIDS in the US, they 'caught on in Ireland because so many intravenous drug users got the virus' and died from AIDS:

> Every February 1st, St. Brigid's Day ... there's a memorial service, cross faith, in what was one of the churches of my childhood, Our Lady of Lourdes, Sean McDermott Street.... I always try to attend even if I am not there as 'poet' – I go to remember my own family members & friends & neighbours who died through addiction. The different family networks (community support groups from all over the island) hang their memorial quilts from the high walls of the church and they are there throughout the service. I think they are the bravest, most powerful, iteration of memory and [they] challenge the official lipservice paid to the deceased.[1]

Irish University Review 47.1 (2017): 10–14
DOI: 10.3366/iur.2017.0253
© Edinburgh University Press
www.euppublishing.com/iur

Integrating the visual and symbolic power of these quilts, *Geomantic* is a series of eighty-one nine-line poetry panels stitched together to form a verbal quilt of memory. The cover design, made from Meehan's own maturing visual art, echoes the volume's structure, with nine squares representing stylized landscapes in vivid rainbow colours, three blocks repeating three times each. Public memorial in these poems is stitched to private memory through a matriarchal line in 'The Quilt', 'a simple affair—nine squares / by nine squares ... my grandmother's quilt I slept under / the long and winding nights of childhood'.[2] The repetition here and elsewhere of the number nine, each nine-line poem with nine syllables per line and the total number of poems divisible by nine, echoes the earth magic of the volume's title. Meehan gives us the definition of 'geomantic' from the Greek as 'Earth divination', 'that interprets markings on the ground or the patterns formed by tossed handfuls of soil, rocks, or sand.' In this organismic worldview, human futures can be predicted through careful attention to the material conditions of the past, 'The Handful of Dirt' 'being composted of our past lives, / the nine years in this house by the sea' (93). The volume's epigraph, Ciaran Carson's 'Indefatigable dazzling / terrestrial strangeness', reinforces the potential for enchantment when confronting a living earth. Meehan suggests in these poems that despite the alienations of modernity, we might remember how to be in dynamic relation with a natural world whose capacity to defamiliarize and dazzle is enduring. Earth memory and magic emerge, Yeatsian fashion, in 'The Moon Rose Over an Open Field', where the moon 'rises with the vowels' and the resulting poem is 'muse magic wrought from the power of nine' (43). Meehan reclaims throughout this volume the mystical power of the number nine, that symbol of wholeness, completion, and fullness throughout world mythology, especially in the stories of the old Norse god, Odin, who gained spiritual insight for transformation by drinking the mead of poetry. Recovering from the past intuitive practices for the present, Meehan in these poems recalls her mentor Gary Snyder's *ars poetica*, 'What You Must Know to Be a Poet', with its injunction that the poet know, among other things, 'at least one kind of traditional magic:/ divination, astrology, the book of changes, the tarot.'[3] By embracing ancient practices for intuitive insight, Meehan's work enacts the kind of generative perspective that ecofeminists Maria Mies and Vandana Shiva have described, combining 'contemporary science, technologies, and knowledge with ancient wisdom, traditions and even magic.'[4] Retrieving the best aspects of premodernity and modernity, the poems in *Geomantic* imagine a future beyond oppressive dualisms and the arid ecological and social landscapes where modernity has landed us.

In these ways Meehan sews the quilt as a powerful material symbol of memory to collective pre-modern memories of magic: Irish mythology incorporates as magical that square root of nine, the number three in the triple spiral of passage graves, the triple goddess Bríd, the tricolor flag, the shamrock. Shored up by 'muse magic', the quilt reverberates as the volume's source and structure, returning to the past in order to serve the present. For Meehan, the quilts embody

> the compassion and desperation experienced, especially by the poorer communities, who have, I believe, been abandoned by successive governments in the face of huge crisis, of which addiction is the most harrowing aspect. I felt, in this year of commemoration, 2016, that these quilts would be my inspiration and source, because they mean more to me, and speak more profoundly to me, than many of the 'official' or state commemorative gestures. If measured by the aspirations of the founding principles of the Republic, these communities have been betrayed.[5]

In *Geomantic*, the aftermath of the Celtic Tiger economic boom is recollected as an abandoned daughter found 'in the Liffey's dark water' on 'the eve of the new austerity' in 'The Trust' (17); the 'junk-dazed eyes' of a 'life in a black plastic bag' in 'The Pinhead' (29); a grandson 'hustling for smack' in 'The Spank' (30). Memorial poems for these young lives lost stand alongside poems like 'The Clouds' where a young generation risks losing embodied memory itself: 'the cloud children of the machines' rely on the technology of the internet cloud to store 'dream song and secret and story' (24). The poet grieves for an unmindful cyborgism, digital clouds 'where the students heads ought to be' (24). Thus, precisely where memories reside affects not only the quality and kind of memories with which we engage, but also our human capacity to remember at all. As in 'Death of a Field', Meehan reverses the usual association of safe storage on hard drives and flash drives by offering as more supple and enduring the poet in the flesh. She alludes to the vocation of the bard as the memory of the tribe, setting the poet as human vessel of memory beside the 'map memory / In some archive of some architect's screen.'[6] In 'Death of a Field', these locations of memory generate quite different realities: the poet's memory provides an elegy for a living field animated by its flora and fauna as well as its dynamic exchanges with humans – 'I might possess it or it possess me' – while the architect's hard drive gives way to nests 'of sorrow and chemical' in yet another housing estate. In *Geomantic*, 'The Memory Stick' reinforces the dangers even to the poet of the new technology as the storing of 'an ode, an elegy, a ballad, / a sonnet' in 'a square inch / cohesion of metal and plastic' puts the work at risk, the poet unable to 'recall where I put it, / the memory stick in its shiny case' (27).

The poems in *Geomantic*, then, represent memory as embodied, personal, communal, transpersonal, multigenerational, earthly, and cosmic. In 'The Mother Tongue' an ancestral memory of Irish collides with the personal memory of being made to learn it – 'Was it beaten into me or out / of me?' – a tension 'that builds and builds and threatens to blow / my head off' (47). Such tensions inform a volume deeply engaged with how a fully rendered collective memory is a necessary condition for going forward into the increasingly uncertain terrain of the 21st century. Bringing those forgotten to the centre of the Irish poem has been, of course, central to Meehan's poems from the beginning. Unapologetically embracing the role of shamanic seer, she continues to recuperate pre-modern ways of knowing, integrating, and incorporating what the global capitalism of modernity has cast out. Performance artist Dominic Thorpe observes that one role of the arts is to situate 'responsibility for action in the present and not only the past', a practice that moves the arts toward having 'a central role in advocating for human rights through engaging ethically with memory.'[7] Just so, Meehan's poem, 'The Commemorations Take Our Minds Off the Now', addresses the forgetting of the dire circumstances of the present. Focussing on the past makes possible the power relations for increasingly insane current conditions for the poor: 'A boon to the Government; they rule / in the knowledge that none can keep track'. In the face of this erasure of the now, the narrator restores the present: 'I commemorate / the poor going round and round the bend. / How mad do you have to be to make / sense of the state of the State we're in?' (58). The neoliberal policies that created the financial collapse of 2008 were followed in Ireland and elsewhere by austerity measures, both intentional and *de facto*, that rewarded elites who continue to plunder both the earth and the populace. The resulting disenfranchisements have created the conditions for dangerous forms of authoritarianism among despairing populations for whom a failure of historical memory could promise social, economic, and ecological catastrophe. Like Yeats's 'Easter 1916' and 'The Second Coming', Meehan's poems now serve an international community with a widespread need for many kinds of historical memory. Here in the US, we have never been so in need of it.

NOTES

1. Paula Meehan, personal email, 29 October 2016.
2. Paula Meehan, *Geomantic* (Dublin: Dedalus Press, 2016), p.90. All other references to this volume are supplied in the body of this essay.

3. Gary Snyder, *Regarding Wave* (New York, NY: New Directions, 1970), p.40.
4. Rosemary Tong, *Feminist Thought* (Boulder, Colorado: Westview Press, 1998), p.272.
5. Paula Meehan, personal email, 29 October 2016.
6. Paula Meehan, *Painting Rain* (Manchester, England: Carcanet, 2009), p.14.
7. See Dominic Thorpe's contributions to the 'Memory Roundtable' in this issue.

Naomi McAreavey

Portadown, 1641: Memory and the 1641 Depositions

The winter of 1641 was the coldest in memory, but in Portadown it is remembered for something else. That year one of the worst atrocities in this island's history took place, when about 100 men, women and children were stripped of their clothes, corralled overnight in a barn and then thrown over the town bridge to drown in the icy waters of the Bann.[1]

The mass drowning in Portadown is the defining cultural memory of the 1641 rebellion, yet it is a little known and highly contested incident. From the evidence of the 1641 depositions we can neither securely date the atrocity nor accurately estimate the death toll; we cannot ascertain whether it was one incident or several; we do not know if the massacre was spontaneous or pre-planned; and we know little of the immediate circumstances of the killings. All we know is that a large number of Protestants lost their lives in the River Bann in the early months of the rebellion.

Portadown remembers 1641, however. Specifically, the Portadown Orange Order remembers 1641. Images of the drownings appear on banners prominently displayed during the Twelfth of July parades. On the 350th anniversary of the rebellion in 1991 the Orange Order staged a re-enactment of the massacre, and commissioned a permanent memorial in the town's Pleasure Gardens, where a wreath continues to be laid during the 'Mini-Twelfth' parade each year.[2] As recently as November 2016 Carleton Street Orange Hall hosted an event marking the 375th anniversary of the drownings.[3] With the Orange Order the main guardians and stakeholders of memories of 1641, and no other atrocity sustaining such a vibrant memory culture, popular memories of the rebellion have for a long time been shaped by the 'siege mentality' of sections of the Ulster Protestant community who believe that throughout their history they have been attacked, oppressed, and marginalized by Irish Catholics. This has led to a 'black and white' account of the rebellion where innocent Protestants were subject to

Irish University Review 47.1 (2017): 15–31
DOI: 10.3366/iur.2017.0254
© Edinburgh University Press
www.euppublishing.com/iur

a brutal, unprovoked, and indiscriminate attack by native Catholics, with the Portadown massacre cited as the worst example of such sectarian violence. Yet if we go back to the earliest recorded memories of the rebellion – the Protestant survivor testimonies that constitute the 1641 depositions, some of which were promptly published by the commissioners responsible for collecting them – the picture is much greyer.[4] In the 1641 depositions we find that the memories of seventeenth-century Protestants were multifaceted, ambiguous, clashing, and significantly richer and more nuanced than what is remembered in Portadown today.

This essay contributes to a growing body of research that considers 1641 in memory and history.[5] But by returning memories of 1641 to their origin in the mid-seventeenth century, I make the case that, in relation to the 1641 rebellion, 'memory too has a history'.[6] In what follows I unpack that history by showing how the Portadown massacre was diversely remembered by survivors of 1641, starting with the imprisonment of Protestants in Loughgall Church, the release of some prisoners with the promise of safe passage, the journey towards Portadown, the murder of a local parson on the way, the mass drowning at the bridge, the few escapees, and finally supernatural activity in the aftermath of the atrocity.[7] I explore how the massacre was remembered by eyewitnesses as well as through rumour and hearsay; by survivors and the bereaved; by refugees speaking within weeks and months of the event, and those recalling the incident over a decade later. Identifying dominant and marginal 'stories' of the atrocity, and considering how they were shaped by time and circumstance, I explore how a range of deponents remembered the Portadown atrocity, and illuminate the tensions, inconsistencies, and contradictions in their memories.

The 1641 depositions are a rich resource for such enquiries, encompassing several thousand witness testimonies made by Protestant settlers in the immediate aftermath of the 1641 rebellion. The collection is diverse, but can be broadly divided into two categories.[8] The first is the core of the collection, the original depositions that were gathered in the early 1640s, primarily in Dublin where refugees had fled from violence elsewhere in the country. They were collected by a commission of eight clergymen led by Henry Jones, Dean of Kilmore, with the threefold purpose of gathering evidence against the rebels, providing a historical record of what happened, and facilitating the relief of victims.[9] The second is the Commonwealth examinations, taken in the early 1650s with the aim of convicting those responsible for violence. Original and Commonwealth materials commingle in the collection, which is now split into separate county groupings. The entire collection was made available online in 2010.[10]

Among the 1641 depositions are forty-four items that mention the drownings in Portadown. Almost all of them can be found among the Armagh depositions (thirty-two items), although there are a small number of depositions from the bordering counties of Monaghan (five), Down (three), Tyrone (two), and Antrim (one). The narrow provenance of memories of the Portadown drownings among the depositions suggests that at the beginning such memories were highly concentrated in and around the plantation towns of Armagh, and did not generally catch hold elsewhere. Given that Armagh Protestants sought refuge in Dublin alongside deponents from other counties, it is surprising that the Portadown drownings were not more widely reported, especially since the commissioners actively sought hearsay.[11] This might suggest that there was little interaction among deponents in what may have been a short stay in Dublin, or that the Portadown atrocity was not considered to be noteworthy except by those connected with the county. There are twice as many depositions from the 1640s (twenty-seven) as there are Commonwealth examinations (thirteen); the remaining three items are undated. Among the deponents there are thirteen women from a range of social and economic backgrounds; two depose with their husbands, and the majority of the rest identify as widows. There are thirty-one men representing a variety of professions including innkeeper, rector, parish clerk, husbandman, tanner, tallow chandler, yeoman, servant, and gentleman. A range of literacies is represented.

The depositions themselves are the textual records of testimonies that were delivered orally before at least two commissioners who posed a series of pre-established questions and recorded the answers.[12] The statements were then read by or to the examinant who made any revisions before adding their signature or mark. Although the depositions followed a standardized format, the evidence suggests that the form was flexible and there is a great deal of variation in the depositions that survive in terms of the length and detail of the evidence recorded. There is also an abundance of material that is not strictly within the remit of the commission, and the commissioners evidently added new questions in response to the type of evidence they received: it seems that they were open to recording whatever memories the deponents brought to them.

Traumatized deponents from Armagh and its border counties delivered their testimonies in the relatively safe but distant and probably unfamiliar capital city. They arrived in Dublin having been robbed and stripped, displaced from their homes, the victims or witnesses of violence, often bereaved of family and friends, and having endured a long and arduous journey through rebel territory in the north.[13] For the lucky ones, their suffering had been relatively short: William Clarke was already in Dublin when the commissioners began their work in January 1642.[14] Elizabeth Price was not so fortunate: she did not reach Dublin until June 1643, having only recently escaped from rebel hands.[15] Deponents spoke to sympathetic listeners, some of whom were also victims of the rebellion. But they delivered their testimonies to men they did not know, who were often their social superiors, and in the imposing surroundings of Dublin Castle or the law courts. The Commonwealth examinations, in contrast, were recorded where the examinants lived, at a time of relative peace and stability, and were more singularly focused on the conviction of rebels. Delivered from a safer and more secure time and place, in general they were less likely to entertain uncertainty than the earlier depositions. In the later examinations there is more emphasis on the guilt of the rebels than the suffering of the victims, and evocative detail tends to be replaced by the bare 'facts' of what happened.

IMPRISONMENT OF PROTESTANTS

Deponents testify that some of those drowned in Portadown had first been imprisoned in Loughgall Church, and there are statements from four people incarcerated there (Clarke, Newberry, Price, Warren). Only Elizabeth Price provides a description of the circumstances of her capture, testifying that the rebels 'tooke and seised on' her and the other Protestants *'in the Church of Armagh'*, where they had found refuge after being cast from their homes.[16] The church that for a short time offered a safe haven is only named in the revised draft of Price's deposition, and the addition of this detail exposes the omission of the location of her subsequent detention, which she names only as 'Prison'.[17] Loughgall Church was only the first place where Price was incarcerated; she would remain in rebel hands for '14 or 15 months together' being 'tossed & halled from place to place in most miserable manner'.[18] The various locations of her imprisonment matter little to Price; what is important to her is the long duration of her captivity, especially compared to the relatively short time (three months) since her freedom was restored.

Manus O'Cane, Brian O'Kelly, and Patrick O'Mallan are repeatedly named as the rebels responsible for the incarceration of the Protestants, but what emerges from the Commonwealth examinations is the claim that they acted under Sir Phelim O'Neill's direct orders. O'Neill had been named as 'the Cheife of these Rebels' in William Clarke's 1642 deposition, but in his examination of 1653 he adds – evidently in response to the promptings of the commissioners, as the transitional phrase 'And he saith', suggests – that 'the Irish gaue out that this was done by by Sir Phill: O Neales comand'.[19] Clarke thus contributes to the mounting evidence being gathered by the Commonwealth commissioners against O'Neill, even though he is careful to stress that 'being kept prisoner & much affrighted he doth not remember what was acted more particularly or by whome'.[20] John Warren, also testifying in the 1650s, had a more vivid memory of O'Neill's involvement, specifying that he and his fellow Protestants were captured by 'the said Sir Phelyms soldiers', and that O'Neill himself ominously 'bid them wellcome' as they were brought to prison.[21] Warren's was one of a cluster of examinations gathered in February 1653 in preparation for the trial of Sir Phelim O'Neill, which began in Dublin on 5 May 1653. No other deponent suggests that O'Neill was physically present as the Protestants were taken to Loughgall Church, but Warren's memory was evidently jogged by the desire to secure O'Neill's conviction.

There are inconsistencies in the depositions about the number imprisoned and the circumstances of their imprisonment. Warren gives the Commonwealth commissioners the largest figure for the number of prisoners, testifying that the final total reached 'seauenscore and ffifteene'.[22] The Commonwealth examinations do not always prompt the highest estimates, however: Clarke testifies in 1642 that 'at the *least* 100 men women and Children' were imprisoned, but by 1653 this figure is reduced to 'threescore persons', without any acknowledgment of the discrepancy between his two testimonies.[23] The lower figure is closest to that provided by other deponents, with Price citing sixty-plus and Edward Saltenstall and George Littlefield seventy.[24] Deponents rarely provide detail about the experience of the prisoners, and Clarke is unusual in testifying (and then only in 1642), that 'manie of them were sore tortured by strongling and halfe hanging and many other cruel*tye* actions'.[25] Price's comparable account of torture during her imprisonment includes testimony about the murder of prisoners, but diverging from Clarke she specifies that it happened to those that 'were stayd behinde'; that is, after Clarke and the others had been released and brought to Portadown.[26] Traumatized survivors such as Clarke and Price cannot be relied upon for the accuracy of their timelines, of course, but for both of them, memories of their incarceration are bound up with memories of violence and torture.

RELEASE OF THE PRISONERS

Deponents testify that prisoners were held for a period ranging between two days and two weeks, after which some of those imprisoned – 'Children & those that they knew hadd noe meanes left', according to Price – were given passes to go to England.[27] Clarke and the Price children were among those released. The depositions are largely consistent in saying that the pass came from Sir Phelim O'Neill, but the strongest evidence against him comes from Warren who once again places him at the scene, testifying that the rebels 'tould the said Protestants *in the examinants* heareing that Sir Phelym was come, and that they had receaued orders to send them away'.[28] Repeated throughout the earlier depositions is the idea that the prisoners 'beleeved that report' (Carlile), 'imbraced' the offer (Price), and went with the rebels 'gladly' (Newberry), with the emphasis on the innocence and naivity of the Protestants.[29] But by the 1650s the rebels' intentional act of treachery becomes the focus, and variants on the word 'pretend' are insistently repeated.[30] Stressing the rebels' duplicity, in the later examinations – which are singularly focused on the conviction of rebels – there is no doubt that the intention of the rebels was always to kill their prisoners.

JOURNEY TO PORTADOWN

Deposition memories of the journey to Portadown vary in terms of the size of the convoy and the conduct of the soldiers. Clarke suggests that 'hee with an 100 men women and Children or therabouts' were in the convoy, whereas Saltenstall and Littlefield and later Warren use the figure of one hundred to name the number of *rebels* leading the group, which suggests that the prisoners were more numerous than one hundred.[31] According to Price, the prisoners were 'brought or rather driven like sheepe or beasts to a Markett', and her language echoes that of other deponents speaking in the 1640s.[32] Her on-the-spot substitution of 'driven' for 'brought' in her deposition reflects a preference for a word that is also used by Clarke and Saltenstall and Littlefield, suggesting that the prisoners were herded to the bridge like animals.[33] Animal similes are used by other deponents to describe the dehumanization of the prisoners: for Clarke they are treated like 'hogs', while for Richard Newberry they are 'like sheepe to the slaughter'.[34] Although similar phrasing is used to describe the prisoners being transported to their deaths, subtle distinctions in the choice of noun – different animals (hogs, sheep, beasts) and different destinations (market, slaughterhouse) – raise and simultaneously undermine the possibility that other deponents influenced an individual's narrative recall. Nevertheless, deponents drew upon similar tropes of Protestant victimhood, using metaphors from their lives and religion to describe the atrocity. Clarke reaches to the foundational myth of Christianity to describe his ordeal and ultimately the martyrdom of his fellow Protestants, claiming that the 'Christians were most Barberously vsed by forceing & *pricking* them to goe fast with swords and pikes thrusting them into theire sides'.[35] With the term 'Christians' a deliberate choice ('Protestants' is the term overwhelmingly favoured by later deponents), the connection Clarke draws between their journey to Portadown and Christ's road to Calvary is impossible to avoid.

This highly evocative description is excised from Clarke's subsequent 1653 examination, however, which replaces such suggestive detail with hard 'facts'. He testifies 'that such English as they mett [the rebels] did take them alongst with the rest', and this information is corroborated by William Skelton and others.[36] Jane Beare suggests that among those later drowned 'were Country people that Ranne Into them vpon the Report thay were to [-] goe to Lisnegarvie thinking to take the benefit off that Convoy'.[37] Warren testifies that he and his parents were also tempted to join the convoy until his father 'asked Manus ô Cahan who then comanded at Loughgall whither or nor hee ~~might~~ and his might not goe along with them to <C> which the said ô Cahan (smileing) said you may goe if you will, but the examjnants father mistrusting thereby, some mischeife did not goe'.[38] These testimonies contradict Clarke's original evidence of the violent mistreatment of the prisoners since no Protestant would have tried to join the convoy if the rebels' malevolent intent was clear.

MURDER OF MINISTER FULLERTON

Seven deponents in the 1640s testify to the murder of William Fullerton and '2 or 3 others' on the journey from Loughgall, with Clarke repeating his evidence in his Commonwealth examination.[39] Clarke does not claim to be an eyewitness to the murders, however, and all the other deponents clearly offer only hearsay accounts ('as I heard', 'as it was related to me'). Minister Fullerton's widow Eleanor also deposes but she was not present at the murders and provides little detail of her husband's death.[40] A few deponents specify that the murdered men were among the prisoners, but no context is given to explain the murders or describe the reaction of other prisoners as they witnessed the killings. Almost all of the deponents describe the murders happening on the way to Portadown, except John Kerdiff who suggests they occurred at the bridge immediately before the drowning of the others.[41] While Fullerton's name and clerical status is repeatedly mentioned – no doubt he was well known to the prisoners from Loughgall – the identities of the other victims are unclear, although the names of Richard Gladwich and Morgan Aubrey are cited.

Deposition memories of the murder of Minister Fullerton seem to be shaped by the social relationships of Protestant settlers in different parts of Armagh. Alongside the depositions that make only the general claim that Fullerton and the others were 'murdered' is Saltenstall and Littlefield's joint pronouncement that Fullerton was beheaded.[42] As a manner of death that was particularly resonant of Irish barbarism in the early modern period, Saltenstall and Littlefield's recording of this detail reinforces their sense of the cruelty of the rebel they identify as primarily responsible for their own suffering as well as the Portadown massacre – their fellow Grange native, Manus O'Cane.[43] That other deponents omit this detail does not necessarily indicate that Saltenstall and Littlefield were mistaken about the manner of the minister's death; instead it might reveal the honour codes underlying the description of the murder of a local cleric. The fact that the only deponents to mention it are two self-professed gentlemen, neither of whom were from Loughgall, suggests that they were less constrained to censor the details of Fullerton's murder than those who knew and respected him.

MASS DROWNING

Although Clarke has been cited as the only eyewitness to the drownings, Portadown resident Phillip Taylor also claims that the atrocity occurred in his 'sight'.[44] The death toll he gives is 196, which is not only among the highest estimates but a figure that the deponent does not produce himself but 'was credibly tould and beleveth'.[45] The gap between his eyewitness account of the drowning of 'a great number of English protestants' and his reliance on hearsay evidence to provide an exact death toll is striking but perhaps not surprising given what he witnessed.[46] In the midst of such chaos it would be difficult to discern the exact number of dead, and Taylor's acceptance of a higher figure reveals his sense of the enormous scale of the atrocity. Clarke offers the lower figure of 100, but there is no reason to accept his estimate any more than Taylor's.

A death toll of 100 is below average for the depositions, in fact. Among the hearsay reports of the 1640s, the figures that most frequently appear fall in the range of 140 to 160. Lower estimates are provided by Price who offers the figure of 115; Dr Robert Maxwell proposes the highest number, 190, which he further inflates by suggesting that there were other atrocities on a similar scale at Portadown bridge, bringing the final death toll to over 1000.[47] The average for the 1650s examinations is similar to that of the 1640s, although there is more consistency: five examinations cite 140 and two quote 100, with Clarke repeating the figure of 100 from his earlier deposition. Although it is tempting to conclude that a hundred or more Protestants died at Portadown Bridge, perhaps the only thing that can be said with certainty is that deponents remembered it as a wholesale atrocity. Whether a hundred died or 196, what matters is that the massacre was perceived as a large and unprecedented assault on the settler community. Perhaps the truth of the experience is best expressed by mother and daughter Ann Smith and Margaret Clarke who 'hadd seuerall of their frends acquaintance & neighbours drowned at the bridg of Portadowne, to the number of one hundreth and fifty att one tyme. Soe as in deed all the full & faire plantacions of protestants in the Cuntry thereabouts, were quite depopulated and distroyed'.[48]

For many deponents, their losses were personal. Like Smith and Clarke, Humphrey and Elizabeth Stewart report that they lost neighbours in the atrocity: they testify that among the dead were 'William Tayler with 4, or 5 Children Alexander Rose, with six or seaven Children; John Johnson, & his wyfe, [Atiles] warde, & his wyfe, Edward Eaten, James Runckard & very many more of this Examinants Neighbours'.[49] There are also four deponents who lost or believed themselves to have lost family members in the drowning: for Price, five children; for George Pipes, three children; for Thomas Taylor, his father, two brothers and three sisters; and for George Tully, his brother, sister-in-law and their two children.[50] What is striking is that among the lists of fatalities, whole families are decimated, and juvenile victims by far outnumber the adult dead. However, there is also a lack of certainty about whether loved ones died. Pipes, for example, says that he had three children taken away with the others to the bridge of Portadown 'where as hee hath credibly heard and thinketh they were all drowned'.[51] There is perhaps a sense that the bereaved use the formality of the deposition process to officially register deaths of which they cannot be certain. Price names each of the children whom she believes to have perished in Portadown as 'Adam John Ann Mary and Joane Price'.[52] Tully names his brother Martin Tully, his sister in law Anne, and his two-year-old niece Elizabeth, but he cannot remember his baby nephew's name and instead compensates by identifying him as 'being of the age of one yeare and a quarter'. Recording the names of their dead might have given these deponents a kind of closure that would otherwise have been impossible.

Most of the deponents who speak of the Portadown drownings provide little detail beyond the number and names of those who died. The two eyewitnesses offer further, if somewhat ephemeral, memories. Clarke suggests that the bridge 'was Cut doune in the midst' of the killings, and in this detail unique to his 1642 deposition, he risks giving the lie to the suggestion by Maxwell and others that there were subsequent drownings at the bridge.[53] But there is an affective power to Clarke's story: Portadown Bridge had only stood for a decade in

1641, and barely older than the town itself, it was a conspicuous sign of the new Protestant settlement of the town. As Clarke recalls the bridge's destruction mere weeks after the event, his memory perhaps betrays his fear that the plantation infrastructure was being demolished by a rebellion that continued to rage through the country.[54]

Clarke and Taylor provide further detail about the fate of the Protestants as they were thrown from Portadown Bridge, with Clarke testifying that the rebels 'striped the said people naked', and Taylor specifying that some of those killed in Portadown were drowned *'with their hands tyed on their backs'*.[55] The stripping of Protestants is ubiquitous throughout the depositions, and many of the deponents speak of stripping elsewhere in their testimony (Price, for example, testifies that she was stripped before being imprisoned).[56] The detail Taylor provides is an interlineal insertion, which suggests that it was added after his deposition had been recorded and read back to him. Important enough for him to add, the detail suggests the hopelessness of the prisoners' situation. This sense is reiterated by Clarke, who (with others) claims that 'those of them that asayed to swim to the shore the Rebel{s} stood to shoot at', and in his 1653 examination Clarke adds that those who tried to swim to safety the rebels 'did either shoot or knock them downe with the oares of their Boats', thus offering bludgeoning as a third way to die.[57]

SURVIVAL

Yet there were survivors of the drownings, including Clarke himself who secured his release by paying £15 to the rebels at the waterside. The account of his narrow escape comes immediately after his description of the many deaths in the Bann, with the transition between the two points marked by the commissioner-imposed statement, so pervasive throughout the depositions: 'further he saith'. This shows how the structure of the deposition prioritizes general accounts of mass murder before personal stories of survival. Even when Clarke describes his escape, the emphasis is on continued trauma as he endures 'many hardships vid stripping hunger Cold nakednes imprissonment in the dungeon at Ardee with 10 more Engleshmen his neighbours'.[58]

The Commonwealth examinations appear more open to survivor stories. In his 1653 examination Clarke shares more of the immediate circumstances of his escape, testifying that on the night of the drownings he was imprisoned in 'an hen roost in an Englishmans house in the Port of Downe & the next morning he came downe & stood at the doore < B > of the said house where he had mett with one that he had prosecuted him at the Asizes who swore he would haue this examinant hanged'.[59] In 1653 Clarke seems to take some pleasure in recalling the drama of his escape. As he recalls anew his ordeal from an Ireland in which the rebel threat had been thoroughly crushed, the more positive spin on his escape perhaps reflects Clarke's new sense of safety.

In earlier and later material there are secondhand accounts of prisoners being rescued by Irish Catholics. In 1642 John Wisdome sources his account of the drownings to a survivor who 'escaped being begd of an Irish man to be his seruante'.[60] Thomas Howard, examined in 1652, testifies that a servant of his household was a child survivor of the drownings 'but by the helpe of one Irishman escaped into an old house and soe was saved'.[61] In 1653 Thomas Taylor recounts how he was saved by the actions of an Irishwoman, a friend of his family, who 'lockt this Examinante in the Roome till night, and then lett him out, and told him that all those English that were sent away in the Morning were put to death at Porte of Downe'.[62] Taylor was subsequently forced to become a servant to his rescuer's brother who 'caused him to woorke for him in a Tannhouse' belonging to the deponent's murdered brother.[63] Taylor also mentions the separate escape of his pregnant mother and five-year-old brother from the waters of the Bann. A neighbour, Elizabeth Stewart, proposes that Taylor's mother survived drowning because she was 'nott ... soe Aptt to sincke; as those that were nott with child'.[64] Her survival was brief, however: Stewart testifies that the woman endured a second drowning attempt that claimed the life of her young son, and which shocked her into a premature labour that resulted in the death of her unborn child and then her own demise. As this woman's fateful story suggests, within the depositions survival is uncommon, difficult, and often temporary.

SUPERNATURAL ACTIVITY

Perhaps the most precarious memories associated with the Portadown drownings concern the sighting of apparitions in the aftermath of the massacre, with uncertainty about their appearance and meaning permeating the depositions. Supernatural activity is described in a significant minority of the 1640s depositions (eight out of twenty-seven), which means that the apparitions are important to the earliest depositions but not those of a decade later. Newberry testifies that apparitions were spotted in Portadown 'within a few dayes' of the massacre, and speaking in June 1643 Price says she saw them 'about Candlemas last', which suggests that there may have been sightings for more than a year.[65] Price and another woman, Katherine Cooke, offer eyewitness testimony, a detail that is emphasized in Cooke's deposition as the words *she sawe* and *as she apprehended* are inserted during the revision process to clarify the source of her evidence.[66] That her account was authorized in this way, and also that Price was allowed to offer such a full and comprehensive description of what she saw at Portadown Bridge, suggests that the commissioners treated these stories, which are in many respects outside the official reach of the deposition commission, as worthy of note. Although Henry Brereton or William Aldrich were signatories to all of the depositions that speak of supernatural activity in the Bann, there is little to suggest that these commissioners invited such stories more than others. But it was possible that they were gathered with print publication in mind, as the warranting of their own sub-section in Sir John Temple's *The Irish Rebellion* (1646) might suggest.[67]

Newberry's deposition is typical in specifying that the evidence comes from the rebels themselves: they saw the apparitions, and the sightings terrified them.[68] He is unusual in naming the rebels to whom he is indebted for his account rather than suggesting that it was 'common report among the rebels' as so many of the other deponents do. He is also unique in suggesting that the sightings led to the repentance of the rebel commanders. Like other deponents, Newberry does not confirm the veracity of the sightings, and also leaves open the possibility of a natural explanation. Since the 'bodyes' first appeared within a few days of the drowning, they might have simply been the floating corpses of the dead.[69] Still, the phrasing of the deposition gives agency to the bodies as they '*showed* themselues'.[70] Newberry does not offer any detail about the figures, and they are mute, their power attributable solely to the responses they evoke in the guilty rebels. Later deponents add to Newberry's account of the rebels' terrified response, almost all saying that they were sufficiently frightened to leave Portadown altogether.

Reverend Maxwell provides a fuller account of supernatural activity in Portadown, which is based on evidence from the rebels themselves amongst whom he suggests the sightings were 'common table talke'.[71] He claims to have deliberately engaged the rebels in conversation about the spectres, and 'obiected vnto them' about the ghosts' existence.[72] He alone testifies to the appearance of the murdered Minister Fullerton among the apparitions; thus his desire to disprove the (Catholic) belief that they were the ghosts of the dead is driven by his need to protect the minister from the suggestion that he was languishing in purgatory rather than enjoying salvation as a Protestant martyr.

Maxwell provides further details about the appearance of Fullerton and the other 'Ghosts'.[73] Their 'singing of psalmes' and 'brandishing of naked swords' are particulars found only in Maxwell's testimony, but his account of the 'horrible scritching' of the apparitions is repeated throughout the deposition evidence.[74] Joan Constable also reports that the apparitions 'did most extreamely and fearfully skrich', but while for Maxwell the supernatural shrieks are wordless, for Constable the apparitions 'cry out for vengeance and blowd against the irish that had murdered their bodies there'.[75] Constable's account of the apparitions at Portadown bridge is included as a postscript, which suggests that it was added later. Whatever the reason for Constable's supplementary hearsay evidence, it was clearly important enough for her and the commissioners to add to the deposition.

A lengthy eyewitness account of a particular vision in the River Bann is at the heart of Price's deposition. She and her companions deliberately seek out the apparitions, visiting Portadown upon 'hearing of divers apparitions & visions that were ordinarily seene neere the port a downe bridg since the drowning of her children And the rest of the Protestants there'.[76] Making a very clear and tangible connection between the apparitions and the drownings they supernaturally memorialize, Price's encounter with the spectre is narratively mediated by the traumatic loss of her five children. I have argued elsewhere that the apparition's appearance in 'the shape of a woman' is significant for Price and her female companions for whom she becomes a symbol of their gendered experience of victimhood and survival, and a powerfully feminized revenge fantasy.[77] Price is alone among the deponents in witnessing a single female apparition, with Constable, for example, offering hearsay evidence that the apparitions were 'somtymes of men & somtymes of ~~children~~ *women*'.[78] Constable adds that the figures appear 'brest highe above the water', and for Price the apparition appears 'waste highe *vpright* in the water'; the word '*naked*' is added in the second draft of her deposition, drawing attention to the bared breasts that are less conspicuously displayed in Constable's account.[79] Price also provides more detail about the figure's pose, which she describes as having 'elevated & closed handes'.[80] Cooke similarly records this detail, having witnessed a figure in the water 'bolt vpright brest high, with elevated and closed handes'.[81] Although the textual echoes are striking, Cooke's apparition is 'in the shape of a man'.[82] William Gore also testifies to the appearance of a male figure, although in his deposition the original use of the gendered pronoun is overwritten by the gender-neutral '*it*' or '*that body*'.[83]

Cooke and Price's accounts of their apparitions' hands closed presumably in prayer share similarities with William Holland's description of the body of a Scottish man who 'was found on his knees holding up his hands in a kind of a religious posture of prayer under the water and thick ice through which ice (being very clear) many discerned him'.[84] This sighting was probably not in Portadown, and was not spectral. Yet there are correspondences between what he sees and what Price and Cooke witness in the River Bann. Price and Cooke's prayerful figures, unlike Holland's, emerge from the frozen waters rather than lying buried beneath them, and while Holland's figure represents the impassive muteness of the victim, in Cooke and Price's account he/she becomes a highly vocal and forceful presence.

Vividly describing the fear evoked by a (natural or supernatural) body floating on the water, Gore recalls how the rebels 'endevoured seuerall tymes to hold ~~him~~ & keepe that body vnder water and make ~~him~~ it sinck yet they could by noe meanes doe it but ~~he~~ it still kept ~~above~~ & floated on the water & cryed for vengeance as afore for a long tyme'.[85] Elizabeth Greene also describes how 'the carcasse of one of the men protestants drowned there would by noe meanes be gotten to sinck nor to goe away with the streame but stayd in one place in the water' until some local Englishmen 'with a boate fetched away the bodie & buried it'.[86] Unlike Gore's account of a body that resists interment, in Greene's account a natural interpretation of the body is foregrounded, as the Englishmen, not afflicted with the same supernatural fear as the rebels, are able to retrieve the body and give it a Christian burial. But Greene quickly adds that the men were by the rebels 'soone after hanged for their paynes'.[87] The ability of the apparitions to protect the Protestants by frightening the rebels is revealed as transient and ultimately impotent, and the Protestants continue to be defenceless against rebel violence.

CONCLUSION

Memories of the Portadown drownings contained in the 1641 depositions are diverse, inconsistent, and even contradictory. They are fundamentally shaped by the way they were collected, recorded, and used, as well as by the identity positions of the deponents and the status of their evidence. As such, the 1641 depositions are a rich resource for memories of the rebellion, but perhaps not for the 'facts' of what happened. Traces of the deposition evidence can be found in the commemorative traditions of the Portadown Orange Order, but the rough edges of the evidence have been smoothed out to tell a simpler story of Irish Catholic violence against Protestant settlers. As such, Orange Order parading banners, re-enactments, and memorial stones propagate a singular memory of victimized Protestants, and cannot accommodate divergent memories of Protestant survivors, Catholic saviours, and vengeful apparitions, much less the messy questions about the number of dead or what actually happened at an unknown date in late autumn 1641. Attending to the history of 1641 memories has the potential to offer a more nuanced picture of the way sectarian violence was experienced in the past and perhaps suggests a way of reconsidering the role of memory and history today in post-conflict Northern Ireland.

NOTES

1. Mary Russell, 'Witnesses to mass murder in the icy Bann', *The Irish Times*, 9 October 2010.
2. Naomi McAreavey, '"Building Bridges": Remembering the 1641 Rebellion in Northern Ireland', forthcoming in *Memory Studies* 11.1 (2018).
3. 'Presentation on the 375th Anniversary of the 1641 Rebellion and Portadown Massacre', 23 November 2016, Carleton Street Orange Hall.
4. The most influential of the early printed texts are Henry Jones, *A Remonstrance of Divers Remarkeable Passages concerning the Church and Kingdome of Ireland* (London, 1642) and Sir John Temple, *The Irish Rebellion* (London, 1646).
5. John Gibney, *The Shadow of a Year: The 1641 Rebellion in Irish History and Memory* (Madison: University of Wisconsin Press, 2013); *Ireland: 1641*, ed. by Micheál Ó Siochrú and Jane Ohlmeyer (Manchester: Manchester University Press, 2013); *The 1641 Depositions and the Irish Rebellion*, ed. by Eamon Darcy, Annaleigh Margey and Elaine Murphy (London: Pickering and Chatto, 2012).
6. Guy Beiner, 'Memory Too Has a History', *Dublin Review of Books*, 1 March 2015 http://www.drb.ie/essays/memory-too-has-a-history.
7. My focus on memory rather than history responds to the forensic historical scholarship best exemplified by Hilary Simms, 'Violence in County Armagh, 1641', in *Ulster, 1641: Aspects of the Rising*, ed. by Brian Mac Cuarta (Belfast: Institute of Irish Studies, 1993), pp.122–38. See also Eamon Darcy, *The Irish Rebellion of 1641 and the Wars of the Three Kingdoms* (Woodbridge: Boydell, 2013), pp.68–72.
8. Aidan Clarke, 'The 1641 Depositions', in *Treasures of the Library, Trinity College Dublin*, ed. by Peter Fox (Dublin: Royal Irish Academy, 1986), pp.111–22, remains the definitive description of the 1641 depositions.
9. Aidan Clarke, 'The Commission for the Despoiled Subject, 1641–7', in *Reshaping Ireland, 1550–1700*, ed. by Brian Mac Cuarta (Dublin: Four Courts, 2011), pp.241–60.
10. The depositions can be accessed online at http://1641.tcd.ie, and in print in *The 1641 Depositions*, 12 vols., ed. by Aidan Clarke and others (Dublin: Irish Manuscripts Commission, 2014–). All quotations from the 1641 depositions are taken from the online transcriptions.
11. Clarke, '1641 Depositions', p.113.
12. Clarke, '1641 Depositions', p.113. See also Marie-Louise Coolahan, '"And this deponent further sayeth": Orality, Print and the 1641 Depositions', in *Oral and Print Cultures in Ireland, 1600–1900*, ed. by Marc Caball and Andrew Carpenter (Dublin: Four Courts, 2010), pp.69–84.
13. For a contemporary account of the experiences of deponents in Dublin, see Jones, *Remonstrance*, pp.105–9.
14. MS 836, fols 002r–003v.
15. MS 836, fols 101r–105v.
16. MS 836, fols 101r–105v (101r).
17. MS 836, fols 101r–105v (101r).
18. MS 836, fols 101r–105v (102r).
19. MS 836, fols 002r–003v (2r); MS 836, fols 177r–178v (177r).
20. MS 836, fols 177r–178v (177r).
21. MS 836, fols 139r–142v (139r).
22. MS 836, fols 139r–142v (139v).

23. MS 836, fols 002r–003v (2r); MS 836, fols 177r–178v (177r).
24. MS 836, fols 101r–105v (101r); MS 836, fols 069r–079v (70v).
25. MS 836, fols 002r–003v (2r).
26. MS 836, fols 101r–105v (102r).
27. MS 836, fols 101r–105v (101v). See also Wisdom, MS 836, fols 014r–015v (15r); and Newberry, MS 836, fols 060r–061v (61r).
28. MS 836, fols 139r–142v (139v).
29. MS 836, fols 101r–105v (101r); MS 836, fols 060r–061v (60v).
30. MS 836, fols 179r–180v (179r), MS 836, fols 161r–162v.
31. MS 836, fols 002r–003v (2r); MS 836, fols 069r–079v (70v); MS 836, fols 139r–142v (139v).
32. MS 836, fols 101r–105v (101v).
33. MS 836, fols 002r–003v (2r); MS 836, fols 069r–079v (70v).
34. MS 836, fols 002r–003v (2r); MS 836, fols 060r–061v (60v).
35. MS 836, fols 002r–003v (2r).
36. MS 836, fols 177r–178v (177r); .
37. MS 836, fols 161r–162v (161v).
38. MS 836, fols 139r–142v (139v–140r).
39. MS 836, fols 177r–178v (177r).
40. MS 836, fols 050r–051v (50v).
41. MS 839, fols 012r–016v (13v).
42. MS 836, fols 069r–079v (71v).
43. Patricia Palmer, *The Severed Head and the Grafted Tongue: Translating Violence in Early Modern Ireland* (Cambridge: Cambridge University Press, 2013).
44. Simms, p.124. MS 836, fols 007r–007v (7r).
45. Simms, p.124. MS 836, fols 007r–007v (7r).
46. Simms, p.124. MS 836, fols 007r–007v (7r).
47. MS 836, fols 101r–105v (101v); MS 809, fols 005r–012v (10v).
48. MS 836, fols 073r–074v (73v).
49. MS 837, fols 082r–083v (82r, 83v).
50. MS 836, fols 101r–105v (101v); MS 836, fols 100r–100v (100r); MS 836, fols 179r–180v (179r); MS 836, fols 224r–225v (224r).
51. MS 836, fols 100r–100v (100r).
52. MS 836, fols 101r–105v (101v).
53. MS 836, fols 002r–003v (2r).
54. For a history of Portadown, see S.C. Lutton, 'The Rise and Development of Portadown', *Journal of the Craigavon Historical Society*, 5.2, available at http://www.craigavonhistoricalsociety.org.uk/rev/luttonriseofportadown.html.
55. MS 836, fols 002r–003v (2r); MS 836, fols 007r–007v (7r).
56. MS 836, fols 101r–105v (101r).
57. MS 836, fols 002r–003v (2r); MS 836, fols 177r–178v (177r). See also MS 836, fols 075r–076v (75v); MS 836, fols 101r–105v (101v–102r); and MS 836, fols 222r–223v (222r).
58. MS 836, fols 002r–003v (3r).
59. MS 836, fols 177r–178v (177r).
60. MS 836, fols 014r–015v (15r).
61. MS 836, fols 147r–148v (148r).
62. MS 836, fols 179r–180v (179r).
63. MS 836, fols 179r–180v (179r).
64. MS 837, fols 082v–083v (82v–83r).
65. MS 836, fols 060r–061v (61r); MS 836, fols 101r–105v (102v).
66. MS 836, fols 092r–093v (92r).

67. Temple, pp.133–36. The apparitions only appear in depositions recorded after the publication of Jones's text in March 1642 so would not have been available for inclusion.
68. MS 836, fols 060r–061v (61r).
69. MS 836, fols 060r–061v (61r).
70. MS 836, fols 060r–061v (61r).
71. MS 809, fols 005r–012v (10v).
72. MS 809, fols 005r–012v (10v).
73. MS 809, fols 005r–012v (10v).
74. MS 809, fols 005r–012v (10v).
75. MS 836, fols 087r–090v (89v).
76. MS 836, fols 101r–105v (102v).
77. MS 836, fols 101r–105v (102v). See 'Re(–)Membering Women: Protestant Women's Victim Testimonies during the Irish Rising of 1641', *Journal of the Northern Renaissance* 2.1 (2010), http://www.northernrenaissance.org/re-membering-women-protestant-womens-victim-testimonies-during-the-irish-rising-of-1641/.
78. MS 836, fols 087r–090v (89r).
79. MS 836, fols 087r–090v (89r); MS 836, fols 101r–105v (102v)
80. MS 836, fols 101r–105v (102v–103r)
81. MS 836, fols 092r–093v (92r).
82. MS 836, fols 092r–093v (92r).
83. MS 837, fols 025r–027v (25v).
84. MS 834, fols 159r–160v (160r).
85. MS 837, fols 025r–027v (25v).
86. MS 836, fols 094r–094v (94v).
87. MS 836, fols 094r–094v (94v).

Oona Frawley

Edmund Spenser and Transhistorical Memory in Ireland

Edmund Spenser has been beleaguered by some critics who deem him to be a willing and active representative of the worst of English colonial aspirations, and defended by others who see him as a humanist poet caught in the closing jaws of an imperial mission. This vacillation of opinion is seen in the rewriting of Spenser by Irish authors over time, from Geoffrey Keating to Peter Walsh, from Sarah Butler to Maria Edgeworth, from W.B. Yeats to Frank McGuinness. At different points, Spenser has drawn the attention of Irish writers; he has also haunted Irish critical work, moving through the contemporary academy in a swift transmission beginning in the 1980s, when 'Spenser and Ireland' became a subject of some significance.[1] Yet now, only thirty years later, that attention has been largely diverted.[2] Certain moments of resurgent interest in Spenser are more easily explained than others. Attention to 'Spenser and Ireland' from the late 1980s onwards, for instance, occurs within the context of postcolonial studies and Irish studies, which were both then in the ascendant. But deferring to such explanations does not give us some of the crucial information we need: if we want to consider how and why it is that Spenser – or any figure – makes a more marked appearance in Irish criticism and creative work at certain points, we need to consider cultural memory. For Spenser to recur in Irish culture as the object of imaginative and critical speculation, a form of memory must be at work: Spenser has been remembered, in effect, on a cultural level. While recent work in the area of memory studies has usefully focused on transcultural memory (and Spenser is also productively considered in those terms) there has been little consideration of the ways in which cultural memory functions transhistorically, perhaps because 'memory' implies interaction over time, and this has allowed us to avoid considerations of how cultural memory moves through decades, through centuries. In this case, there is a sense that the cultural memory of Spenser is transferred through textual sources that revive and reinterpret his work, his life, and his image through rewriting.

Irish University Review 47.1 (2017): 32–47
DOI: 10.3366/iur.2017.0255
© Edinburgh University Press
www.euppublishing.com/iur

In one of few interventions on the subject of transhistorical memory, Plate and Rose have named the concept of 'rewriting' as vital:

> As process and as product, rewriting is engaged in cultural transmission and inheritance. Like translation, commentary, exegesis ... it adapts culture to preserve it, re-producing it to keep it alive. In this sense, rewriting's teleology is conservative: although it is a transformative process, its re-productive capacity produces tradition, the semblance of things eternally present and unchanged, carried on across time and space. Yet rewriting may also be primarily vested in change. Its interest, then, is not so much in preserving culture as it is in transforming it, directing its look at what might be, rather than to what is or was.[3]

The 'rewriting' of Spenser might, in some contexts, amount to a cultural preservation; in an Irish context, however, this rewriting seems to have a more radical intent of reevaluating the relationship to the colonial occupation and not simply preserving difficult historical moments. Spenser, I suggest, comes to function as a 'coming to terms' with aspects of the Irish historical past. While in an English context Spenser was, early on, interpreted as an impoverished poet forced by rebels to flee inhospitable Ireland, in an Irish context Spenser becomes, in a wonderfully appropriate turn of events, allegorized in Irish culture over time. Seen in a certain light, the 'story' of Spenser in Ireland is one of an Englishman who comes to Ireland and is, after a long period in the country, driven out again by the Irish. This interpretation immediately suggests a reason for Spenser's recurrence in Irish literature and criticism over the centuries: he can so easily be shaped into a narrative that serves the Irish cultural imagination's sense of putting paid to the invader and usurper of power. Rather than the various unsuccessful rebellions that saw Irish hopes of independence quashed, the 'Spenser narrative'[4] is one that relies upon the story of a coloniser who is, eventually, uprooted and driven from Ireland. Read this way, 'Spenser' is a potent icon for the Irish imagination, and one that might be called upon at particular historical moments in order to 'remember' Irish rebelliousness, if not independence. It would thus seem no accident that Spenser reappears in Irish cultural memory at heightened moments in Irish history, when the culture is either under colonial pressure or recovering from it. While it is impossible to present a thorough survey in so brief a space, this essay considers key moments or changes in the rewriting of Spenser's cultural memory in Ireland, attempting to consider the long duration of his figuring in Irish literature and culture as a case study of transhistorical memory processes.

EARLY REWRITINGS: KEATING, WALSH, BUTLER

The first to claim Spenser as an opponent in a forum that was consciously attempting to shape Irish identity, Geoffrey Keating – a learned and prolific Jesuit priest – refuted Spenser and other planters' descriptions of Ireland in *Foras Feasa ar Éirinn* (c.1634). Because Keating's history circulated at around the same time as Spenser's *A View of the Present State of Ireland* (belatedly published in 1633), Keating must have had access to a manuscript version of the *View*.[5] Just as extant manuscript copies of Spenser's *View* suggested the text's impact, the many seventeenth-century manuscript copies of Keating's text testify to its own rapid success. 'Keating's history', Bernadette Cunningham writes, 'was immediately accepted as authoritative by Ireland's professional scribes'.[6] If his English contemporaries were prepared to draw upon ancient history to justify their claims about the Irish, Keating would do the same by transforming Irish manuscript and oral traditions into an exhaustive written history of Ireland. But Keating also drew upon continental source material, which distinguished his history from earlier attempts to employ Irish manuscript material in an overarching history, and which spoke of his continental education. Bede, Nennius, Geoffrey of Monmouth, John Speed, Raphael Holinshead, William Camden, George Buchanan, John Mair, Edmund Campion, Meredith Hanmer and Richard Stanihurst are all discussed – in addition to Spenser. Even a cursory glance at this list makes clear that Spenser was situated in a line of authors, and, more particularly, was only one of many English authors who had written prose tracts on Ireland – several of whose works were in fact included in James Ware's 1633 edition with Spenser's *View*.

Keating's dismissal of Spenser and other planters' assessments of Ireland occurs in the preface, suggesting that Keating has been sparked to his task by those very assessments; Cunningham notes that Ware's volume 'may well have been the catalyst that led Keating to add an historiographical preface'.[7] If a sense of outrage is taken as the starting point for Keating's monumental work, *Foras Feasa* becomes, ideologically at least, a postcolonial text in its reclamation of culture, identity, history, and doctrine. By refusing to write his history in English, Keating takes a crucial step towards what would later be recognized as a postcolonial mindset: he claims the Irish language as his medium, refuting the ascendancy of the English language in Ireland and instead focusing on native cultural traditions. This led to his being seen as the 'symbolic personification' of the language revival of the late nineteenth and early twentieth centuries.[8]

Interestingly, for Keating it is not Spenser who is singled out for the greatest attack, but other planters. Keating's refutation of other

English writers is much more ferocious than that of Spenser; Richard Stanihurst, like Keating a Catholic who claimed Norman heritage, comes in for the sharpest critique. Keating certainly dismisses Spenser's *View* and the attitudes it expresses towards Ireland and the Irish, but he does not focus relentlessly on Spenser as the principal icon of Elizabethan colonial administration and abuse in Ireland. Keating's text thus establishes quite clearly that Spenser, in the 1630s, had not yet become the solitary representative of a widespread phenomenon. So when does Spenser become something other than one of several, or many – when does he move beyond the fold of James Ware's 1633 collection of tracts on Ireland, beyond Keating's assessment that considers Spenser as one, and certainly not the worst, of many Englishmen who misappropriated and condemned Irish culture? The 'Spenser narrative' that recurs in Irish culture in later centuries, in other words, had not yet been shaped three decades after his death. Indeed, there seems not enough material in *Foras Feasa* to justify the *Oxford Companion to Irish Literature*'s claim that Keating viewed Spenser as 'a leading calumniator of Irish culture and society'.[9] Keating does lay down a cornerstone, however, for the construction of what functions as a transhistorical Spenser script. Spenser's analysis of the Irish and Irish culture, Keating concludes, is the fancy of a poet too used to indulging his imagination:

> I am surprised how Spenser ventured to meddle in these matters, of which he was ignorant, unless that, on the score of being a poet, he allowed himself license of invention, as it was usual with him, and others like him, to frame and arrange many poetic romances with sweet-sounding words to deceive the reader.[10]

In mentioning Spenser's status as a poet, Keating establishes a pattern that will be frequently followed; when Spenser reappears in Irish literature in the coming centuries, his *View* will not be read or interpreted as the work of a mere planter, but as the work of a poet, the author of *The Faerie Queene*, the laureate buried in Westminster.

Following Keating's interpretation of Spenser, there are a handful of Irish texts in the 17th and 18th centuries that mention Spenser and reveal the ways in which subtle changes occur to the cultural memory of Spenser in both English and Irish contexts. Peter Walsh – described as 'conciliatory' by Leerssen[11] and self-described as 'no Irish man by blood, but English, though born in Ireland'[12] – discusses Spenser in the preface to his *Prospect of the State of Ireland* (1682) and, like Keating, corrects Spenser's excesses to a degree: 'in writing his Faerie Queen he had the right of a Poet to fancy anything; nevertheless, in the Historical part of his Dialogue ... [h]e should have follow'd other Rules'.[13] This is fairly typical of 17th century appraisals of Spenser, in that Spenser's contribution to the body of written work on Ireland is acknowledged, but he is a diminishing figure. Spenser is eclipsed in Walsh by Keating, whose careful history of Ireland is far more credited; the reader is even reassured that Walsh will only mention Spenser one further time.[14]

Something changes, however, in the early 18th century, with the preface to Sarah Butler's *Irish Tales* (1714). The text drew heavily on Keating himself to present a version of Irish history 'cloath'd ... with the Dress and Title of a Novel'.[15] In the preface, Spenser is mentioned alongside Camden, but rather than condemning Spenser's position on Ireland, Butler instead deploys Spenser as part of a defense of Irish writing and culture: '[B]oth *Camden* and *Edmund Spenſer* in his *View of Ireland*, page 29. do acknowledge, *That our Anceſtors in* Great Britain *learned the very form and manner of framing their Character for Writing, from* Ireland'.[16] Butler's text, sympathetic to the Catholic platform of Jacobitism, was published at a moment of uprising and at a time when Spenser would still have been linked in a triumvirate with Shakespeare and Milton as the greatest of English writers; therefore to deploy Spenser's own claims in defense of Irish culture was both to acknowledge his position and to use it to raise the status of Irish history and literature. Taken as an attempt to revive interest in the Irish past from a sympathetic, even pseudo-nationalist point of view, Butler's text is important in signalling a changing usage of Spenser in an Irish context. It is important, though, that Spenser still figures as one of several chroniclers named as representative of an ideological position.

REWRITING SPENSER IN THE 19TH CENTURY:
EDGEWORTH, SIGERSON, YEATS

Spenser moves out of the preface and into the text several decades later, and is named individually, without mention of other of his contemporaries. Maria Edgeworth will name Spenser on the opening page of *Castle Rackrent* (1800), her well-known novella about one Irish estate and its changing fortunes. In the second line of the book, narrator 'Honest Thady' describes his 'greatcoat' as fastening 'cloak fashion'; this leads to a long footnote that quite overwhelms the book's first page. The footnote begins by citing Spenser as an expert of some reliability in establishing the 'high antiquity' of the garment, and proceeds to quote from *A View* a passage in which Spenser describes the potential treacherous usage of the cloak by the Irish: 'for it is a fit house for an outlaw, a meet bed for a rebel, and an apt cloak for a thief'.[17] The note's reverential tone is of course undercut by the central text, in which Thady, whose narratorial reliability is questionable, repeatedly demonstrates his own wherewithal as opposed to the inanity and ignorance of the estate's owners. Spenser's expertise as a colonial occupier, then, is called upon by Edgeworth in ironic fashion to underline the distinctly inexpert management of his fictional colonial successors, while also potentially implicating 'Honest Thady's' role in his masters' downfall. That this commentary appears just as the Act of Union comes into force suggests that, at a moment of political crisis, previous English commentators on the Irish situation remain important; in fact, in terms of the textual presentation and the space given to the note citing Spenser, it would seem that the past is overwhelming the present. However, if Spenser has been consigned mostly to the preface, his position here in a footnote does suggest that, in cultural memory in Ireland, 'Spenser' is something that has gone before that must be dealt with, and however marginal he and those with similar ideas might be perceived, their impact continues to be felt. The conclusion that we can begin to draw, then, is that 'Spenser' remains in memory, and remains because narratives concerning him travel through time. 'Spenser' offers an example of a specific process of memory, a transhistorical version of 'postmemory', in which what is experienced is not the direct, personal memory of the individual, but an inherited (and in this case cultural) version of memory. While 'Spenser' is not remembered firsthand, the transmission of his literary and cultural legacy suggests that transhistorial memory, like postmemory, travels and moves across generations.[18]

There are several curious traces in the next century that tell us something about the way in which Spenser's memory moved across time after the Act of Union. One of these comes in the first epigraph[19] to George Sigerson's *Bards of the Gael and Gall* (1907). Like Butler's two centuries before, Sigerson's citation of Spenser comes as a support for his own claims and precedes his main text; he chooses to cite Irenius from *A View* on the merits of Irish poetry.

> Eudoxus. But tell me (I pray you) have they any art in their composition? or bee they anything wittie or well savoured, as poemes should be?

> Irenaeus. Yea truly, I have caused divers of them to be translated unto me, that I might understand them, and surely they savoured of sweet wit and good inventon ... sprinkled with some pretty flowers of their naturall device, which gave good grace and comelinesse unto them. – Edmund Spenser, *A View of the Present State of Ireland*, 1596[20]

This is an extraordinary epigraph to have chosen for an important Revival text that made available translations of bardic poetry. Spenser's name is invoked as almost ultimate proof, as if to say – if *even Spenser* could praise Irish literature and culture, it must indeed be worthy of praise. There is thus an odd, colonial nod to Spenser – an acknowledgement that he retains a priveleged position in British literary culture and history – with his 'Irish connection' no doubt encouraging the citation of his work as evidence of the merit of Irish cultural heritage.

Yeats, writing on the eve of Irish independence and picking up on the threads left by Sigerson, takes things further. Yeats's engagement with Spenser is prolonged and cannot be fully treated in so short a space, but it is important to note the shift that occurs through his rewriting of Spenser.[21] Yeats acknowledges the prestige retained by Spenser because of his poetic capacity, but returns to Keating's tone of rebuke: despite his fondness for Spenser's poetry and its impact on his work, Yeats chastises Spenser for his overfondness of the state and queen. At this point, as the momentum for home rule and independence increases, it is clear that Spenser cannot be wholly approved of; nor can his political stance be ignored and simple positives focused on as in Butler's preface or Sigerson's epigraph. Instead, Spenser comes in for critique as an able poet who lost his way in the maze of colonialism. If Spenser, willing colonial servant and national poet, is deployed in defense of Irish culture in the earlier part of the Revival, he is symbolically disempowered by Yeats, with a lasting impact.

LATE 20TH-CENTURY REWRITINGS OF SPENSER: HEANEY AND MCGUINNESS

In addition to Yeats's rewriting of Spenser, the 20th century saw other high profile Irish literary engagements with Spenser.[22] Two of these occur far later in the century, when Ireland was again under pressure due to mounting difficulties in the North. Seamus Heaney's is a cautious rewriting; Spenser occurs not as a persona for the poet to inhabit – as he does Sweeney, for instance, in the same period[23] – but as a distant figure of the past. Heaney's subdued engagement stands in contrast to several other poetic responses, such as the challenging rendition of Spenser in Brendan Kennelly's *Cromwell* sequence a decade later, in which Spenser is represented as an alcoholic auctioneer wishing to escape 'fucking Cork';[24] but Heaney, as Ireland's most prominent late 20th century Irish poet, is important to examine. Heaney's caution might be ascribed most straightforwardly to the political and social situation in which he wrote, on the heels of Bloody Sunday, and in the midst of an unfurling civil crisis.

In 'Bog Oak', one of his much-analysed series of bog poems, Heaney presents images that grow out of the raising from the bog of an ancient oak, a 'black,/ long-seasoned rib' (ll.3-4).[25] As the 'mizzling rain/ blurs the far end/ of the cart track', the poet knows that the track will lead 'back to no / "oak groves"' (ll.17-8). It is in this state of being able to only half see into the past that Heaney writes:

> Perhaps I just make out
> Edmund Spenser
> dreaming sunlight,
> encroached upon by
>
> geniuses who creep
> 'out of every corner
> of the woodes and glennes'
> towards watercress and carrion.

Quoting from Spenser's *View*, Heaney confronts Spenser not as a poet, but as the author of an infamous tract that among other things recommended the felling of the oak trees, which both impeded travel and hid rebels, and centuries later turn up in bogs. If in earlier incarnations, in Keating, say, Spenser the poet is admonished for his colonial role, here Spenser's poetic function has all but disappeared; he is merely one who suggested starving the Irish out of the forests. Despite the planters' takeover of the land, it is not the Irish but Spenser who is 'encroached upon' – a choice of words that captures the Elizabethan belief in England's right to Ireland. However, while the presence of the colonizer is manifested through the citation of Spenser's own words and that sense of colonial entitlement, the 'creep' of 'geniuses' – whether defined in contemporary usage or in the medieval sense of the spirits or sources of inspiration – undercuts that presence and the force of the colonizing agenda. The colonizing presence in the poem is not given the last word; in the end, the will to survive – and Heaney is aware of the dire circumstances that drove survival in many periods of Irish history, the 'watercress and carrion' – closes the poem. Just as the oak has persisted in the bog despite its felling, so does genius – we might say Heaney's own – continue.

Heaney's concern with memory and metaphors of memory during this period is well known: the bog itself acts as a preservative, a medium through which to read the past, as so compellingly described by Stuart McLean.[26] When we talk about Heaney's concern with memory during the 1970s, we are immediately dealing with a form of memory that goes beyond the personal: the bog remembers for the culture, for the tribe, to use a term to which Heaney has recourse to use in this same period – even at times when the culture is preoccupied with forgetting, as Guy Beiner has argued, there is a sense in which memory persists and is 'regenerated'.[27] If the bog preserves physical objects like that oak beam, it also functions as a preservative of ideas that, Heaney's poetry considers, we might be better off forgetting: this is because the physical preservation disallows social forgetting, with the object functioning as both a revenant and a placeholder of memory.[28] Heaney is thus aware of the possibility of being bogged down, as the phrase goes, in memories, in the past. This is a particularly important crux for postcolonial cultures[29] and suggests why Spenser inserts himself into this era of Heaney's poetry: how does one ensure that rituals and traditions are preserved, heritage maintained, without preserving too what Heaney in 'North' deems 'the hatreds and behind-backs' of the past (1.25)?[30] For a poet writing in 1970s Ireland, this was a vital question – and for one from the North of Ireland, it was near unavoidable. Jane Grogan notes that a particular phase of 'Spenser's Irish legacy is dominated by the emerging northern poets of the day: John Montague, Seamus Heaney, and Derek Mahon'.[31] If postcolonial cultures felt themselves in the earliest stages to be struggling against the absence or the loss of memory,[32] Northern Ireland – neither clearly a colonial nor postcolonial space – seemed to suffer from a surfeit of memory, an excess so great that it was spilling over in two nations.

Frank McGuinness's *Mutabilitie* (first performed in 1997) continues the rewriting of cultural memory by deploying and transforming Spenser at another critical moment in Irish history, when the Good Friday Agreement was being composed and the cultural memory of the Troubles was beginning to be acknowledged and sifted through. It is this dramatic rewriting that most extensively deploys Spenser as a way of getting to grips with the colonial relationship between England and Ireland, with the implication that this deployment mirrors a present moment when the relationship was yet again being redefined, and for what many hoped was the last time, as a form of reconciliation was broached. Where Spenser had been kept at a distance by Heaney, McGuinness enters Kilcolman Castle and imagines Spenser's life within its walls as his time in Ireland draws to a close. In McGuinness's play, Spenser and his wife Elizabeth have opened their doors to a family of Irish servants who are linked to the medieval story of *Buile Suibhne*, in which king Sweeney has been usurped and forced out into the natural world. The allusions make clear that McGuinness's once royal family has also been displaced by the colonial occupation.

It is through this family that *Mutabilitie* settles on a symbol of importance to both Irish mythology and *The Faerie Queene* – the fostered babe. In taking up this topic, McGuinness draws on a famous aspect of Spenser's biography: Ben Jonson's reported claim that 'The Irish ... robd Spensers goods, and burnt his house and a little child new born'.[33] McGuinness transforms this child lost to the fire into a child who has lost his way, only to be found by the dispossessed Irish royal family and its powerful File who will become Spenser's child's foster-mother.[34] Confused and frightened by the flames, McGuinness's child emerges as an apt summation of a play that has dwelt on the complex interactions necessitated by colonial expansion. The child functions as an allegorical symbol for what happens between a colonial occupier and occupied, a figure who bridges while also representing those gaps it is impossible to bridge. The colonial occupier – Spenser – might flee, might be run out by the rebellion of native landholders, but he will always leave something of himself behind: ways of thinking, ways of life, ways of being.

Beyond the child's use as an allegorical symbol of the results and inheritances of colonialism, the fact of the child's fosterage opens onto a theme of significance in Irish lore as well as in Spenser's epic. Within Irish mythology, Cuchulain and Finn are both given over to foster parents to be raised;[35] fosterage remained an integral part of early and medieval Irish culture, in all likeliness reflecting a response to demands that multiple children placed on parents.[36] For exceptional figures like Cuchulain and Finn, fosterage also meant exposure to people or environments that teach the hero crucial things – Cuchulain learns to bear arms from his foster father, while Finn learns about the natural world through his fosterage in a forest. In terms of narrative, then, fosterage provides an explanation of various factors that may not be available simply out of a given character's birth.

Spenser himself deployed fosterage for its narrative possibilities. Several times in *The Faerie Queene* knights are required to rescue infants from dead parents, as in Book 2, when Sir Guyon fosters a 'lucklesse babe, borne under cruell starre'[37] to Lady Medina. A second fosterage occurs in Book 6, when Sir Calepine rescues a babe from a bear. Calepine chances afterwards on the weeping Matilda, whose husband lacks an heir and who is thus the perfect foster mother. Besides commenting on the anxieties at Queen Elizabeth's own lack of an heir, the episode allows Spenser to gesture towards the baby's future. Matilda passes the child off as their own to her husband, with the result that 'it in goodly thewes so well upbrought, / That it became a famous knight well knowne / And did right noble deedes, the which elsewhere are showne'.[38] There is a certain poignancy in this, because the babe that Spenser evidently intended to grow up and host another book of the projected back half of *The Faerie Queene* remains a babe and does not go on to adventures of his own; his 'noble deedes' are not 'elswhere showne', since the writing of *The Faerie Queene* was halted. There is a sense in which Spenser's writing – like memory by rewriting or through the physical preservation of artefacts – itself is fostered, in the end – given over to control other than the author's own. Chance, as so often happens in this epic, intervenes, and Spenser's intention of a twelve-book poem was thwarted.

If Spenser's circumstances in a colony struggling with rebellion contributed to the fact of *The Faerie Queene* never being completed, there is a way in which the unfinished business that was his literary legacy and his political one has been taken up by Irish writers in the four centuries since his death. Just as Spenser's child in *Mutabilitie* is fostered, so too has Spenser been fostered: adopted by authors whom he never envisioned as his audience or the interpreters of his legacy, of which McGuinness is one of the most recent. Spenser, as is so frequently noted, set out in *The Faerie Queene* to show how to 'fashion a gentleman', and the figure of Spenser in McGuinness is, indeed, gentle; he is not blameless, but he is not savage in the way that earlier writers might have imagined him. Spenser is greatly to be pitied, in McGuinness's version of him, in a significant break from previous anticolonial versions of Spenser: a man defeated by his own inspiration, whose zeal has created the gaps in his thinking that will be his downfall. Pity and imaginative empathy with a clear 'other' would seem to represent a distinctive postcolonial remembering, at a point when imaginative engagement with the 'other' in Northern Ireland was actively encouraged society-wide: this is the kind of empathetic leap that makes possible the idea of 'healing through remembering'.[39] Spenser's desire to convert the Irish, to reform them in McGuinness's play, is itself fascinating: McGuinness's Spenser requires the Irish to change, to mutate, just as, ultimately, 'Spenser' himself has become a mutable narrative in Irish culture. And yet, ironically, in *Mutabilitie,* the very instability of Spenser's situation – its changing, mutating nature – is what he cannot bear.

And one of the worst things for Spenser to bear would surely have been the idea of a child of his being rescued by the Irish, by the kernes – foot-soldiers – that kept the woods. McGuinness's play employs this scenario as a resolution to the colonial context and the workings of empire, and as a contemporary plea for reconciliation, it would appear. But if we imagine that Spenser might have dreaded the notion of his child fallen to the hands of the savage Irish, he could have seen the irony that is apparent in the play in his child being rescued by a royal family. For the court-conscious Spenser, this is an appropriate and savagely warranted turn of fictional events: in McGuinness's version of it, Spenser's middle-class English son will be raised by the Irish nobles who live in a wood.

McGuinness's knowledge of Spenser's writing is apparent throughout the play, and there are echoes of many aspects of *The Faerie Queene*. In Book 6, noble-born Tristram is sent away by his mother to keep him safe from his uncle, who has usurped Tristram's power (6.2.28-9). She sends him to 'some forrein land' (6.2.29), where, like Finn and like a Robin Hood figure, he learns to live as an exceptional hunter in the natural world, away from cultural corruption and devoted instead to nature. Sir Calidore is immediately impressed with the courtesy and vigour of the youth, and makes a squire of Tristram, with the implication that noble birth will eventually reveal itself in greatness. The narrative echo of greatest import between McGuinness's fostered child and Spenser's epic is that of Arthur, whose birth is of an origin unknown to him. Like Tristram, he was removed from his family, while only a babe – but unlike Tristram, is unaware of his ancestry. When Una asks him to outline his background, he replies:

> Faire virgin (said the Prince) ye me require
> A thing without the compas of my wit:
> For both the lignage and the certain Sire,
> From which I sprong, from me are hidden yit.
> For all so soone as life did me admit
> Into this world, and shewed heavens light,
> From mothers pap I taken was unfit:
> And straight delivered to a Faery knight,
> To be unbrought in gentle thewes and martiall might. (1.9.3)

Reared by 'old Timon' (1.9.4), Arthur was also visited frequently by Merlin, of whom the child prince enquired his beginnings, only to be told 'That I was sonne and heire unto a king, / As time in her just terme the truth to light should bring' (1.9.5). Merlin's involvement with Arthur's upbringing, as well as Arthur's childhood home on the river Dee – which in Spenser's marriage of the rivers is described as a river 'which Britons long ygone / Did call divine' (4.2.3) – suggests an origin beyond the merely human. The fact of his fosterage thus confirms his mysterious, wondrous origins, as is the case with Finn as well: the semi-divine and mythological origins of the hero imply the greatness that is to come.

If Arthur is brought up by a man representing earthly wisdom and ability in arms and by a magician with all the power of good, the figure of Spenser's child in McGuinness's *Mutabilitie* will be reared by a poet-sorceress with extraordinary strength of will and by a gentle man of wisdom. The parallel and allusion McGuinness no doubt intends us to note; and yet it is a parallel that problemetizes our reading of *The Faerie Queene*, and provides a comment on the prophecies that Spenser lays out in the poem. Arthur's fated greatness is firmly pronounced at every opportunity in the six existing books of *The Faerie Queene*, even though we are not privy to any passage in which his eventual meeting with the Faerie Queene herself takes place. In this sense, the epic ends without the crucial union – on which the fate of the nation rests. McGuinness's employment of a parallel to Arthur complicates this, challenging the very notion of prophecy by denying its possibility from an *English* perspective – for in his play the child's arrival has been prophecied, of course, by the File. Knowing that no heir was produced to follow Elizabeth, and knowing that the British empire as Spenser imagined it has now come apart, McGuinness's version of Spenserian prophecy is definitively postcolonial; it is denied except within the context of the Irish family. McGuinness thus problematizes our view of *The Faerie Queene*'s close, since – if we consider the possibility of an intentional abandonment of the poem by Spenser – *Mutabilitie*'s ending suggests that Spenser himself had come to doubt his own prophecies and leaves Arthur unfulfilled, having failed to make a union with Gloriane and produce an heir.

Of all of the literary rewritings of Spenser in an Irish context, McGuinness's is, to my mind, the most successful: notably engaged with Spenser's poetry, prose, and, crucially, with Spenser criticism. It is this last element that, as Grogan has noted, distinguishes the play from other versions of Spenser in Irish literature, for McGuinness consciously writes in the context of the revived interest in 'Spenser in Ireland' that was apparent by the time of the play's composition.[40] *Mutabilitie* is conscious of its allegorizing not only of Spenser but also of the colonial encounter, and thus mirrors the milieu in which McGuinness wrote, conscious of ongoing negotiations of English, Irish, and Northern Irish identities. 'Spenser', in his four-hundred year presence in Irish literature and culture, has moved from functioning as one of many English chroniclers and essayists on Ireland and as a lauded poet to a representative figure who stands in and, true to allegory's roots, speaks otherwise – of the past, of the colonial relationship, and of the shifting perception of that colonial relationship in the present. In this recent versioning of Spenser, we find Spenser still speaking otherwise, still functioning allegorically, but simultaneously returned to himself, a lone poet, for whom Ireland is indeed a Den of Errour.

Spenser, I have suggested, functions as a revealing case study of transhistorical memory since his presence in Irish literature is of such duration. Of course, Spenser is also functioning in the realm of transcultural memory, with his literary legacy stretching across at least two national spaces. As the Republic of Ireland, England, and Northern Ireland enter into a new and unknown stage of relations following Britain's 'Brexit' vote in June 2016, we face further questions about how both transhistorial and transcultural memory will function on these islands. While McGuinness's play seemed in some sense to signal a reconciliation of memory and a literal performance of it, it is not clear, in the new political climate, how the intertwined histories of the three geographical spaces will be negotiated. Spenser might, even after four hundred years, find himself called upon yet again to allegorically represent the past and speak to the present.

NOTES

1. See, for instance, Ciaran Brady, 'Spenser's Irish Crisis: Humanism and Experience in the 1590s', *Past and Present* 111 (May 1986), 17–49; Anne Fogarty, 'The Colonization of Language: Narrative Strategies in *A View of the Present State of Ireland* and *The Faerie Queene*, Book VI', in *Spenser and Ireland: An Interdisciplinary Perspective*, ed. by Patricia Coughlan (Cork: Cork University Press, 1989), pp.75–108; Richard McCabe, 'The Fate of Irena: Spenser and Political Violence', in Patricia Coughlan, ed., *Spenser and Ireland*, pp.109–25; Clare Carroll, 'The Construction of Gender and the Cultural and Political Other in *The Faerie Queene* and *A View of the Present State of Ireland*: the critics, the context, and the case of Radigund', in *Criticism* Vol. XXXII, 2 (1990), 163–192; Richard Rambuss, *Spenser's Secret Career* (Cambridge: Cambridge University Press, 1993); Andrew Hadfield, *Edmund Spenser's Irish Experience: Wilde Fruit and Salvage Soyl* (Oxford: Clarendon Press, 1997); Willey Maley, *Salvaging Spenser: Colonialism, Culture and Identity* (London: Macmillan, 1997); David Gardiner, *Befitting Emblems of Adversity: A Modern Irish View of Edmund Spenser from W.B. Yeats to the Present* (Omaha, Nebraska: Creighton University Press, 2001); Richard McCabe, *Spenser's Monstrous Regiment: Elizabethan Ireland and the Poetics of Difference* (Oxford: Oxford University Press, 2002).
2. A notable exception is Andrew Hadfield's biography, *Edmund Spenser: A Life* (Oxford: Oxford University Press, 2012), and the Fifth International Spenser Society conference, 'The Place of Spenser/ Spenser's Places', which took place at Dublin Castle 18–20 June 2015.
3. Liedeke Plate and H.G. Els Rose, 'Rewriting, a Literary Concept for the Study of Cultural Memory: Towards a Transhistorical Approach to Cultural Remembrance', *Neophilologus* 97 (2013), p.613.
4. I have used this phrase in 'Spenser's Trace', *New Hibernia Review* 12.1 (2008), to describe the way in which a story of Spenser extends itself across time.
5. Bernadette Cunningham, *The World of Geoffrey Keating* (Dublin: Four Courts Press, 2004), p.59.
6. Cunningham, p.181.
7. Cunningham, p.86.
8. Cunningham, p.14.
9. Robert Welch, ed., *The Oxford Companion to Irish Literature* (Oxford: Oxford University Press, 1996), p.52.

10. Geoffrey Keating, *Foras Feasa ar Éirinn* (Dublin: Irish Texts Society, 1902), Volume I, p.31.
11. J.T. Leerssen, *Mere Irish and Fíor-Ghael* (Cork: Cork University Press, 1996), p.321.
12. Peter Walsh, *A Prospect of the State of Ireland From the Year of the World 1756 to the Year of Christ 1652* (London, 1682), p.8.
13. Walsh, p.405.
14. Walsh, p.405.
15. Sarah Butler, *Irish Tales, or, instructive histories for the happy conduct of life* (London: E. Curll and J. Hooke, 1714), Preface, n.p.
16. Butler, Preface, n.p.
17. Maria Edgeworth, *Castle Rackrent: A Norton Critical Edition*, ed. by Ryan Twomey (London: W.W. Norton & Co., 2004), p.11.
18. On 'postmemory', see Marianne Hirsch, *Family Frames: Photography, Narrative, and Postmemory* (Cambridge, Massachusetts: Harvard University Press, 1997).
19. There are two others: the second cites Wordsworth's 'The Solitary Reaper' in which the speaker listens to a 'Highland lass' singing; the last is a Fenian poem spoken by Oisin.
20. George Sigerson, *Bards of the Gael and Gall* (London: T. Fisher Unwin, 1907), n.p..
21. On Yeats and Spenser, see Oona Frawley, *Irish Pastoral* (Dublin: Irish Academic Press, 2004); Oona Frawley, '"Who's He When He's at Home?" Spenser and Irishness', in *Affecting Irishness*, ed. by J. Byrne et. al. (Bern: Peter Lang, 2009); Jane Grogan, 'Spenser's Lost Children', *Spenser Studies* Vol. XXVIII (2013), 1–54.
22. On poets' treatment of Spenser, see David Gardiner, *Befitting Emblems of Adversity: A Modern View of Edmund Spenser from WB Yeats to the Present* (New York: Fordham University Press, 2001), and Grogan, 'Spenser's Lost Children'.
23. Tales of 'mad Sweeney' thought to have been composed between the 12–15th centuries and written down in the 17th and 18th century were published as *Buile Suibhne*, ed. by JG O'Keeffe (Dublin: Irish Texts Society Volume 12, 1913). Sweeney was cursed by a priest and, transformed into a bird and, suffering from madness, he subsequently flitted about Ireland uttering poems. As a figure of inspiration who was also placeless and on the edges of society, Sweeney intrigued Heaney enough to publish a translation of *Buile Suibhne*, *Sweeney Astray*, in 1983 (Dublin: Field Day Publications, 1983). He later published a series of poems inhabiting the character of Sweeney as part of *Station Island* (London: Faber and Faber, 1984).
24. Brendan Kennelly, *Cromwell: A Poem* (Eastburn: Bloodaxe Books, 1987 (1983)), p.28.
25. Seamus Heaney, 'Bog Oak', in *Wintering Out* (London: Faber, 1972).
26. McLean, *The Event and its Terrors: Ireland, Famine, Modernity* (Palo Alto: Stanford University Press, 2004).
27. Beiner, 'Making Sense of Memory: coming to terms with conceptualisations of historical remembrance', in *Remembering 1916: The Easter Rising, the Somme, and the Politics of Memory*, ed. by Richard Grayson and Fearghal McGarry (Cambridge: Cambridge University Press, 2016), p.21.
28. Marianne Hirsch has described the effects of the preservations of, among other material artifacts, photographs, and their impact on the resulting cultural memory (see Hirsch, 1997).
29. In fact, postcolonial trauma is a new and exciting realm within memory studies, with Stef Craps arguing that western-derived conceptions of individual traumatic experience cannot be applied wholesale to postcolonial cultures, which not only experience trauma in different ways but also *culturally* rather than strictly individually. See *Postcolonial Witnessing: Trauma Out of Bounds* (London: Palgrave Macmillan, 2013).
30. Heaney, 'North', in *Opened Ground* (London: Faber, 1998).

31. Grogan, p.5.
32. This notion was at the implied backbone of many classic postcolonial texts, from Edward Said's *Culture and Imperialism* (London; Vintage, 1994) to, in the Irish context, Declan Kiberd's *Inventing Ireland* (London: Vintage, 1996).
33. *Ben Jonson's Conversations with William Drummond of Hawthornden*, ed. by R.F. Patterson (London: Blackie and Son Limited, 1923), pp.16–17.
34. The File is a poet figure based on the important medieval Irish bards, whose compositions documented a family's history, and who wielded great power – bards were feared for their ability to satirise and undermine a family's position, and so treated with tremendous respect. See Osborn Bergin, *Irish Bardic Poetry* (Dublin: Dublin Institute for Advanced Studies, 1970).
35. Cuchulain spends time with foster parents who each teach him a different skill, while Finn is similarly fostered and raised by two women warriors, Liath Luachra and Bodhmall.
36. See, for instance, T. Charles-Edwards, *Early Irish and Welsh Kinship* (Oxford: Oxford University Press, 1993).
37. Edmund Spenser, *The Faerie Queene* (London: Penguin, 2003), 2.2.1.
38. Spenser, 6.4.38.
39. The Northern Irish charity, Healing Through Remembering, was established in 2001 following a report composed by the head of the South African Truth and Reconciliation Commission. The charity's goal is to promote reconciliation through shared acknowledgement and remembrance.
40. Grogan, p.37.

Marguérite Corporaal

Moving towards Multidirectionality: Famine Memory, Migration and the Slavery Past in Fiction, 1860–1890

Current debates on the dynamics of memory over time and space have increasingly engaged with the ways in which the past is reconfigured under conditions of emigration and transcultural contact. Thus, Andreas Huyssen's groundbreaking scholarship on perceptions of a shared cultural past by migrant communities foregrounds the question whether diaspora communities, with a 'tenuous and often threatened status within the majority culture' that are moreover subject to 'stereotyping of otherness combined with ... exclusionary mechanisms' tend to 'create a unified or even mythic memory of the lost homeland'.[1] Susannah Radstone points to the influence of nostalgia on the recollections of migrant communities, wondering how their experiences of 'social change and upheaval' may have affected the memories they transfer to their new host societies.[2] More recently, Aleida Assmann and Sebastian Conrad have raised the issue of what happens to memories which are transferred to 'new social constellations and political contexts', when migrants carry their heritage and pasts with them to their receiving countries and when transcultural networks that connect home and host land subsequently emerge.[3]

While these significant contributions to memory studies have mainly examined how memories move in relation to contexts of emigration, scholars today also tend to investigate the transnational transmission and transformation of memory through the lens of transcultural contacts in a broader sense. The essay collection *The Transcultural Turn* is such an example of this new direction in transcultural memory studies, for its editors, Lucy Bond and Jessica Rapson, seek to define the notion of transcultural memory as 'the travelling of memory *within* and *between* national, ethnic and religious collectives',[4] thereby applying a scope to memory transfer that moves beyond the context of emigration. Similarly, Astrid Erll's

Irish University Review 47.1 (2017): 48–61
DOI: 10.3366/iur.2017.0256
© Edinburgh University Press
www.euppublishing.com/iur

contribution to the recently published volume *Transcultural Memory* exposes the traditional 'container-culture approach' in memory research as 'epistemologically flawed', because it erroneously ties memory to 'clear-cut territories and social formations.' Espousing the 'transcultural turn', Erll endorses the fluidity and transportability of 'travelling' memory *'across* ... and also *beyond* cultures'.[5]

The increased attention for processes of recollection as transcultural phenomena nevertheless leaves many territories open for further examination. One such issue that requires more profound research and that will be central to this article is the ways in which memories that have migrated to different cultural communities develop when they interact with the cultural legacies of other communities. What patterns emerge during the encounter between different mnemoscapes; for example, when the cultural memories of migrants interact with the memory cultures of communities in the country of settlement? This question will be addressed by an analysis of fiction written about Ireland's Great Famine (1845–50) – a bleak period marked by mass-starvation, caused by a pervasive potato disease, and resulting in the wide-scale eviction of impoverished tenants,[6] as well as mass emigration.[7] Fiction that remembers Ireland's Great Famine and which was written between 1854 and 1890 provides an interesting case study to explore questions about the ways in which 'travelling' memories intersect with sociocultural issues as well as mnemonic repertoires of other communities, for various reasons. Many novels and short stories that recollected the Famine were written and published in North-America, the continent where the largest percentage of emigrants of the Famine generation settled. These early works of Famine fiction frequently testify to the dynamic transfers between the memories of migrants and those of host societies, in that their reconfigurations of the Famine past interact with memories of the Middle Passage and current as well as past debates on slavery in the American South.

Following John Mitchel's comparative discussion of slavery and the conditions of Ireland's Famine-stricken peasantry in *Jail Journal* (1854), some of these novels and stories evoke analogies between the Famine and the plight of Afro-American plantation slaves to critique the land system in Ireland in the present. Often, these Famine narratives contain intertextual allusions to Harriet Beecher Stowe's novel *Uncle Tom's Cabin* (1852). Furthermore, recollections of the transatlantic crossing undertaken by Famine migrants on board the so-called coffin ships are often placed in the context of slaves that were transported from Africa to North-America. Interestingly, these references to the slavery past do not only figure in diaspora Famine fiction, but also in novels written in Ireland, thereby testifying to the transcultural publishing infrastructures in which many of these texts emerged in print, as well as the transcultural constellations in which Famine memory circulated.

Discussing a wide range of Famine narratives, written at home and in North America, in which memories of Ireland's bleak past overlap and intersect with Afro-American legacies, this article will moreover engage with recent theoretical frameworks concerning the dynamics of memory across cultural communities. Michael Rothberg's seminal study *Multidirectional Memory* considers the public sphere 'as a malleable discursive space in which groups do not simply articulate established positions but actually come into being through their dialogical interactions with others'. According to Rothberg, we should move beyond the idea of 'competitive memory' in which 'already-established groups engage in a life-and-death struggle', to account for the complexity of 'dynamic transfers that take place between diverse places and times during the act of remembrance' and that are manifested in translations of one 'figure of memory' into the images and discourses of another remembrance.[8] A similar suggestion has recently been made by Charlotte McIvor who employs the term 'analogy' to point to comparisons made between memories belonging to different pasts, different settings and different cultural groups, as a strategy to assert 'historical duty'.[9] The following analyses will assess this terminology in connection to early literary Famine texts.

'BLACK STARVATION': DEBATES ON THE FAMINE AND SLAVERY

The Great Famine triggered controversy about the condition of the Irish rural poor and the responsibility of the landed class that was believed to be responsible for their well-being. During the Famine years and their aftermath, several treatises were printed which took issue with the frequent absenteism of landlords and accused them and their agents of unfair treatment and even oppression of their tenantry, who were often evicted from their homes when they could no longer pay the rent or when the profit-seeking landlord decided to convert acres into pasture.[10] Thus, the author of *What Have the Whigs Done for Ireland?* (1847) complains about the 'improvidence' and 'reckless and extravagant habits' of the gentry which results in 'their systematic inattention to the duties' they owe to their starving and impoverished tenants.[11] In the same year, Rigby Watson in a letter to Prime Minister Lord John Russell accused the Ascendancy of 'imprudence' and overlooking that 'property has its duties as well as rights'.[12] C.A Rawlins'poem *The Famine in Ireland* (1847) states that those 'whose castles proudly crest the vale' forget that they are 'parents on a larger scale',[13] and F.B. Ryan's poem *The Spirit's Lament, or the Wrongs of Ireland* (1847) exposes the average landlord as a gentleman who 'finds other use for his gold/Than feeding the hungry or helping the old'.[14]

Ryan's poem not only fulminates against the landed class, but also against the British crown, stating that under its imperial rule Ireland is suffering from '[t]he festering imprints of slavery's band'.[15] This idea of Ireland's bondage to England, as well as the rural labourer's enslavement to his landlord, featured frequently in writings about and during the Famine, and often analogies were drawn between the plight of the cottier and the dire fate of the African-American or Caribbean plantation slave. For example, Thomas Doolan's *Practical Suggestions on the Improvement of the Present Condition of the Peasantry of Ireland* (1847) likens the extensive mortality and destitution in Ireland with the past outrages 'in the West Indian and other colonies ... where slavery reared its black front.'[16] These texts, which argued for a better treatment of the Irish peasant, would not necessarily convey sympathy for the suffering of the slaves, especially those in the American South. Well-known examples are the writings of John Mitchel, *Jail Journal* (1854) and *The Last Conquest of Ireland (Perhaps)* (1861), which, in the aftermath of the Famine, argued that it was 'better to be the slave of a merciful master and just man' than 'a serf to an Irish land appropriator'.[17] Mitchel, who himself was unsympathetic to the Abolitionist movement, and in favour of ownership of slaves in the American South,[18] pointed to the unfairness of the plight of a white race 'of the highest and purest blood and breed of men', living, in his view, in greater distress than the black plantation slaves.[19] In a similar vein, the poem 'Famine and Exportation' that appeared in *The Boston Pilot* on 10 January 1846 invokes the image of the 'black Virginian slaves' who are '[b]ound and bruised with thongs and staves' to intimate that their treatment is even better in comparison with the ways in which the famishing Irish are abused by their English 'masters'. While the slaves are at least fed, England abandons the subjugated Irish to '[b]lack starvation'.[20]

Why were these comparisons between the starving Irish peasant and the plantation slave so prevalent? And how can we account for the fact that, especially in texts written in the American context, these common analogies are often rooted in competitive claims for social improvement that are legitimised by ethnicity? An explanation lies in the racialisation of the Irish both in Britain and North America. Edward G. Lengel's *The Irish Though British Eyes* points out that in the mid-nineteenth century the Irish were perceived by the British as racially other, hence black.[21] This point is underscored by David Lloyd's observation that the Irish were ethnically compared to the former West Indian slaves as a similarly regressive tribe with the dangerous potential for unsettling Britain's supremacy – a conclusion he derives from, amongst others, Thomas Carlyle's portrayal of the Irish as white negroes in his novel *Sartor Resartus* (1836), as well as John Stuart Mill's expressive concern in *England and Ireland* (1867) that both the Irish cottier and the black slave 'lacked the motivation required for sustained and improving labor'.[22] While analogies between the Irish peasantry and black slaves may seem evident at first glance, they were also highly problematic in light of the fact that these comparisons were often imbued with rhetoric that legitimised imperial superiority.

The fact that slavery was an ongoing source of income in the American South at the time of the Great Famine evoked analogies between the conditions of the black plantation labourers and Ireland's suffering tenantry. However, at the same time, identification of the Famine-stricken Irish with the exploited Afro American slaves was also complicated by the ethnic bias towards the Catholic Irish newcomers. Studies by, amongst others, David Roediger and Noel Ignatiev show that, well into the era of post- Civil War Reconstruction, the readiness of Irish immigrants to take on underpaid work resulted in their caricaturization as a breed racially inferior to the Anglo-Saxon Caucasian Americans and similar to Afro Americans.[23] Their claims are illustrated by cartoons such as Thomas Nast's 'The Ignorant Vote', published in *Harper's Weekly* on 9 December 1876, which puts the Irish and the American blacks on a par as threats to America's political stability. Faced with racial stigmatisation, many American Irish therefore sought to dissociate themselves from their coloured fellow citizens: in spite of Daniel O'Connell's ardent anti-slavery speeches, many of his supporters in the New World 'took an anti-abolitionist stance'.[24]

'LASHED TO MADNESS BY THOSE MERCILESS LEGREES': MULTIDIRECTIONAL FAMINE MEMORY IN FICTION

In view of the ethnic stereotyping in both Britain and North America, which systematically categorized the Irish among the lowest ethnic classes, it appears indeed, as Peter O'Neill and David Lloyd have suggested, naive to assume that 'the Irish should have identified with another people who were undergoing dispossession, exploitation or racism—or, indeed, shown solidarity with oppressed people in general'.[25] Nonetheless, literary recollections of the Great Famine written on both sides of the Atlantic between 1860 and 1890 go back to the similarities that were displayed between black slaves and Irish tenants in public discourse during the Famine years, and they strongly engage with the recent experiences and cultural memories of slavery in the Americas and Indies, to evoke further sympathy for the malfunctioning of England's colonial administration. By using what McIvor calls the mnemonic strategy of 'analogy',[26] these works of fiction appear to summon support for ongoing, post-Famine struggles between tenantry and landlords in Ireland, in a period covering national war over abolition as well as the integration of liberated slaves in the reconstructed union. Tapping into cultural memories of slavery, as embodied, amongst others, by Harriet Beecher Stowe's novel, these narratives evoke parallels between both mnemonic legacies, probably in order to foreground the 'historical duty' of ending the oppression of the Irish cottiers at a time when abolition was or had been high on the political agenda.

One Famine novel is Allen Clington's *Frank O'Donnell* (1861), which was initially published for the Irish market by James Duffy at the onset of the American Civil War (1860–65), but later serialized in *The Pilot* from January till July 1863, as well as reissued under the title *The O'Donnells of Glen Cottage* for American and Canadian markets by D. and J. Sadlier in 1874. This text draws explicit parallels between the situation of Ireland's tenantry and the cruelty inflicted upon slaves. Clington's text emphasises the 'unchristian conduct of Irish landlords' such as Lord Clearall 'in laying waste the country, in levelling the poor man's cabin, and sending him and his family to a pauper's grave', solely for the purpose of exploiting the mineral resources of the soil.[27] While the tenantry are 'lying prostrate with fever and famine', Clearall shows no compassion with them: he continues his campaign of violent evictions, and forces the poor to earn food by '[b]reaking stones ... in the middle of a severe winter ... from morning until night', while their bodies are 'half naked, and the rain and snow and sleet pouring upon them'.[28]

In one of the many digressions on the part of the omniscient narrator, this suffering during the Famine is not only shown to form a continuum with the present harsh conditions of the tenantry, so that memory is transgenerationally evoked to challenge present societal wrongs: in a footnote, the narrator comments on the tenant rights which have not greatly improved since the Famine, judging 'from the numerous evictions and agrarian crimes still perpetuated there'.[29] The novel also moves Famine memory into the transnational debate of slavery at several stages: a discussion about the 'boasted laws of England' between the main protagonist, farmer's son Frank O'Donnell and Mr Maher, turns to '[t]he slaves of America', which, in Frank's view 'are a thousand times better off than the Irish serfs', because their master has an interest in them. When Maher refutes this point, because 'parents and children' are separated among the American slaves, Frank counters this by suggesting that 'stern necessity compels Irish families to separate as much as the slaves', due to the laws of poorhouses.[30]

The scene is imbued with analogy, primarily to make an equally strong case for the Irish poor as subjects of political interest, that are nevertheless often neglected in contemporary debates. As such, the passage implicitly conveys a sense of 'historical duty'[31] towards its present-day audiences who, if sympathising with the abolitionist cause, should also join the campaign for tenant rights.

Similar analogies between the fate of the Irish rural labourer during and after the Famine and black slaves recur in fiction from later dates. While *Frank O'Donnell* incorporates these mnemonic analogies in semi-political extrapolations that are not strictly embedded in plot development, Charles Joseph Kickham's *Sally Cavanagh* (1869) does so through the representation of landlord Oliver Grindem's treatment of the eponymous heroine. Published in Dublin, and dedicated to one of the key figures in the Irish Republican Brotherhood, John O'Leary, the novel depicts Grindem as a despicable tyrant who has Sally and her starving infants removed from their cabin, because they refuse to convert to Protestantism and Sally 'would not endanger the faith of her children, even to save their lives'.[32] Sent to the poorhouse and separated from her young children, who all succumb to fever and famine, Sally loses her mind, escapes from the asylum, and looks for shelter in an old ruin of an abbey. The passage which describes how Grindem attempts to chase Sally, the 'dangerous lunatic', away from these devotional premises, hints at cultural memories of slavery. Looking quite ferocious himself, ironically, with 'red glassy eyes' that 'glared hideously' in the middle of his deadly pale face, Grindem violently trashes Sally 'with the butt end of his whip' and strikes her in the face.[33] Grindem's cruelty is reminiscent of former slave owners in the West Indies or on the plantations in the American South, who would frequently lash their slaves; a reading which seems justified in light of the fact that, earlier on in the narrative, Sally's husband Connor Shea feels so hunted down by this demanding landlord that he compares himself to a 'galley slave' wearing 'the flesh off my bones' in his toil.[34] In the novel, then, Famine memory appears to overlap and intersect with recollections of transatlantic slavery, thereby transforming into what Rothberg would call 'multidirectional memory'.[35]

The massive transatlantic emigration of Irish during the Great Famine meant that recollections of this dire event in Ireland's history were literally relocated to different social settings and communities, and there became further modified by reconfigured cultural memories that were already circulating through their new host society. The fact that the campaign for the liberation and emancipation of slaves was concurrent with the settlement of a flood of Irish newcomers to the United States, must certainly have impacted the interaction between

Famine memory and the realities as well as past legacies of black slavery. This interaction is not exclusive to texts written in the North-American diaspora, as the novels by Clington and Kickham reveal. This demonstrates that emigration generates transnational spaces 'shared by both immigrants and natives'[36] in which memories freely flow between the native country and the new homeland and transcend national borders.

This fluidity of memory is, in the case of literature, further manifested by the ways in which texts that are important carriers of Famine memory,[37] travelled across communities on both sides of the Atlantic, through various republications. We have seen that *Frank O'Donnell* was issued for readerships in Ireland and the United States. Kickham's *Sally Cavanagh* was first serialised in *The Hibernian* in 1864 and subsequently in *The Irish American* from March 1866 onward; the narrative was then issued in book form in Dublin by W.B. Kelly in 1869, and serialised in *The Pilot* in the late summer and autumn of the same year. There are many more examples that could be cited to show the ways in which texts about the Famine were not limited to a certain audience, espcially also because many North-American periodicals tended to reprint articles and narratives from the Irish press and vice versa; a circulation that was expedited by 'the technology of mass production' and cheaper mass distribution, as Richard Gray observes.[38] In other words, Famine memory, as transferred by fiction, operated in an essentially transnational infrastructure that stimulated intersections with other memory cultures.

While this is the case, it must be noted that Famine memory is especially infused with cultural recollections of African American slavery in narratives written and exclusively published in North America. An example is *Scenes and Incidents in Irish Life* (1884) by Irish-Canadian writer F.H.Clayton, a novel which laments the transplantation during the Famine of an old stock of debt-ridden landlords[39] by a new class of

> English speculators, tradesmen, shopkeepers, weavers and innkeepers, who come over from time to time to gather the pounds of flesh from the bodies of the poor hardworking Irishmen and women, widows and orphans, in exorbitant rents, which if not paid ejection follows, thereby destroying effectually all feeling of security and idea of permanency.[40]

Published almost twenty years after the abolition of slavery in the United States, Clayton's novel evokes an analogy between the deprived Irish poor in both Famine and post-Famine Ireland and the past suffering of black slaves, clearly with the purpose of drawing public attention to the often neglected issue of Ireland's Land Question. The narrator states that 'the Irish poor have experienced more pain' than 'the negroes of the southern plantations', but that '[t]he negroe [sic] was commiserated, but Ireland's population was not'.[41] The novel thus explicitly connects Ireland's past and present with American cultural memory, thereby trying to convince its readers that a 'historical duty' to the distress of the Irish peasantry is called for.[42] At the same time, Clayton's novel points to the hypocrisy of England which 'boasted of setting free the slaves of her West Indian possessions', but keeps the Irish, 'a nobler race, far nearer to the Throne, if not to the heart of it' in imperial fetters.[43] The suggestion that the Irish tenantry are enslaved by their landlords runs parallel to the idea that Ireland is in bondage on an imperial level, to Britain, which has a long history of colonial slavery.

'LOOK AT THIS MRS. STOWE': INTERTEXTUALITY AND MULTIDIRECTIONAL MEMORY

In a similar vein, Dillon O'Brien's Famine novel *The Dalys of Dalystown* (1866), published in the immediate aftermath of the American Civil War, borrows from abolitionist discourses to expose England's abuse of Irish agricultural labourers. Through intertextual references to Harriet Beecher Stowe's international bestseller *Uncle Tom's Cabin* (1852), the narrator emphasizes the 'Maudline' hypocrisy of the English. They were wont, he states, to 'weep over slavery in the South' of America, but simultaneously ignore the slavery in their own colony in which they are implicated: 'the lot of the Irish peasant, robbed, enslaved, lashed to madness by those merciless Legrees', the landlords, whose power is 'spawned and nursed by your English laws'.[44] O'Brien's novel clearly responds to recent developments in American society, employing the legacy of American abolitionism to outline a picture of Britain's enslavement of the Irish lower classes, and thereby exemplifying how the heritage that migrants carry with them can become re-articulated through these cultural legacies and the discourses of the host society. At the same time, O'Brien's text bears witness to processes of memory transfer that are implicated by intertextuality: the reference to the landlords as 'merciless Legrees' is an explicit reference to the cruel and violent slave master that Stowe's protagonist is forced to work for. As Renate Lachmann maintains, the memory of a text lies in its intertextuality:[45] it is a literary device which disseminates cultural recollections across generations and spaces, to audiences for whom certain pasts are only 'prosthetic', indirectly experienced forms of memory.[46] I would like to expand upon this valid notion by suggesting that intertextuality is a process which enhances memory's multidirectionality, because it merges and recontextualises various forms of memory.

Interestingly, similar intertextual, multidirectional allusions to *Uncle Tom's Cabin* can be found in several Famine novels, including those published in England or Ireland. Thus, *Frank O'Donnell* likens the Irish tenantry's cirxumstances to that of slavery, stating that while in Ireland there may be 'some good, kind masters, such as St. Clair', there is sufficient plea against the present system because there are also many 'white slaves of Ireland' left 'at the mercy of men as cruel and hardened as the brutal planter, Legree'. While these landlords may not whip their tenants, they still 'manage to kill the body by a slow process of petty persecution, by energies crushed', in a seemingly more civilised, but not less cruel form of coercion.[47] William C. Upton's novel *Uncle Pat's Cabin* (1882), which was initially published in Dublin by McGill, but later reissued in an edition for the American market in 1914 after its author had emigrated to New York, also clearly resonates with Stowe's *Uncle Tom's Cabin*. Depicting a tenant farmer who has to bear with the hardships he suffers through his landlord and agent, during and after the Famine, at the time of the Land Wars, the title suggests that we should interpret Pat's plight as analogous to that of Stowe's slave protagonist. This analogy is further emphasised by the character of Dr O'Leary who declares to Father O'Mahony: 'I have seen the negro slave of the Southern States of America whipped at the post; I have seen him chained like a wild beast; I have seen him guarded like a criminal; I have seen him hunted down with bloodhounds, but I fearlessly assert, from all I have studied of the treatment the Irish agricultural labourers are subjected to, they are in as hapless a state as were the slaves of America'.[48] This Dr O'Leary, as a traveller between two continents, personifies the encounter between and even conflation of different cultural memories, as a natural process of movement across borders.

As becomes clear from the above discussions, Famine fiction mainly develops analogies between the Irish tenant and the plantation slave as land labourers that have to toil away for the profit of their inconsiderate masters. The parallel between the Irish Famine emigrant, who had to survive his transatlantic journey on board the so-called coffin ship, notorious for the high death toll among passengers,[49] and the many slaves who lost their lives during transportation across the Middle Passage would be evident, as Robert Whyte's fictional autobiographical account, *The Ocean's Plague* (1848) intimates: '[t]he worse horrors of that slave-trade which it is the boast or the ambition of this empire to suppress, at any cost, have been reenacted in the flight of British subjects from their native shores'.[50] However, in Famine fiction this comparison is, surprisingly, hardly ever made.

Reginald Tierney's Famine novel, *The Struggles of Dick Massey* (1861) is an exception. The novel contains references to Stowe and her work, likening the common landlord to a 'Simon Legree',[51] stating that 'for the one slave that has been lashed to death by his master, there have been a hundred Irishmen drowned by their landlords',[52] and even addressing Stowe to direct her attention to the memory of the Irish Famine emigrants whose miserable conditions on the coffin ships may supply harrowing material for another bestseller:

> Mrs. Stowe; quail not; you will not, I am certain, because you are good and gentle, and therefore marvellously strong. You need all your heroism now, for this is a scene upon which devils would rather not gaze. Lo, where are we! Down in file steerage of a plaguestricken ship, that is tossed like a nut-shell on the angry billows. Dead and dying men, women, and, alas! little children, are wallowing around in filth and wretchedness.[53]

Although this passage does not mention the Middle Passage explicitly, it reverberates with cultural memories of loss, death, and disease associated with slave transportation. This single text in which the Green and Black Atlantic are implicitly compared, constitutes a node of multidirectional memory notably absent from other early Famine fiction – a fact that may perhaps be explained by Irish-American immigrants' ambition to be classified as white, an ambition that made an analogy between the Irish emigrant passengers as new American citizens and the African Americans inconvenient.

By drawing a parallel between Irish suffering during (and after) the Famine and slavery, Tierney's novel transforms the coffin ship into a site of transition which figuratively transports cultural recollections of the motherland across the Atlantic and by so doing connects the traumatic Famine past with a troublesome past with present implications over which the American republic was divided. Famine fiction, inextricably connected as it was to contexts of transnational relocation, displays the complex ways in which memory moves, both transgenerationally as well as across communities. Fusing two significant painful cultural memories, these literary texts not only created connections between different episodes in history, but also bonds between audiences at home and in diaspora communities, and, even more significantly, between reading communities that were not necessarily bound by shared, though similar, memories. As such, early Famine fiction presents an interesting early case study that legitimises a transnational outlook on memory, and that also encourages Irish studies to pursue its present transcultural movements.

ACKNOWLEDGEMENTS

The research for this article was financed by an ERC Starter Grant [Grant agreement no. 262898-FAMINE]. The author would like to thank Lindsay Janssen for directing her attention to F.H. Clayton's *Scenes and Incidents in Irish Life*.

NOTES

1. Andreas Huyssen, 'Diaspora and Nation: Migration into Other Pasts', *New German Critique* 88 (2003), 149–50.

2. Susannah Radstone, *The Sexual Politics of Time: Confession, Nostalgia, Memory* (London: Routledge, 2007), p.115.

3. Aleida Assmann and Sebastian Conrad, 'Introduction', in *Memory in a Global Age: Discourses, Practices and Trajectories*, ed. by Aleida Assmann and Sebastian Conrad (Basingstoke: Palgrave Macmillan, 2010), p.2.

4. Lucy Bond and Jessica Rapson, 'Introduction', in *The Transcultural Turn: Interrogating Memory Between and Beyond Borders*, ed. by Lucy Bond and Jessica Rapson (Berlin: De Gruyter, 2014), p.19.

5. Astrid Erll, 'Travelling Memory', in *Transcultural Memory*, ed. by Rick Crownshaw (London: Routledge, 2014), pp.20–24.

6. See, amongst others, Christine Kinealy, *This Great Calamity: The Irish Famine, 1845–52* (Dublin: Gill and Macmillan, 1994); James S. Donnelly Jr., *The Great Irish Potato Famine* (Stroud: Sutton Publishing, 2003); and Peter Gray, *Famine, Land and Politics: British Government and Irish Society, 1843–50* (Dublin: Irish Academic Press, 1999).

7. See, for example, Charles Fanning, *Exiles of Erin: Nineteenth-Century Irish-American Fiction* (Notre Dame, ID: University of Notre Dame Press, 1987); Kerby Miller, *Emigrants and Exiles: Ireland and the Irish Exodus to North America* (Oxford: Oxford University Press, 1985); Donald MacKay, *Flight from Famine: The Coming of the Irish to Canada* (Toronto: Natural Heritage Books, 1991); Kevin Kenny, *The American Irish: A History* (London: Longman, 2000); and Donald MacRaild, *The Irish Diaspora in Britain, 1750–1939* (Basingstoke: Palgrave Macmillan, 2010).

8. Michael Rothberg, *Multidirectional Memory: Remembering the Holocaust in the Age of Decolonization* (Stanford: Stanford University Press, 2009), pp.5, 11.

9. Charlotte McIvor, 'Historical Duty, Palimpsestic Time and Migration in the Decade of Centenaries', *Irish Studies Review* 24.1 (2016), 49–66.

10. David S. Jones, 'The Transfer of Land and the Emergence of the Graziers during the Famine Period', *The Great Famine and the Irish Diaspora in America*, ed. by Arthur Gribben (Boston: University of Massachusetts Press, 1999), p.93.

11. A Barrister, *What Have the Whigs Done for Ireland? Or the English Whigs and the Irish Famine.* (Dublin: Edward J. Millihen, 1851), p.38.

12. Rigby Wason Esq., *Letter to the Right Honorable Lord John Russell, M.P.* (Edinburgh: W. F.Watson, 1847), p.6.

13. C.A Rawlins, *The Famine in Ireland; a Poem* (London: Joseph Masters, 1847), p.15.

14. F.B.Ryan, *The Spirit's Lament, or the Wrongs of Ireland* (Montreal: n.p., 1847), p.31.

15. Ryan, p. 10.

16. Thomas Doolan, *Practical Suggestions on the Improvement of the Present Condition of the Peasantry of Ireland* (London: George Barclay, 1847), pp.9–10.

17. See John Mitchel, *Jail Journal; or, Five Years in British Prisons* (New York: Office of 'The Citizen', 1854), p.170

18. Bryan P. McGovern, *John Mitchel: Irish Nationalist; Southern Seccesionist* (Knoxville, TN: University of Tennessee Press, 2009), p.150. See also chapter three of Christine

Kinealy, *Daniel O'Connell and the Anti-Slavery Movement: 'The Saddest People the Sun Sees'* (New York: Routledge, 2015).

19. See Christine Kinealy, *Repeal and Revolution: 1848 in Ireland* (Manchester: Manchester University Press, 2009), p.257; see also McGovern, *John Mitchel*, pp.126–129 and 136–137; and Peter O'Neill, 'Memory and John Mitchel's Appropriation of the Slave Narrative', *Atlantic Studies* 11.3 (2014), 321–43.

20. 'Famine and Exportation', *The Boston Pilot*, 10 January 1846.

21. Edward Lengel, *The Irish Through British Eyes: Perceptions of Ireland in the Famine* (Westport, CT: Praeger, 2002), p.3.

22. David Lloyd, 'Black Irish, Irish Whiteness and Atlantic State Formation', in *The Black and Green Atlantic: Cross-Currents in the African and Irish Diasporas*, ed. by David Lloyd and Peter O'Neill (Basingstoke: Palgrave Macmillan, 2009), p.10.

23. See David Roediger, *The Wages of Whiteness: Race and the Making of the American Working Class* (London: Verso, 1999); and Noel Ignatiev, *How the Irish Became White* (New York: Routledge, 1996).

24. Angela Murphy, *American Slavery: Abolition, Immigrant Citizenship, and the Transatlantic Movement for Irish Identity* (Baton Rouge, LS: Louisiana State University Press, 2010), p.3.

25. Peter O'Neill and David Lloyd, 'The Black and Green Atlantic: An Introduction', in Lloyd and O'Neill, p.xvii.

26. McIvor, 'Historical Duty', p.49.

27. Allen Clington, *Frank O'Donnell* (Dublin and London: James Duffy, 1861), p.187.

28. Clington, pp.274, 300.

29. Clington, p.189.

30. Clington, p.300.

31. McIvor, 'Historical Duty', p.49.

32. Charles Joseph Kickham, *Sally Cavanagh; or the Untenanted Graves of Tipperary* (Dublin: J.J. Lalor, 1869, p.152.

33. Kickham, pp.195–96.

34. Kickham, p.16.

35. Rothberg, *Multidirectional Memory*, p.5

36. Thomas Faist, *The Volume and Dynamics of International Migration and Transnational Social Spaces* (Oxford: Oxford University Press, 2000), p.240.

37. For further elaboration upon this function of texts in memory transmission, see Astrid Erll and Ann Rigney, 'Literature and the Production of Cultural Memory: Introduction', *European Journal of English Studies* 10.2 (2006), 111–15; and Ann Rigney, 'Portable Monuments: Literature, Cultural Memory, and the Case of Jeanie Deans', *Poetics Today* 25.2 (2004), 361–96.

38. Richard Gray, *A History of American Literature* (Malden, MA: Blackwell, 2004), p.249. See also David E. Sumner, *The Magazine Century: American Magazines Since 1900* (New York: Peter Lang, 2010).

39. Although of an entirely different proportion and smaller scale, hardship was also suffered by the gentry, especially as many landed families had already become heavily indebted, having upheld a lavish lifestyle in times of economic depression, and, as James Donnelly has observed, 'defective laws ... permitted their accumulation of debts far beyond the value of security'. See Donnelly, *The Great Irish Potato Famine*, p.162. The financial prospects of the gentry received a further blow by the outbreak of the blight: as Thomas Benningham remarked in 1847, 'when the payment of rents has been (and is likely still to be) so difficult' due to the failure of the potato crops, 'the total ruin of many proprietors and occupiers of land must ensue'. See *The Thames, the Shannon and the St. Lawrence, or The Good of Great Britain* (London: Messrs. Fores, 1847), p.iv. For further details on how the burden of Famine

relief affected the incomes of the landed class, and eventually led to the forced sale of many properties during the Encumbered Estates Act of 1848 and changes in proprietorship of land, see Peter Gray (1999).

40. F. H. Clayton ('An Irishman'), *Scenes and Incidents in Irish Life* (Montreal: John Lovell, 1884), pp.172, 92. Lindsay Janssen's PhD dissertation, *Famine Traces*, discusses multidirectional comparisons between the Irish poor's condition and slavery at greater length for Famine fiction in the period 1871–91. See the section 'Multidirectional Suffering: The Irish Slave', pp. 137–47. http://repository. ubn.ru.nl/handle/2066/155659

41. Clayton, p.81.

42. McIvor, 'Historical Duty', p.149.

43. Clayton ('An Irishman'), *Scenes and Incidents in Irish Life*, pp.42–43.

44. Dillon O'Brien, *The Dalys of Dalystown* (St. Paul: Pioneer Printing, 1866), p.57.

45. Renate Lachmann, *Memory and Literature: Intertextuality in Russian Modernism*, trans. by Roy Sellars and AnthonyWall (Minneapolis, MN: University of Minnesota Press, 1997).

46. Alison Landsberg, *Prosthetic Memory: The Transformation of American Remembrance in the Age of Mass Culture* (New York: Columbia University Press, 2004), p.3.

47. Clington, *Frank O'Donnell*, p.199.

48. W.C. Upton, *Uncle Pat's Cabin; Or, Life among the Agricultural Labourers of Ireland* (Dublin: M. H. Gill, 1882), pp.157–58. For a very detailed discussion of slavery in Upton's novel, see Janssen, *Famine Traces*, pp.137–47.

49. Robert Whyte's account of a journey on a coffin ship alleges that '[i]n only ten of the vessels that arrived at Montreal in July' of that year 'out of 4,427 passengers, 804 had died on the passage, and 847 were sick on their arrival'. See Robert Whyte, *The Ocean's Plague; or a Voyage to Quebec in an Irish Emigrant Vessel* (Boston: Coolidge and Wiley, 1848), p.15. See also Marguérite Corporaal and Christopher Cusack, 'Rites of Passage: The Coffin Ship as Site of Immigrants' Identity Formation in Irish and Irish-American Fiction, 1855–1885', *Atlantic Studies* 8.3 (2011), 343–59.

50. Whyte, *The Ocean's Plague*, p.15.

51. Reginald Tierney, *The Struggles of Dick Massey; or The Battles of a Boy* (Dublin: James Duffy, 1860), p.376

52. Tierney, p. 376.

53. Tierney, p.374.

Joseph Lennon

'Dreams that hunger makes': Memories of Hunger in Yeats, Mangan, Speranza, and Irish Folklore

In W.B. Yeats's play *The King's Threshold* (1904), the court poet
Seanchan protests King Guaire's elimination of the hereditary position
of prominence for poets at the King's banquet table by refusing food.
This protest represents an 'old custom' of fasting, which Seanchan
performs on the doorstep, or threshold, of the King.[1] The custom of
fasting on someone was practised when the Brehon laws were in use,
as late as the early seventeenth century and at least as early as
St. Patrick's time when they were codified in accord with ecclesiastical
law. The practice had become an integral part of making a case against
someone else; in principle, one with legal standing in the community
(e.g., not a slave) had to sit on another's doorstep and fast from sun-up
to sun-down to demonstrate the justness of one's suit. The defendant
was required to offer food to the plaintiff, who was required to refuse
the offering in order to move the case forward. One might assume that
many conflicts ended over thresholds with shared food, but certainly
many also must have rejected the proffered hospitality and continued
to fast.

Yeats knew of this practice from translations of legends by Lady
Jane Wilde ('Speranza'), whom he visited as a young man, and from
the play of his friend Edwin Ellis, 'Sancan the Bard' (1895), as Declan
Kiely and others have scrupulously documented.[2] The young Yeats
also knew and admired Lady Wilde's poetry, particularly her famous
poem, 'The Famine Year', which opens her collected *Poems* of 1864.
As a nod to Speranza's nationalist articulations in that poem, Yeats
publicly dubbed Maud Gonne, the most important nationalist woman
in his life, 'the New Speranza.'[3] Yeats frequented Lady Wilde's salon
in London as a young man, and her *Ancient Legends, Mystical Charms
and Superstitions of Ireland* (1887) inspired his own first commercially
successful book, *Irish Fairy Tales* (1892), in which he retold a related

Irish University Review 47.1 (2017): 62–81
DOI: 10.3366/iur.2017.0257
© Edinburgh University Press
www.euppublishing.com/iur

story, 'Seanchan the Bard and the King of the Cats.' Of the Irish poets who had written about hunger, however, it was James Clarence Mangan who most influenced Yeats in style and form; Yeats once described his poetry as 'as near perfection as anything that has ever been written' and referenced one of Mangan's Famine poems, 'Siberia', more often than Mangan's popular poems such as 'Dark Rosaleen'.[4] To represent the Famine, as Yeats did in his aristocratic-leaning play, 'The Countess Cathleen', the young poet drew on 'a West of Ireland folk tale' and peppered it with 'both fantastic and human' imagery inspired by William Carleton's *The Black Prophet* (1846).[5] The resulting play, with its strange bat-like imagery (of both men's ears and souls), differed greatly from the more noble fasting imagery of the later *The King's Threshold*, yet both drew on Ireland's social memory and literary culture.[6]

Linked to travel, pilgrimmage, religion, and tenets of hospitality (and criticisms by unhappy guests), fasting and famine shared associations in many medieval and early modern texts, which were written when hosting and eating with gift-bearing guests were regular expectations.[7] Visionary depictions of hunger – at times overlapping with legal authority – point to how fasts referenced the hospitality custom. For example, the Middle Irish satire *Aislinge Meic Conglinne* interweaves supernatural stories of fasting and feasting with the background threat of famine, which the fasting of the hero staves off.[8] In this vision and Land of Cockaygne tale, a travelling poet, Aníer Meic Conglinne, is inhospitably received and badly fed at a monastery's guesthouse in Munster.[9] When he lampoons it for their lack of welcome, the abuse increases. But as he is whipped, he has a dream vision about how to cure the local king, Cathal Mac Finnguine, from his insatiable feasting. In Mac Finnguine's stomach a demon of gluttony had taken up residence, causing the king to steadily devour the supplies of the countryside. Fasting becomes the hero's manner of combatting the demon of gluttony; he sits with the king but refuses to take the first bite, binding the king to stand on custom and not begin without his guest. Aníer requests mounds of food to be set before them and models fasting for the king, who remains honour-bound to refrain from partaking. Eventually the demon leaps from his hungry gullet and escapes into the air.

Customs and expectations surrounding the offering and refusing of food in Irish texts and in later folkloric accounts provide the context for a study of the visions of hungry voices. This essay surveys experiences of the hungry in order to better understand the widespread reception of the modern hero of hunger, the hunger striker, which Yeats's *The King's Threshold* presaged at its first London performance in 1903. These perspectives, particularly the dreams of the hungry, reveal how social memories of hospitality and starvation challenged and indicted audiences.

In this regard, *An Gorta Mór*, the Famine of 1846–50, is the great touchstone. Following the Famine, representations of hunger implicitly evoked that catastrophe. In texts that remember hunger from the nineteenth and early twentieth centuries, safe narratorial distances usually exist between speakers and the famished, keeping readers and writers at a remove from what David Lloyd has termed, 'the indigent sublime'.[10] The indigent sublime awed, terrified, and held readers in thrall but at a safe distance. Memories of hunger in folklore and imaginative lyric poetry do not evoke the sublime as much as brim with indictment and mourn the collapse of hospitality. As I will discuss, lyrical accounts of the Famine, particularly those of James Clarence Mangan and Speranza, (the pen name then of the Protestant Unionist Jane Elgee, who became Lady Wilde in 1851), evoke the politics of proximity between the urban reader and imagined rural and hungry voices, bringing the reader close to the speaker. In contrast, narrative recollections of famine tend to keep hunger in the third-person and at a distance. Clearly, most Famine victims did not write first-hand accounts of their tribulations. Most representations were written by journalists, travel writers, missionaries, doctors, and local leaders.[11] Nevertheless, stories of cataclysmic hunger entered the repertoires of storytellers and lasted for generations, often becoming entwined with memories of fasting.

The second half of this essay looks to the 1930s, when thousands of stories were taken down during the effort to create the Schools' Collection in the National Folklore Archives. Yeats's *The Countess Kathleen* had been 'founded on a West of Ireland folk tale', but the 1930s efforts asked the listeners to record the tales as they heard them.[12] Memories of hunger inscribed in these tales share themes with earlier literary texts about hunger and (in)hospitality, but they differ from other narrative and historiographic accounts of the Famine. Such narratives offer broad sociological perspectives while these shorter stories focus on specific and local memories. If, at times, they convey common images found in literary culture narrative accounts such as the collapsed cabin, devoid of hospitality, in William Carleton's *The Black Prophet*, they more often describe the experience of witnessing hunger, casting light on hospitality's imperative to feed the hungry.

LYRICAL INDICTMENTS OF HUNGER

Lyrical Famine poems represent hunger and its affective emotions with an immediacy not seen in historiographic accounts. James

Clarence Mangan was well acquainted with hunger, poverty, and visionary states and died of cholera on the streets of Dublin in 1849. Many of his poems examine dreams, both hunger-induced and related to prophecy. One of his first Famine related-poems, 'The Warning Voice', published in *The Nation* in February of 1846 at the outset of the second year of blight, declares that dreams may be all that survive the present generation. Mangan signed the poem, 'J.C.' for James Clarence but also with the unmistakeable allusiveness to Jesus Christ. The poem addresses 'Ye Faithful!—ye Noble!' in the opening line, situating his audience on 'blasted' earth:

> O'er once greenest path,
>   Now blasted and sterile,
>   Its dusk shadows loom –
> It comes with Wrath
>   With Conflict and Peril
>   With Judgment and Doom!
>   . . .
> You have dreamed of an era
>   Of Knowledge, of Truth,
>   And Peace, the *true* glory.
> Was this a chimera?
>   Not so! – but the childhood and youth
>   Of our days will grow hoary
> Before such a marvel shall burst on their sight!
>   On *you* its beams glow not –
>   For *you* its flowers blow not![13]

Addressed to the dying, the beams and flowers of the dreamed era will exist for a later generation, the poem claims. Melissa Fegan has written that the poem, published 'long before the second failure [of the potato crop] made deaths almost inevitable', is 'terrifyingly prescient'.[14] The form of the poem – a dialogue with those dying – pushes the intensity of the message upon the reader, the subtextual 'you' addressed in the poem. The prophetic voice of the poem speaks to Famine victims, who do not have voices themselves in the poem. Yet they have a presence unlike other accounts.

As the blight returned in the spring of 1846, a long speech by Daniel O'Connell to the Loyal National Repeal Association was published in the 18 April issue of *The Nation*. In it, 'the Liberator' recounts how he tried to convince Parliament of the existence of the Famine and press 'the necessity of relief'.[15] Like many 1846 narrative accounts, his language does not yet evoke the scale of the catastrophe and remains distant from the indigent, pushing off the language of despair:

> It is not a permanent evil – God forbid it should be: it is not an evil that could be foreseen by man, or prevented by human exertion; it is a visitation of Providence, to which we should bow down with awe and humility. (Hear, hear.) We have this consolation – we can hope it will be but short and transitory. (Hear, hear.) Though the disease is afflictive, we have the period of its termination in prospective. [sic] There is no reason to despond or to despair – there is no reason not to hope that the Powerful Being whose holy will it is to afflict a faithful people, will permit that the period for their relief shall not be remote – (hear, hear) – and that they shall not continue to suffer under the hand of Divine Providence to a point beyond the capacity of human endurance.

The oratorical voice performs confidence, contrition, and endurance to the clear approval of the crowd. The afflicted 'faithful' appear at a distance, not as speakers or addressees. The tone markedly differs from Mangan's speaker in 'The Warning Voice', which, though sounded at the distance of prophecy, articulated the emotions of the victims.

In greater contrast to O'Connell's speech, another poem by Mangan, signed 'Clarence Mangan', appeared a few pages after O'Connell's account in the same April issue of *The Nation*. 'Siberia', one of Yeats's favorite poems, conveys not only hunger but also the pain and narrowing of the will that accompany an ongoing trauma. The poem speaks of a distant place with a vivid immediacy:

> In Siberia's wastes
>   No tears are shed,
> For they freeze within the brain.
> Naught is felt but dullest pain,
>   Pain acute, yet dead;

> Pain as in a dream,
>   When years go by
> Funeral-paced, yet fugitive,
> When man lives, and doth not live
>   Doth not live – nor die.[16]

In dreams pain disassociates from a reality that cannot be wholly comprehended. The unconventional rhyme structure – ABCCB – in which the first line has no echo, puts the speaker's lack of comprehension into a form in which 'dreams' has no rhyme at the stanza's end. Hunger's 'dullest pain' is juxtaposed with its 'Pain acute' in the following line. Its contradictory feeling, both dull and acute, is reconciled in the line 'Pain as in a dream', where pain is complex, and time is slow and slippery.

The poem ends by explaining, 'Therefore, in those wastes, / None curse the Czar' – pain, survival, and endurance remain the realities. For the imagined victims of hunger and cold, the pain subsides as bodies becomes less electric and conserve energy until life is finally spent:

> And such doom each drees,
> Till, hunger-gnawn,
> And cold-slain, he at length sinks there,
> Yet scarce more a corpse than ere
> His last breath was drawn.

The isolation, exile, and climate silence these speakers – 'Each man's tongue is cloven by the North Blast, who heweth nigh / With sharp scymitar' – preventing them cursing the Czar. Again, here their voices go unheard, but Mangan's mention of their lack of political invective does not obviate its necessity; it underscores their accusal.

Other writers from the late 1840s, such as the young 'Speranza', imagined Famine speakers more directly. In 1846 Speranza used heroic couplets to represent the doom of the famished, who respond to a visionary speaker in the dialogic poem. The six-stanza poem 'The Famine Year', first published as 'The Stricken Land' in *The Nation* on 23 January 1847, has become one of the best known Famine poems, primarily because it contains a political message about culpability later developed into clearer nationalist form by John Mitchell, as Christine Kinealy has noted.[17] Christopher Morash has explained how the poem's prosopopoeia allows the absent dead to speak through the voices of the poem, and Amy Martin has commented on the narratorial switches and layered multiple voices that distinguish the poem.[18] The lyrical indictments uttered by imagined Famine victims demonstrate hunger's implicit charge.

At its outset, the poem's narrator controls the possible meanings in the first stanza with a series of questions ('There's a proud array of soldiers – what do they round your door?') addressed to several groups that the speaker sees or envisions in a sort of dream parade – 'weary men', 'fainting forms', and 'pale mothers' – who answer each in succession.[19] The second stanza begins with a similar catechetical rhythm, addressing a group of 'little children' whose 'tears are strange upon your infant faces'. The multiple voices respond in an urgent unison for four lines, speaking their crisis at length, and eventually overwhelm the narration.

> Little Children, tears are strange upon your infant faces,
> God meant you but to smile within your mother's soft embraces.
> Oh! We know not what is smiling, and we know not what
>   is dying;
> But we're hungry, very hungry, and we cannot stop our crying.
> And some of us grown cold and white – we know not what
>   it means;
> But as they lie beside us, we tremble in our dreams.
> There's a gaunt crowd on the highway – are ye come to pray
>   to man,
> With hollow eyes that cannot weep, and for words your
>   faces wan?

The sixth and shortest line ending 'we tremble in our dreams' closes the speech of the children, yet the lack of attributions in the poem encourages an interpretive confusion about who speaks the stanza's remaining lines. At first read, the children's narration seems to continue as their description enters an interior and doubly visionary world. In this double reading of 'There's a gaunt crowd on the highway', the shadowy figures exist within the children's dreams. The sense of the line soon becomes clearer when the original speaker poses another (and final) question: 'are ye come to pray to man... ?' In either reading, the dreams of the 'very hungry' children function as a transition for the largest speech in the poem, of the 'gaunt crowd', who offer the most biting indictments of the narrator and the reader explicitly framed in terms of the custom of hospitality.

The remainder of the poem constitutes an answer and a reversal of the roles of interrogator and respondent in which the interrogator becomes the accused. The voice of the final four stanzas is that of the chorus, the collective crowd. The original narrator's voice goes silent for the remainder of the poem yet remains addressed. This collective voice offers a first-person account of hunger founded in traumatic memories of the recent past, delivered in images more than narrative: 'we left our infants playing with their dead mother's hand'. The voices clamour to be heard, if not by their 'fellow-men' who have deserted them, then by the Divine: 'God will hear our groan'. Yet their questions continue to implicate those who should have been responsible for offering hospitality to the starving as they wander 'houseless'.

> O Christ! how have we sinned, that on our native plains
> We perish houseless, naked, starved, with branded brow,
>   like Cain's?
> Dying, dying wearily, with a torture sure and slow –
> Dying, as a dog would die, by the wayside as we go.

The fifth, penultimate stanza focuses on the absences of a human audience and evokes the immemorial social duty of burying the dead:

> One by one they're falling round us, their pale faces to the sky;
> We've no strength left to dig them graves – there let them lie.
> The wild bird, if he's stricken, is mourned by the others,
> But we – we die in Christian land – we die amid our brothers,
> In the land which God has given, like a wild beast in his cave,
> Without a tear, a prayer, a shroud, a coffin, or a grave.
> Ha! but think ye the contortions on each livid face ye see,
>
> Will not be read on judgment-day by eyes of Deity?

The voice of the 'gaunt crowd' at this stage has fully overtaken the initial speaker of the poem, who is now interrogated as one of 'ye', along with the audience of the poem. The hungry are no longer questioned, and the final stanza uncomfortably lessens the distance between the audience of the poem and the indigent sublime.

> We are wretches, famished, scorned, human tools to build
>   your pride,
> But God will yet take vengeance for the souls for whom
>   Christ died.
> Now is your hour of pleasure – bask ye in the world's caress;
> But our whitening bones against ye will rise as witnesses,
> From the cabins and the ditches, in their charred,
>   unconfined masses,
> For the Angel of the Trumpet will know them as he passes.
> A ghastly, spectral army, before the great God we'll stand,
> And arraign ye as our murderers, the spoilers of our land.

The army addresses the living readers and seeks justice for the hungry who synecdochally become their whitening bones before arraigning the 'spoilers of our land.' Such images became aide-memoires for the

Famine when, in the twentieth century, new performances of hunger emerged.

TRACES OF SOCIAL MEMORY IN THE FOLKLORE ARCHIVE

Famine memories give structure to many subsequent hunger references in Irish social memory, as scholars have been ably demonstrating for two decades. These memories do not blot out distinct chains of references to fasting, however. A set of folklore texts held in the National Folklore Collection demonstrate how these co-referential memories work. Within this two-million text archive housed at University College Dublin, 64,000 texts have recently been made available in a digital archive. The stories were written down by school children from informants, and compiled in a scheme developed by the Irish Folklore Commission.[20] The physical texts are collected in the Schools' Manuscript Collection: 500,000 pages of text collected by 5,000 children across twenty-six counties in an effort to preserve folklore in their home districts between 1937–39.[21] These are post-famine stories and post-hunger strike stories that can be read in terms of social memory – against historiography and the demands of source criticism and *post hoc* logic – as they enfold social memories of hunger, fasting, and hospitality. By the 1930s, they had absorbed the idea of the hunger strike, as one story in particular reveals. The stories were told to school children (aged twelve to thirteen usually) by an adult, usually a close relation, concerning an event in the community. The children recorded the stories in neat handwriting while they listened to these prominent local stories, at least a half a dozen of which reference hunger and fasting. In Dublin, the written texts were classed into a wide variety of folklore categories, including 'local history and monuments, folktales and legends, riddles and proverbs, songs, customs and beliefs, games and pastimes, traditional work practices and crafts.'[22] In most of the stories, implicit lessons are delivered, but these are not simple fables with simple lessons.

Folklore presents problems: it conflates, distracts, and misplaces. It collapses time and obfuscates authority. What is often presented in folklore on the topic of hunger resembles a complex filled with justifications, elaborations, and digressions, rather than a carefully constructed set of voices, images, and themes such as exist in lyrical poetry. Guy Beiner has argued that folklore collects, reshapes, regenerates, represents, and repackages memory in contrast to invented modern traditions (along the lines Eric Hobsbawm explored in the metropolitan development of Scottish and Welsh national cultures).[23] Moreover they differ from professional historiography in the way events and chronology are jumbled.[24] Beiner suggests the term 'social memory' when he analyzes folklore, which he describes as dynamic in its construction and analyzable for communal discourses:

> Social memory is collective insofar as it is neither the exclusive property nor the faculty of one individual, but commonly shared by a community. It is a discursive reconstruction of the past performed and promulgated by multiple agents and relating to numerous participants. Members of a society draw and contribute to a communal body of cultural knowledge relating to the past.... Social memory is an organic and dynamic synthesis rather than an eclectic compilation. It does not merely reflect the total sum of individual memories in a community at any given time, but is grounded in a set of frames of reference by which individuals can locate and reinterpret their own recollections.

Beiner argues that history and memory are structurally linked, and reviews how modern historians have long held memory and folklore in opposition to historiography.[25] Since the late eighteenth century and the battles between historiography and antiquarianism, modern history often required a kind of cultural forgetting, relying more upon source criticism and bracketing local memories as legend and fanciful lore.[26] As a result, in the nineteenth century oral narratives and traditional manuscripts were increasingly disregarded as reliable sources. Indeed, folk materials were seen as contributing to the assumed problem of Irish fantasy, another symptom of the supposed Celtic reaction to what Matthew Arnold called the despotism of fact.[27] Texts with unverifiable accounts and local stories have since been revalued for the social memories they contain, moving beyond debates about objectivity to consider how individual memories are shaped by public memories as well as individual performances.[28]

The old divide between memory and history remains a practical quandary for researchers in the humanities. Memory studies, like cultural studies, has encouraged researchers to move beyond historical and literary texts to study intangible, fragile, less verifiable texts reliant on individual memories – folklore, in particular. On several levels, however, interpreting folklore in terms of memory requires our credulity – the recorded memories given by the story-tellers do not also record the questions of the listeners, nor do they cite sources or include references. We are also asked to suspend disbelief of the normal order to things in order to enter the story. Finally, the written memories in the Schools' Collection have multiple ascriptions, to borrow from Paul Ricoeur in his discussion of personal and collective memories; that is, their sources spring from not only personal but also familial and social memories.[29] The story's authorship is not a single person but belongs to the repertoire of the community.

Much of what exists in the repertoire of a story-teller or within a local memory is only manifest in performance, and enters the archive, in this case the Schools' Collection, sporadically and in disembodied form. Still, in the archive we find repeated relationships, well-worn understandings, and rehashed tales, all of which point to patterns and contours of social memory and cultural scripts. The traces of these oral performances, and the shadows of the dynamics between informants and collectors, listeners and storytellers, echo the lessons of hunger in these texts, namely that audiences, like witnesses, always have a role to play. Further, the publication of this particular archive on the website of the National Folklore Archive has created new audiences for these stories and may help reveal how archives and repertoires overlap.[30]

HUNGER IN THE REPERTOIRE

Three stories from the Schools' Collection suggest how hunger and fasting had long been imagined in Ireland and continued to be remembered. The first passage concerns St. Patrick, who was perhaps the most celebrated hero of hunger in nineteenth-century Ireland.[31] St. Patrick's legendary powers of fasting reflect his supposed integration of Brehon and ecclesiastical law, as well as religious and legal fasting. The verb 'to fast' here is only partly adequate as a translation from Irish and Latin. Fast in English connotes how hunger functions as determination; the Old English word *fæst* emerged from a Germanic root that signifies the sense of fastening oneself solidly to a pledge. The weakened, fasting body thus has long resonated an idealistic resolution. But in Latin the common noun for fasting *ieiunium* or *jaiunium* also suggests boundless hunger, emptiness, or esurience – from which English also derives words that both carry connotations of emptiness: jejune (as in naïve) and jejunum (the part of the small intestine that connects the duodenum and the ileum, so named because it is usually empty during autopsies because its peristaltic motion continues after death). The Irish verb that signifies fasting (*troscud* or *troscadh*) is distinct in Middle and Old Irish from the loan word, *óine*, for a religious type of fasting, derived from the Latin *ieiunium*. It signifies a spiritual connection to God, an emptying of early passions, and serves as the root of the Irish words for the fast days, Wednesday and Friday (*Dé Céadaoin, Dé hAoine*). *Troscud*, in contrast, denotes fasting as a legal practice with a moral, ethical imperative; it also resembled the medieval Irish word for lepers, *troscu*, often, particularly then, associated with Jesus's mission.

Sources of Patrick's life include legendary accounts, some collected in *The Tripartite Life of St. Patrick* (once a source for feast-day patterns) and historical texts such as Patrick's *Confessio*. In the many biographies and hagiographies that were published in the nineteenth century, St. Patrick repeatedly uses fasting as a quasi-spiritual-legal weapon to damn and curse his enemies in God's eyes. St. Patrick's fasts then exist in both senses, alternately using the verbs for religious and legal fasting, and occasionally uniting the meanings of both *troscud* and *óine*. The following story from the Schools' Collection, recorded in Leitrim, resembles other stories collected and translated in the nineteenth century, but the focus on St. Patrick's fasting is remarkable. The tale is also replete with imagistic mnemonic devices to help generations of storytellers keep it in their repertoire and recall the punishments (there are three) meted out to an inhospitable host of the peripatetic saint.

> When Saint Patrick was passing through Tullaghan he came to the Duff river. He asked the fisher men for a salmon. The fisher men [sic] would not give him a salmon. Saint Patrick was very hungry and the fisherman was roasting a salmon at the foot of the tree near a precipice at the river edge. The saint begged a portion of the fish to appease his hunger, but was ungenerously refused; whereupon he prayed that the fisherman would not long enjoy prosperity. The latter frightened at the appearance of the saint, climbed up the tree. At once the fire spread to the tree and it took the flames, fell over the edge of the precipice. The fisherman after hanging some time from the branches fell into the water: and thus the prayer of the saint was heard for the *inhospitable* victim was burned, hanged and drowned. The saint journeying onwards met two miles farther eastward at Bundrowes a fishery man named Cassidy also roasting a salmon to whom he made a similar request. The compassion and generosity of this man so pleased the saint that he prayed that the fishery at the place might long prosper with Cassidy and his descendants.[32] [emphasis added]

In this story, likely a favourite with the Cassidys, the expectation of hospitality exists before and after the telling of the tale, where the villain is the 'inhospitable victim'. St. Patrick's triple retribution and violence may seem extreme but is not uncommon to medieval legends collected in the *Tripartite Life*. Hospitality is not merely a vague notion here, but a set of explicit expectations for food to be offered to the hungry. The offer of food is rewarded and the refusal to offer food to the hungry meets with severe communal disapproval, a reminder to the listeners to help the hungry. Hunger serves as the prompt for moral, divine, and social contracts.

A second story, recorded in Donegal, exhibits an opposing side of fasting literature – that of the unjust faster who abuses the custom and fasts falsely. Notably, because it was recorded in the 1930s, the fasting is called 'hunger striking', but the tale appears to predate its later redaction. This form of fasting directly echoes the earlier known legal version of fasting, *troscud*. Here, as in the tale of St. Patrick, hunger becomes the force that chastises deprivation, both moral and physical. Although the tale was written down after the hunger strikes of the early twentieth century, it appears to have emerged from an older tradition with both oral and textual influences. The story exists, in a sense, within a legendary fold of time outside history. The historical reference to a 'hunger strike' only emerges once the expectations of story-telling traditions have been established by the opening phrase, 'Once upon a time', and by naming the main character simply 'a great miser.' Listeners are asked to suspend disbelief and accept generalities and absolutes in place of verifiable detail and historical fact, even more so as a hungry man's dream is recounted.

> Once upon a time there lived a man who was a great miser. He never gave anything to charity and it is believed that he would go on hunger-strike for days and even weeks in order to save his money. One night this old miser had a great dream.
>
> He dreamt that he was wa[l]king down the town and that he turned down a small side-street which he knew to be the slums, where the poor people live. He thought that he stopped to look into one of the houses and this is what met his eyes.
>
> In the house was a man, a woman, and a child. In the badly kept house was a bed and in the bed lay the woman, looking very ill, with the child in her delicate arms. The man was kneeling on the floor beside a half-dead fire trying to keep it lit. When the fire was lit the poor man rose to his feet and went over to the press, but as he opened it he saw to his great dismay that there was not a scrap of food in it. The next thing the man knew was that his dream was ended and that he was awake. He got up out of bed on the moment, and dressed as quickly as he could, and went to the priest's house. When he was shown into the priest's house to the priest's surprise the old miser handed him one hundred pounds to give to the poor.[33]

The empty press or cupboard is a common symbol in hunger narratives and reflects an emptiness at the centre of their home, echoing that of the stomach. Notably, the empty press appears in a dream as the miser's conscience; it contrasts his hunger with that of the famished family. To the miser, hunger is a way of saving money until he dreams of others who have no choice but to be hungry. As with the other folk stories, the hunger of the main character is not the main point of the story; his unnecessary hunger is not a protest or appeal, nor is it a physical emptying for spiritual fulfillment. The dream of hunger challenges his own moral deprivation. His decision to become generous and donate to the poor emerges because he envisions the hunger of others and his responsibility to them. The hunger-induced dream, like that of Seanchan and Aníer Meic Conglinne, emerges from his own fasting – a dream made by hunger.

A third story from the Schools' Collection, recorded in Kerry, presents another transformation around hunger, this a fairy or miraculous one, itself a kind of dream narrative. Notably, the miracle only occurs once the custom of hospitality is fulfilled. At the outset of this story, we are given a historical time frame, with a specific Famine year, and an actual place – near the Ferry Bridge outside Ballyduff in north Kerry – in part to ground the miraculous events within actual history. But hunger here operates in a legendary manner, where images signal recurrent themes and memories. The threshold of the door functions as the metaphor of the social contract, where starving people await welcome.

> In the year 1846 in the famine days, the people of this district like all others were dying with the hunger. They were forced to eat raw turnips and cabbage. In this locality lived a family named Joyce, who lived near the Ferry Bridge about a mile from the village of Ballyduff. The Joyce family sold the farm about nineteen years ago and the present owner is a man named Patrick Dunne. One member of the family was a nun in the Mercy Order in Tralee and lived to be over ninety years.

> The Joyce family were very generous to the poor and needy in the famine days, and these came long distances to get food. Many a time on getting up in the morning they found dead bodies in their yard or at the door – people who died of hunger.

> One evening an old woman came to the door and asked for a few leaves of cabbage but there was not a leaf in the haggard. Old Billy Joyce told his daughter to go out and cut the cabbage stumps. The woman filled her apron with the stumps. Next morning when they got up the haggard was full of cabbage, on which a shower of honey had fallen during the night, and all the neighbors came and collected it. Some went on their knees

sucking the honey. An old woman named Bridget Power, who died last year was said to be one hundred and fourteen years and was in service in Joyce's house at the time this event happened. She often told how people buried the dead during the famine. They tied a rope round the dead persons and carried them on their backs just as they were without shroud or coffin.

This story I got from Richard O'Gallagher Ballyhorgan, who spent many a night in Joyce's house.[34]

We hear the lineage and provenance of the story, pointing us back to a reality of other listeners, closer to the Famine, and to its place in a wider network of social memory. The references to actual people in the story suggest an anxiety about relaying a miraculous story within an historical frame, but it also points to the presence of the storyteller's repertoire, a kind of social memory in which legends and stories spread throughout cultures and over time. The bridge between the miraculous and the historical is created through the performance of telling the story.

Notably, the living persons in this story bear a striking intimacy with and responsibility for the dead, carrying them on their backs, collecting bodies from the yard or doorstep in order to bury them. Such an intimacy reinforces hunger's social contract with the living, one that extends beyond life and death. The extraworldly and miraculous appearance of a 'shower of honey' on the cabbage leaves suggest that a reward for feeding the hungry is both forthcoming and sweetly abundant. The transformation of the empty 'haggard' or press in the centre of the home to a full one mirrors the deeper recompense given to the Joyces, resembling that which St. Patrick gives to the Cassidys: a favoured place in story and social memory.

Stories concerning the catastrophe of the Famine echo the role of (in)hospitality, even when fasting as an ancient cultural practice reborn is recalled. They also often treat hunger as belonging to others, and rare are hungry voices with their own memories. Nevertheless, these stories underscore the imperative to feed the hungry. In the script of hospitality, proffering food is the cardinal expectation and being unable to do so amounts to a failure. These hungry people differ greatly from those of another tradition, namely that which includes *Piers Plowman* and Adam Smith, where hunger primarily serves as a lesson for the lazy and a prompt for the animal in us.[35]

DIVIDING SALMON BY A POOL

The legendary Seanchan, depicted in Lady Wilde's folktales (also collected by Yeats in *Irish Fairy Tales*) and in several earlier scholarly publications, is a false faster, who impetuously fasts because of his jealousy and imperiousness. But as the old man in the Prologue to the first edition of the play notes, 'he who told the story of Seanchan on King Guaire's threshold long ago in the old books told it wrongly.... But he that tells the story now, being a poet, has put the poet in the right'. The king, known in Irish folklore and legend as 'Guaire the Hospitable', is the fitting host for Seanchan's fast.[36] Yeats's Seanchan describes the vision he had during his own 'dream that hunger makes'. In this dream Seanchan places himself into one of the stories from his repertoire, one he would have performed as the King's poet and storyteller. He thus envisions himself inside the repertoire as one of a gathering in legendary time at a feast of Finn and his son Oscar (Osgar in the play):

> I was but now
> At Almhuin, in a great high-raftered house,
> With Finn and Osgar. Odours of roast flesh
> Rose round me and I saw the roasting spits,
> And then the dream was broken, and I saw
> Grania dividing salmon by a pool,
> And then I was awakened by your voice.[37]

Seanchan embodies fasting as he recalls a shorthand dreamscape version of the legend of Diarmuid and Grania. The tale is redolent of hospitality and rejection; it begins with a vision of a scene of feast being prepared by Finn and Osgar as they await Grania, who has agreed to marry Finn.

Significantly, Seanchan envisions the moment of hunger, of anticipation, before the feast begins. But the feast will not begin because Finn will start instead on his epic jealous pursuit of Grania and her new lover, Diarmuid, the man Finn sent to collect her. Instead of arriving at Almhuin for the wedding feast, the lovers have fled into the woods to live like hunted animals. In the legend, Diarmuid is advised to not eat food where it has been cooked, nor to sleep where he and Grania eat, but to keep moving always without human hospitality. In Yeats's play, Seanchan envisions Finn's planned hospitality—'Odours of roast flesh/Rose around me and I saw the roasting spits' – but it is broken by the desultory realization that Grania has fled – 'and then the dream was broken'. In place of sensory evocations of the feast, Seanchan sees Grania dividing salmon by a pool, an image that contrasts pointedly with hearth and home.

Grania divides the salmon, as if at an absent table, in order to share them with Diarmuid. Her hospitality remains in the sharing connotation of 'divide'. The two lovers' desire correlates with the interrupted feast, unsatiated hunger turned to desire. Hunger therefore forms the enclosing dream of the court poet where the rules of hospitality are breached and a refusal to eat is suggested by their legendary abandonment of their homes. The section ends when Seanchan wakes fortified by his dream in order to continue his fast to its conclusion. In the end of Yeats's first published version, Seanchan lives and King Guaire recognizes 'the greater power' of his fast as he hands Seanchan his crown.[38]

But in 1920 Yeats rewrote the ending of *The King's Threshold* following the advent of the modern hunger strike and the death of the Lord Mayor of Cork, Terence MacSwiney, on hunger strike in Brixton Prison, as numerous scholars have examined. He did so in order to give the play a more 'tragically appropriate' ending, as Yeats wrote to Lady Gregory.[39] The appearance of a starved man on stage when the Abbey Theatre performed the play again in 1920 echoed the image that had been appearing in daily newspaper accounts, both of which resonated with the social memories of hunger, (in)hospitality, and fasting.

Hunger in Irish social memory is more than a prompting to eat or work. It exists in a relationship between the hungry and the witnesses, where hunger is hospitality removed. It requires not only an individual to be deprived of sustenance, but also others to witness that deprivation, others with implicit responsibility. Irish memories of hunger can be considered also in terms of their 'articulation' – to borrow from Chiara De Cesari and Ann Rigney's formulation that suggests both voiced (articulated) memories and how expectations articulate or link up with one another in social memory, linking 'individuals and groups through their common engagement with [shared] narratives'.[40] Memories of fasting and hunger might be effectively understood as such articulations of (in)hospitality, particularly as revealed through 'the dreams that hunger makes'. These performances of hunger in folklore, lyrical poetry, and drama, exist as forerunners to later hunger-strike narratives and depict hunger in opposition to hospitality, giving agency to the hungry and assuming the responsibility of the witnesses. To some extent, the distinctions between the speakers for hunger in these readings can be classed according to genre and period distinctions. But the shared visions of hunger and hospitality across such divergent selections suggest a cardinal relationship between the satiated and the hungry within Ireland's social memory of hunger. To restate a truism, no one can be perilously hungry without the implied inaction of others; today no one starves because no food exists, but because no food has been made available.

NOTES

1. W.B. Yeats, *The King's Threshold and On Baile's Strand; Being Volume Three of Plays for an Irish Theatre* (London: Bullen, 1904), p.15.
2. Declan Kiely, ed., *The King's Threshold: Manuscript Materials* (Ithaca, NY: Cornell UP, 2005), pp.32–39.
3. Roy Foster, *W.B. Yeats: A Life; I: The Apprenctice Mage, 1865–1914* (Oxford: Oxford UP, 1997), p.93.
4. Foster (1997), pp.90, 558.
5. W.B. Yeats, *The Countess Kathleen and Various Legends and Lyrics* (London: Unwin, 1892), p.139; Foster (1997), p.97.
6. The play begins with a speech from 'Teig': 'Strange things are going up and down the land / These famine times. By Tubber-vanach crossroads / A woman met a man with ears spread out, / And they moved up and down like wings of bats.' Later in the play, one of the wicked merchants describes the souls of Famine victims: 'on all sides, / Bat-like, from bough, and roof, and window ledge, / Clung evil souls of men, and in the woods, / Like streaming flames, floated upon the winds / The elemental creatures.' W.B. Yeats (1892), pp.14, 48.
7. See Catherine O'Sullivan, *Hospitality in Medieval Ireland 900–1500* (Dublin: Four Courts, 2004).
8. See Lahny Preston-Matto, *Aislinge Meic Conglinne; The Vision of Mac Conglinne* (Syracuse, NY: Syracuse UP, 2010).
9. Medieval Land of Cockaygne stories featured carnivalesque elements such as power reversals and depicted environments composed of food; for instance where buildings were made of bread and milk lakes were lined with sausage trees.
10. See David Lloyd, 'The Indigent Sublime: Specters of Irish Hunger', *Representations* 92 (Autumn 2005), 152–185.
11. For an instance of an account written by a local leader, see Catherine Gage's *A History of Rathlin Island* (1851), ed. by J. Margaret Dickson (Coleraine: Impact, 1995), pp.87–9, in which she describes the Rathlin's conditions during the Famine years. Her husband, both the local rector and landlord, Rev. Robert Gage, led Famine relief efforts both to feed locals and to speed their emigration.
12. Yeats (1892), p.139.
13. James Clarence Mangan, 'The Warning Voice', *The Nation* 21 February 1846, p.297.
14. Melissa Fegan, *Literature and the Irish Famine 1845–1919* (Dublin: Clarendon, 2002), p.195.
15. "For my part I confess that my first great business in going to London, and leaving my duty here, was to work out something for the people of Ireland as a protection against the famine which is pressing upong them." Daniel O'Connell, 'The Famine', *The Nation* 18 April 1846, p.418.
16. Mangan, 'Siberia', *The Nation* 18 April 1846, pp.212–13.
17. Christine Kinealy, 'The Stricken Land: The Great Hunger in Ireland', *Hungry Words: Images of Famine in the Irish Canon*, eds. George Cusack and Sarah Goss (Dublin: Irish Academic Press, 2006), pp.7–28, p.21.
18. Morash, Christopher. *Writing the Irish Famine* (Oxford: Clarendon, 1995), p.182; Amy E. Martin, 'Victorian Ireland: Race and the Category of the Human', *Victorian Review* 40.1 (Spring 2014), 52–47.
19. Speranza (Jane Francesca Elgee), 'The Stricken Land', *The Nation* 23 January 1847, p.11.
20. Seán Ó Súilleabháin, 'Forward to the Repring Edition [1970]', *A Handbook of Irish Folklore (Scríbhinní Béaloidis/ Folklore Studies* 22) (Kindle Locations 103–105). Comhairle Bhéaloideas Éireann. Kindle Edition.

21. According to a University College Dublin press release, 'Materials from one of world's largest folklore collections now available online', http://www.ucd.ie/news/2013/12DEC13/231213-Materials-from-one-of%20worlds-largest-folklore-collections-now-available-online.html, visited 20 August 2016.

22. "National Folklore Collection (NFC); The Schools' Collection" http://www.duchas.ie/en/info/cbe, accessed 30 March 2016. Also, see Séamas Ó Cathain, 'Súil siar ar Scéim na Scol 1937–1938', *Sinsear* 5 (1988), 19–30.

23. Guy Beiner, 'Intra-Community Remembering and Forgetting: Commemorative Possessiveness and Envy in Ulster', University College, Dublin, Irish Memory Studies Network podcast, available at http://irishmemorystudies.com/index.php/memory-cloud/#beiner, accesssed 15 March 2016.

24. Guy Beiner, *Remembering the Year of the French: Irish Folk History and Social Memory* (Madison: University of Wisconsin Press, 2007), p.12.

25. Beiner (2007), p.31.

26. For an overview of this, see Joep Leerssen's *Remembrance and Imagination Patterns in the Historical and Literary Representation of Ireland in the Nineteenth Century* (Cork: Cork UP, 1996), pp.68–156.

27. Matthew Arnold first published his famous formulation of the Celts a 'passionate, turbulent, indomintable reaction against the despotism of fact' in 'The Study of Celtic Literature, Part IV—Conclusion', *Cornhill Magazine* 14.79 (July 1866), 117.

28. Lynn Abrams's chapter, 'Memory', in *Oral History Theory* recounts the struggles over using memory in folklore scholarship: 'researchers are now able to say that an oral history source based on memory offers up insights into the interplay between self and society, between past and present and between individual experience and the generalised account; in addition it will often provide emotional content that a written version of the same story will not' (New York: Routledge, 2010), p.81.

29. Paul Ricoeur, *Memory, History, Forgetting* (Chicago: University of Chicago Press, 2004), p.132.

30. Diana Taylor has explored such complex relationships in her work, *The Archive and the Repertoire: Performing Cultural Memory in the Americas* (Durham: Duke University Press, 2003), pp.1–52.

31. See Joseph Lennon, '"A Familiar Kinde of Chastisement": Fasting in the Nineteenth-Century', *Victorian Literary Cultures: Studies in Textual Subversion*. (New Jersey: Farleigh Dickinson Press, 2016). The paragraph that follows this note condenses some of the argument from this previous essay.

32. The informant is cited as Edward Connolly, 'Aged 60 years' of Tullaghan, Co. Leitrim. Its title is given as 'St. Patrick and Fasting': *The Schools' Collection*, vol. 190, pp.86–7. http://www.duchas.ie/en/cbes/4602725/4598519, accessed 8 January 2017.

33. The informant is cited as Mrs J. Cunningham 'Aged (39)' and the collector, Joan Cunningham 'Aged (13)' of Killybegs, Co. Donegal. *The Schools' Collection*, vol. 1039, pp.286–7. http://www.duchas.ie/en/cbes/4428304/4393110, accessed 8 January 2017.

34. The informant is cited as Richard O'Callaghan of Ballyhorgan, Co. Kerry, and the collector as Mrs B. Lawlor 'teacher' of Ballyduff, Co. Kerry. *The Schools' Collection*, vol 415, pp.209–10. http://www.duchas.ie/en/cbes/4666610/4666477, accessed 8 January 2017.

35. See Adam Smith's *The Theory of Moral Sentiments* (1759), http://www.econlib.org/library/Smith/smMS6.html, accessed 8 January 2017.

36. For one account of the legend, see Eleanor Hull's *Early Christian Ireland* (Dublin: Gill, 1905), pp.55–61.

37. W.B. Yeats, *The King's Threshold and On Baile's Strand; Being Volume Three of Plays for an Irish Theatre* (London: Bullen, 1904), p.18.

38. Yeats (1904), p.65.

39. R.F. Foster, *W.B. Yeats: A Life: Volume II The Arch Poet 1915–1939* (Oxford: Oxford University Press, 2003), p.182. Tom Paulin has written astutely about Yeats's response to MacSwiney's strike, 'Yeats's Hunger-Strike Poem', in *Minotaur: Poetry and the Nation State* (Cambridge, MA: Harvard UP, 1992), pp.133–50. Also see: Declan Kiely *The King's Threshold: Manuscript Materials* ; Roy Foster, 'Yeats at War: Poetic Strategies and Political Reconstruction from the Easter Rising to the Free State', in *Transactions of the Royal Historical Society* (Sixth Series, Vol. 11, 2001), pp.125–45; and Joseph Lennon 'The Starvation of a Man: Terence MacSwiney's Hunger Strike and Famine Memory', in *Memory Ireland: The Famine and the Troubles*, Vol. 3, ed. by Oona Frawley (Syracuse: Syracuse University Press, 2014), pp.59–90.

40. '[A]cts of remembrance involve "articulation" in the sense of "giving expression" to events in the form of a narrative. Cultural memories are "articulated discourses" (see Hall in Grossberg 1986) made up of heterogeneous elements, borrowings, and appropriations from other languages and memorial traditions that are assembled together into narratives. But acts of remembrance, as the second section emphasizes, also involve "articulation" in another sense: they help to link up ("articulate") individuals and groups through their common engagement with those narratives.' Chiara De Cesari and Ann Rigney, eds., *Transnational Memory Circulation, Articulation, Scales* (Boston: De Gruyter, 2014), p.15.

Graham Dawson

The Meaning of 'Moving On': From Trauma to the History and Memory of Emotions in 'Post-Conflict' Northern Ireland

'Trauma' has become established as a pervasive trope in discourse and practice concerned with the affective legacies of the Northern Ireland Troubles, providing a popular as well as a critical framework for understanding the effects of political violence during the conflict and memories of that violence during the peace process. The concept has proved highly productive in identifying the problem of the past in Ireland as a painful and troubling history that remains unresolved in the present and requires acknowledgement and redress. It has also generated new kinds of cultural and psychosocial analysis, encouraging engagement with questions of feeling and affective states marked by pain, distress, and disturbance. However, I argue in this article that its productivity may have become exhausted as the concept itself congeals into normativity, whether homogenised as the trace of an unspeakable wound or medicalised as 'PTSD' (post-traumatic stress disorder). Placing emphasis on psychic entrapment within states of affect derived from experiences 'in the past', 'trauma' is open to accusations of being backwards-looking rather than illuminating the possibilities and means of transformation in subjectivities shaped by experiences and memories of violent conflict – or of conceiving such transformation in the questionable language of 'healing', 'closure', and 'moving on'.

In the first part of this article, I draw on existing critical studies to identify a number of problematic assumptions within now-orthodox understandings of trauma promoted in what has become known as 'trauma theory' in the Humanities, and in the therapeutic culture centred on the treatment of PTSD. The analysis here focuses on the constraining effects of these understandings in three areas of debate and practice concerned with legacies and memories of the Troubles,

Irish University Review 47.1 (2017): 82–102
DOI: 10.3366/iur.2017.0258
© Edinburgh University Press
www.euppublishing.com/iur

namely academic studies of history and memory, victims' support, and storytelling conceived as an aspect of peacebuilding. In the second part, I make a case for shifting the frame for investigation of subjective experiences and 'psychological' legacies of the conflict, away from trauma and towards the history and memory of emotions. Here I identify critical resources in theory and history that enable interesting alternative conceptions of the internal world of embodied feelings and the meanings ascribed to them, that recognise the complex temporalities of emotional experience and that explore the shifting modes of management and containment, expression and performance of emotions within social and political relations and practices. Focusing on object-relations psychoanalysis, Raymond Williams' cultural materialism, and the emerging field of emotional history, I tease out key concepts and insights with the potential to inform new ways of thinking about the affective legacies of the Irish conflict and the possibilities of their transformation – of 'moving on' – in 'post-conflict' Northern Ireland.

THE TROUBLE WITH TRAUMA

In an essay problematising what she calls 'the apparently oxymoronic "popularity" of trauma' in academic debate in the Humanities, Susannah Radstone traces 'the rise of what is becoming almost a new theoretical orthodoxy'; that of 'trauma theory' as articulated in seminal and widely cited texts by Cathy Caruth, Shoshana Felman, and Dori Laub.[1] Subjecting this body of work to wide-ranging critical analysis, Radstone begins by contextualising its origins and founding assumptions as a marriage between theories of representation and subjectivity developed in deconstruction, post-structuralism, and psychoanalysis, on one hand, and '(mainly US-based) clinical work with survivors of experiences designated as traumatic', including the Vietnam War, the Holocaust, and sexual abuse, on the other.[2] This clinical work is itself informed by the diagnostic categorisation of post-traumatic stress disorder (PTSD), one of various 'mental conditions and disabilities' recognised (since 1980) by the American Psychiatric Association (APA); and also by a 'neuroscientific approach to memory disorders'.[3] According to the APA's widely cited definition, PTSD is diagnosed on the basis of psychological and somatic symptoms produced in response to 'an event out of the range of ordinary human experience in which one's life or the lives of one's family are endangered', generating overwhelming feelings of helplessness and fear.[4] The shocking, wounding event is considered to be 'unassimilable or unknowable' by the conscious mind[5] and to give rise to a 'dissociation' from the self of its traumatic experience, which 'comes to occupy a specially designated area of the mind that precludes (its) retrieval' in memory.[6] This idea meshes with the argument made in neuroscience, that 'the traumatic event is encoded in the brain in a different way from ordinary memory'.[7] Leaving gaps without trace in memory, the 'unexperienced' trauma[8] manifests subsequently in recurrent symptoms that include re-experiencing of the event (for example, in flashbacks or nightmares), the numbing of general responsiveness, and hyper-arousal to certain stimuli that evoke associations with the event.

While unrepresentable and incommunicable, the 'experience' of trauma is held to find displaced expression not only in these psycho-somatic symptoms but also in forms of testimony and other cultural representations in literature, film, art, and the media. 'Trauma analysis' of such representations in the Humanities has tended to take its lead from Caruth's oft-quoted argument that trauma is 'more than a pathology or a simple illness of a wounded psyche: it is always the story of a wound that cries out, that addresses us in the attempt to tell us of a reality or truth that is not otherwise available'.[9] Manifesting in this way an 'impossible history' that 'they cannot entirely possess',[10] utterances of the traumatised subject call for acts of listening and witnessing whereby 'some testimony can be made to trauma's "traceless traces"', in an 'act of "recovery"' that represents traumatic experience of the event whilst 'acknowledg(ing) the gaps and absences' in memory and representation.[11]

Radstone identifies a number of theoretical problems with academic discussions of trauma conducted on these terms, which tend to be overlooked when the value of trauma theory becomes taken for granted.[12] I will focus here on three of these problems. Firstly, in understanding the 'wound' of trauma to be caused by an extraordinary event, trauma theory proposes a model of the traumatised subject that reintroduces into the Humanities a distinction between the 'normal' and the 'pathological': 'One has either been present at or has "been" traumatized by a terrible event or one has not.'[13] This dichotomy runs counter both to a fundamental tenet of psychoanalytic thinking that rejects these categories and understands forms of psychic disturbance as a continuum, and to the model developed in cultural theory of the 'de-centred subject ... engaged in processes of (fear), desire and meaning-making over which it lack(s) full conscious control'.[14] Secondly, in ascribing the sole cause of trauma to an event in the external world, the significance of its mediation in the internal world and the meanings conferred on it by the subject afterwards is evaded: this is to 'attribute all badness to the world outside' at the expense of recognising, for example, aggression and violence within the subject.[15] Thirdly, the emphasis placed by trauma theory on 'the role of the listener or witness in the bringing to consciousness of previously unassimilated memory' is doubly problematic: it contradicts another of its central tenets, namely the neuroscientific pathology of dissociation that happens to a 'passive victim',[16] whilst also inscribing a privileged position and role to the trained cultural analyst. It is this analyst who is invested by trauma theory with the authority to identify and select for critical attention those cultural texts 'that are most likely to reveal trauma's absent traces', to exercise empathy in discerning what is unspeakable in those texts, and to interpret their wider significance.[17] This is to abandon the emphasis placed by cultural studies on 'the situated, local and multiple readings of historically specific readers and audiences', thereby avoiding questions of 'for whom, when, where and in what circumstances are particular texts read or experienced as trauma texts?'[18] 'Trauma criticism', concludes Radstone, 'arguably constructs and polices the boundary of what can be recognised as trauma'.[19]

Trauma theory derived from the medical discourses of PTSD and neuroscience, often in productive combination with other theoretical frameworks, has been taken up in Irish Studies and underpins a valuable body of scholarship on memory and the Irish past, including the Troubles. In her Introduction to *Memory Ireland: The Famine and the Troubles*, for example,[20] Oona Frawley quotes Caruth to ground the volume's framing argument that, 'since the traumatic event is not experienced as it occurs', trauma disrupts but also stimulates the desire to shape linear temporal meaning of the event in narrative.[21] Tracing the shift in interest stimulated by trauma theory, from individual to *collective* experience of trauma', Frawley identifies the initial application of this idea to the legacies of the Great Famine, and 'ways in which it is possible to move forward and let go of that perceived trauma'[22] through representation and commemoration, in the context of its 150th anniversary in the mid-1990s. Subsequently this same model has been applied to the recent history and living memory of the Troubles. Stefanie Lehner, for example, uses Caruth, Felman, and Laub – together with Jennifer Edkins' work on the political implications of trauma theory and Berber Bevernage's concept of 'irrevocable time' (referring to 'a "haunting" past' that 'got "stuck" and persists into the present')[23] – to 'expose the troubled position that the traumatic past occupies in present Northern Ireland'.[24] Lehner's argument is developed through analysis of two novels produced following the ceasefires of 1994 and explores in Caruthian terms '(l)iterature's potential to make "unthought knowledge" ... and the "unclaimed experience" of trauma ... available and indirectly accessible to us as readers' in encodings that 'enable an empathic witnessing'.[25] Fionna Barber makes similar use of Caruth to ground her study of art practice in Northern Ireland before and after the Belfast Agreement of 1998.[26]

Generative and subtle as such analyses have often been, they are vulnerable to Radstone's critique of the trauma theory underpinning them, for its inherent pathologising of the subject as traumatised under the impact of a determining external event, which has been selected and interpreted as such by cultural analysts trained in deciphering its unspeakable effects. Moreover, in applying a singular Caruthian model to very different historical contexts and cultural practices, the specificity of events and their 'wounding' effects upon meaning and subjectivity tend to be reduced to so many instances of 'Ireland's traumatic past'. A further inherent problem, identified by some working within this paradigm, concerns how 'collective trauma', held to affect entire communities or nations and to have transgenerational impact, might be conceptualised 'while avoiding the danger of ascribing to that group a collective psyche ... as if it were *like* an individual'.[27]

A second orthodox discourse of trauma has flourished in policy and practice concerning provision of support for victims of Troubles-related violence. Originating in an expansion of services for increasing numbers of people seeking professional help in the early years of the peace process, the idea of 'conflict-related trauma'[28] was promoted by a wide range of organisations in civil society and a conventional view became mainstream in public debate. This was institutionalised by the British Government's victims strategy from 1998 (subsequently continued under the devolved administration from 2007), involving the construction of an infrastructure to implement policy and channel significant sums of public money into PTSD counselling and other services offered by the statutory and voluntary sectors and grassroots victims' organisations.[29] Chris Gilligan identifies the underlying assumptions of this conventional view stemming from the medical model of PTSD: that 'an event, or events, in the past *causes* the symptoms in the present';[30] that 'trauma is *created* by conflict, but more likely to be *manifested* in a period of peace';[31] and that the provision of public services offering treatment for trauma in the post-conflict present furthers the restoration of psychological healing whilst also addressing the 'psychosocial dimensions' of peace-building, thereby enabling both traumatised individuals and the wider society to move on from the past.[32]

The normative temporality implicit in what Allan Young calls the 'architecture of traumatic time',[33] envisaged as a binary, linear relation between past and present, is particularly problematic in the context of 'transitional' societies like Northern Ireland. When causation and 'healing' of suffering are mapped too neatly onto a simplistic view of 'war as bad and peace as good' for mental health,[34] more complex temporalities are obscured; as when time flows backwards from disturbing experiences in the present to past events, illustrated by the question asked post-Agreement by retired RUC officers, 'What was it all for?'[35] For Brandon Hamber, alignment of the recovery of victims of violence with the politics of peace-building fails to recognise how individual experience may be 'out of sync' with what is happening collectively, and be '"moving" at a different pace'.[36] This gives rise to 'political and social pressure upon victims to remain "in step" with the national or political process' and demands that they 'move ... forward' in their psychological healing through what is termed 'closure'.[37]

The associated 'medicalisation' of distress is especially pernicious in a context of political violence since it 'pathologises a social phenomenon'.[38] Those diagnosed as suffering from PTSD are constructed as 'passive victims overwhelmed by their experiences in the past'[39] and offered a therapeutic solution that avoids, and displaces attention from, political considerations of responsibility for violence, of justice, and of overcoming divisions in the making of an agreed future society. Hamber argues that the 'concept (of) trauma and PTSD specifically, drives thinking towards homogeneity, as if all experiences of violence have the same outcome or need the same treatment'.[40] In Northern Ireland as in other 'post-conflict' societies, the discourse of trauma works performatively 'to change the personal and local language of suffering; that is, victims start to express themselves in medical language ("I am suffering from PTSD") rather than express how they really feel'.[41] According to Gilligan, the professionalisation of care associated with PTSD undermines the 'informal social support networks' grounded in 'protective community bonds' that previously provided adaptive resources to deal with and absorb the effects of violence;[42] and sustained what might now be described as resilience.[43] Hamber calls instead for close attention to 'the context of violence (and) its cultural specificities',[44] including the ways political violence works to alter and destroy existing 'individual and community meaning systems' as well as social bonds and relations.[45] Understanding the 'distinctive political, social and cultural meanings, and, thus, specific impacts' of 'different violent and political incidents' is therefore essential.[46] This requires recognition of those affected as 'active agents who are involved in giving meaning to their experiences'[47] and engaging in forms of 'social action' in pursuit of their own goals according to their own articulated needs and desires.[48]

A third area of activity engaged with trauma in the context of the Northern Ireland Troubles and the peace process concerns practices of popular and grass-roots storytelling. These have flourished in post-ceasefire Northern Ireland in close proximity to public debate and politics about dealing with the 'legacies' of the conflict in terms of truth, justice, and reconciliation. An orthodoxy has emerged here too, in the notion of the 'healing' potential of storytelling in relation to the trauma of a still-present past. Derived from the discourse of 'healing is revealing' which emerged in debates surrounding the South African Truth and Reconciliation Commission in the mid-1990s,[49] this was taken up in Northern Ireland notably by the Healing Through Remembering (HTR) organisation formed in 2001. In its wide consultation about how people could best 'remember the events connected with the conflict . . . and in so doing, individually and collectively contribute to the healing of the wounds of society', HTR discovered popular support for the idea that those telling their stories, 'if listened to empathically could experience a degree of healing'; as well as concerns that 'recounting painful experiences could . . . "reopen old wounds"'.[50] This discourse influenced the subsequent development of storytelling practices and 'the recording of trauma memories from conflict'.[51] For example, the film-maker and founder of the Prisons Memory Archive, Cahal McLaughlin, while sensibly cautious about 'claim(ing) any healing potential' for his own films, has situated his practice in relation to a range of critical writing on trauma and 'reparative memory' which includes that of Caruth and Laub.[52] It has also found its way into policy formulations on 'dealing with the past', such as the Report of the Consultative Group on the Past, which recommends storytelling as 'a process designed to facilitate individual and societal healing and to break the cycle of conflict'.[53]

Running through these debates, and widely deployed in media reportage and popular understandings of traumatic experience, is another conventional assumption: that of 'closure'. The desire for closure, in the sense of a wished-for ending to emotional distress, is routinely expressed by those harmed by political violence, whether sought through storytelling or, alternatively, through campaigning for truth and justice in unresolved cases of killing from the conflict.[54] In the words of Gillian Grigg of the War Widows' Association of Great Britain, in her evidence to the House of Commons Northern Ireland Affairs Committee in 2005: 'While you have unfinished business, whatever it happens to be, to do with what happened, then you cannot have closure; you cannot completely move forward; you cannot take a second new life.'[55] This vocabulary of closure contradictorily echoes both exhortations to victims to keep 'in step' with the requirements of peace-building, and concerns about the difficulties encountered in attempts to 'move forward and let go of' a traumatic past. The popularity and concomitant instability of this idea of closure signals a set of issues concerning emotional and affective experience and how it is lived, handled, and potentially transformed, that the PTSD paradigm – with its emphasis on linear temporality and a clear demarcation between past and present on one hand, and its homogenising tendencies on the other – is ill-equipped to address.

FROM TRAUMA TO FEELING AND EMOTION IN HISTORY: SHIFTING THE FRAME

Running through critiques of trauma theory and practice grounded on the diagnostic of PTSD and ideas from neuroscience is a set of concerns about its lack of detailed attention to the substance of 'traumatic experience' (if indeed we can so name a condition that is by definition 'unexperienced') involving a range of human feelings and emotions as these are embodied and made meaningful within specific historical cultures. In this second part of the article, I advocate making a shift in the analytical framework we use to think about the affective legacies of the Irish Troubles and their relation to 'post-conflict' activity to 'come to terms with' or 'deal with the past' in the Irish peace process, away from trauma and towards the domain of emotion, feeling, and affect in history.

To open up this kind of enquiry is to move beyond the particular framing emphases and circumscriptions of trauma, in four main ways. Firstly, freed from trauma's focus on pathological affective states implicitly counterposed to an 'untraumatic' norm, more inclusive consideration could be given to emotions and feelings in times of war, conflict, and political violence, utilising more open, less rigid categorisations of what these consist in, what they mean, and how they work within historically specific cultures that pre-exist and continue after violent events. Secondly, moving beyond explanations of the effects of violent conflict on emotional life that reduce this to external causation by 'the event', richer, more complex, and nuanced accounts of the relation between external and internal worlds are required. These would enable emotional experience to be considered not only as a wound crying out, but as the medium for a range of interactions as well as 'disconnects'[56] between historical subjectivities and socio-cultural worlds consisting not only of events but also of frameworks of meaning. Thirdly, by acknowledging the active engagement of those affected by 'trauma' in making sense of and representing their own emotional experiences, work on the interpretation of states of feeling need no longer be restricted to analysis undertaken by professional authorities (the cultural critic, the trauma counsellor, the academic historian), but would seek understanding of how emotional life within a society is recognised and 'felt' by situated individuals and social groups. Critical enquiry could then focus its attention on 'the real feelings and desires of actual victims'[57] – or, to avoid the exclusive and politicised connotations attached to this term in Northern Ireland, of those who have been subjected to, or harmed by, or engaged in political violence (or all of these) – when freed from hegemonic silencing and the pressure to represent themselves as trauma victims. Fourthly, abandoning linear conceptions of temporality and socio-political imperatives for 'premature closure'[58] points to the need for investigations of the complex temporalities of emotion and feeling within structures of power, compliance, and resistance; and of the activisms that seek transformation of conflict-related emotions through future-oriented efforts 'to change social reality, forge new connections and align inner reality with what is happening externally'.[59]

In my thinking about these issues, I am finding resources for a new analytical framework in three areas of investigation which propose distinct though in certain respects overlapping approaches. These are the tradition of object-relations psychoanalytic theory derived from the work of Melanie Klein and associated in the UK with the Tavistock Institute in London, cultural materialist analysis centred on Raymond Williams' conception of 'structures of feeling', and work developed since the turn of the century on emotional histories. In what follows I discuss each in turn.

Object-relations theory 'holds out a perspective for the construction of a psychoanalysis that takes account of social relations',[60] and demonstrates 'a potential willingness to investigate psychic life in terms of the particularity of (actual) social relationships ... located historically within a specific culture'.[61] Embodied emotional and psychic life is understood as a dynamic process occurring within a person's inner world, largely unconscious, peopled by imagined objects or 'imagos' with which the self interacts to establish various kinds of internal object relations. These imagined objects partly derive their character from, but also affect perceptions of, external others and social situations, which are experienced according to internal psychic reality. Expressions of feeling, behaviours, and relationships in the social world thus become vehicles for 'acting out' internal object relations, managing internal disturbances and conflicts, and controlling or managing emotions.

This kind of psychoanalytic thinking offers more dynamic conceptions of the emotional substance of psychic and social life than those found in conventional trauma theory. Indeed, much of the critique presented earlier in this article is informed by this tradition. In making her argument that 'the traumatization effect does not appear to reside in the nature of the event ... but (in) what the mind later does to memory', Radstone quotes the object-relations psychoanalyst, Caroline Garland:

> Whatever the nature of the event ... eventually (the survivor) comes to make sense of it in terms of the most troubled and troubling of the relationships between the objects that are felt to inhabit his internal world. That way the survivor is at least making something recognisable and familiar out of the extraordinary, giving it a meaning (original ellipsis).[62]

Hamber's thinking about extreme political violence, trauma, and victimhood is also rooted in object-relations theory derived from his training as a clinical psychologist and psychotherapist, as he encountered a 'tidal wave of emotion' in local meetings with victims of apartheid-era violence whilst preparing for the South African Truth and Reconciliation Commission in 1995.[63] The object-relations model complements and may be integrated into cultural and historical approaches to feeling and emotion, and opens up ways of thinking that understand these phenomena as a medium through which the interconnections between internal and external worlds are produced, regulated, contested, and transformed.

Raymond Williams' cultural materialism is also centrally concerned with the agency of historically-situated people in the making of meanings, the articulation of the felt texture of personal and social experience, and the challenging of received understandings and dominant frameworks for making sense. Williams proposes the concept 'structures of feeling'[64] to think about 'meanings and values as they are actively lived and felt, and the relations between these and formal or systematic beliefs' – relations which may range from assent or dissent to more complex interactions and negotiations.[65] It draws attention to what he calls 'characteristic elements of impulse, restraint, and tone; specifically affective elements of consciousness and relationships: ... thought as felt and feeling as thought', often 'at the very edge' of 'practical consciousness' and not yet fully recognised or articulated within existing frameworks of understanding.[66] For Williams, 'this felt sense of the quality of life at a particular place and time' is the medium of a 'community of experience' linking those who share a class position and belong to a generation.[67] It is hard to pin down and study, especially '[o]nce the carriers of such a structure die'.[68] But what Williams calls these 'social experiences *in solution*' can be discerned in the *'precipitated'* form of cultural representations, the stories and images that we make of our lived experience.[69] Williams here identifies a gap between lived experience and its representation, and invites further reflection on how this is mediated and how emotions 'in solution' might be accessed. Critical attention can then focus on the quality of the precipitating voices, the forms they create to articulate 'embryonic' or 'emergent' new structures of feeling, with their limitations and achievements, and the social positions from which they speak.[70]

As Harding and Pribram have argued, Williams' concept brings the emotions into focus 'as rich, complex sociocultural practices' that are 'culturally constituted and culturally shared', with ascertainable effects;[71] and enables us to ask 'what new or changing formations of emotion has it become possible to think or feel at a given moment?'[72] According to their useful critique, these possibilities are limited by Williams' tendency to homogenise 'vast singular structures of feeling reflecting unified configurations of subject positions – class or generational – at a particular historical moment or location', and an insufficiently developed sense of 'conflict, competition or struggle between the structures of feeling of any epoch'.[73] Revised, as they suggest, to refer to 'a multiplicity of structures of feeling that operate in a complex interactive web' that is 'interactional ... (and) historically changing',[74] 'structures of feeling' provides a valuable conceptual basis for analysing the configuration of felt experiences that manifested in Northern Ireland in response to the violence of the Troubles, and the shifts that have occurred 'post-conflict'. These include the emergence of social interest in trauma, therapy, and healing, and also how the so-called ceasefire generation post-1994 has 'respond(ed) in its own ways to the world ... feeling its whole life in certain ways differently, and shaping its creative response into a new structure of feeling'.[75]

More variegated accounts of the contingency, context, and social dynamics of feeling can be found in recent studies of the history and politics of emotion, including work that is directly concerned with emotional life in times of war and conflict. While emphasising emotional life as a cultural and social phenomenon, historians of emotion have to confront its intersection with the felt energies and affects arising in what Joanna Bourke terms 'the emotional body',[76] evident in the 'fight or flight' reactions to fear in combat situations,[77] and in the prevalence of stomach aches and upsets amongst soldiers on the Western Front during the First World War identified by Michael Roper.[78] However, caught in a tension between embodiment and signification, our own affective experience is not self-evident and transparent but requires 'emotional labour' to understand and interpret what goes on inside, in the internal world, at the 'boundaries between "bodily space" and social space"'.[79] We discover, reflect on, and may attempt to articulate, what it is that we feel on the basis of a 'vocabulary of emotion'.[80] These words have, as the much-quoted anthropologist William Reddy puts it, a 'unique capacity to alter what they "refer" to or what they "represent"'; so, for example, 'the *sensation of fear*' may be conjured, or altered, by 'acts of speaking (or writing) one's fear'.[81] 'As the words change, so too does the meaning of the emotion within a particular culture'.[82]

The prevailing languages of emotion are imbricated with social norms and what Claire Langhamer calls 'dominant emotional codes and standards', which also form and shift historically in relation to changing conditions of life.[83] For Barbara Rosenwein, 'emotions have social functions and follow social rules', providing 'tools with which we manage social life' and conduct our relations with others.[84] She proposes the concept of 'emotional communities' to refer to the 'systems of feeling' that are active within social institutions and networks – 'families, neighbourhoods, parliaments, guilds, monasteries, parish church (congregations)' – and which establish 'what these communities (and the individuals within them) define and assess as valuable or harmful to them; the evaluations that they make about others' emotions; the nature of the affective bonds between people that they recognize; and the modes of emotional expression that they expect, encourage, tolerate and deplore'.[85] Rosenwein argues that multiple emotional communities jostle and overlap within a society at any particular historical moment, constituting conflicting and sometimes contradictory common sense about the meaning and value of an emotion such as hatred;[86] and that 'people move (and moved) continually from one such community to another', adjusting their emotional expression accordingly.[87] This can be seen in Roper's analysis of the emotional survival skills that soldiers exercised during the First World War, which demonstrates how 'models of care' derived from their 'closest emotional bonds' within the family, particularly between mothers and sons, provided soldiers with 'emotional reference points' to draw on in their relationships within the institution of the Army at the front.[88] In an analysis that suggests how we might think concretely about Gilligan's 'informal support networks' and the resilience of those affected by the violence of the Troubles, Roper explores how soldiers tried to 'keep their spirits up', took care of each other, and coped with 'emotions like fear, anger, love and loss', which were shaped 'according to particular class and family cultures and idioms of expression'.[89]

In handling feelings such as loss or love within social life, then, while we 'exercise … emotional agency', we are not free agents.[90] Rather, we situate our own feelings in relation to cultures – or 'structures of feeling', used by both Rosenwein and Roper[91] – that shape patterns, expectations, and models of experience. Emotional communities and cultures with specific locations in time and space develop particular ways of organising felt subjectivity, enabling us to recognise and communicate our emotional lives and interactions. On this basis our emotions are felt to be validated by, or to be transgressive of, cultural norms and values. Thus they have political implications. Handled in culturally sanctioned ways according to 'feeling-rules' that govern their expression or concealment, emotions are subject to repression, restraint, and sanctioned release.[92] The gendering of such rules is demonstrated in Lucy Noakes' study of 'the management of female grief' in anticipation of, and response to, air raids on Britain during the Second World War.[93] This explores how a long-established 'emotional economy ... emphasiz(ing) stoicism and reticence' as the '(desirable) codes of behaviour' for men was extended to women as a means of curtailing the 'disruptive' and 'destabiliz(ing)' impact of mass bereavement on national morale and the war effort.[94] In wartime British culture, the requirements of emotional restraint, whether internally adopted through engagement with popular cultural texts or externally imposed by national and local state authorities, policed public expressions of emotion whilst constituting the private sphere as the location of greater licence, and responsibility, in emotional life. However, the negotiation of felt experience between people and social institutions is never only about emotional control, but also involves the social and political 'evoking' of emotion, as in the case of fear, which Bourke shows to have been incited historically in relation to shifting social anxieties from the afterlife of hell to terrorism.[95]

Emotions may be felt collectively, even contagiously, by people in social groups undergoing a common experience, including those recognised as a 'traumatized community'; and such collectivities themselves become the object of emotional management, as in official strategies for avoiding panic in crowd control.[96] Yet varied and unexpected emotional reactions also arise within groups, which are never homogeneous; as can be seen in the diverse expressions of happiness, fortitude, and a sense of reassurance perversely derived from the recognition that other people are also worried, reported in response to the danger of bombings during the Blitz.[97] This leads Bourke to conclude that, far from belonging to any pre-given collective entity such as a class, emotions work to 'align people with others', thereby constituting them as a social group (and, as Sara Ahmed argues, organising their felt relation to others);[98] so 'fear places people', sorting them into positions within a social hierarchy.[99] The question for historians of emotion, then, is 'what is (an emotion such as) fear *doing*?'[100] Applying this argument to Northern Ireland since the Troubles, Bourke suggests that the 'invention of trauma society' has 'framed, created and managed extremes of anxiety' at the cost of recognizing people's resilience, creativity, and courage.[101] 'The issue', Bourke concludes, 'is not whether we are traumatised, but how we are transformed'.[102] This suggests other ways of thinking about the temporality of emotions and the meaning of 'moving on'.

Historians of emotion offer complex models of emotional life and temporality, sensitive to what I have called the 'afterlife' of emotion and the ways in which feelings 'live on' and move dynamically in time.[103] In one sense, following the temporal architecture of conventional trauma theory, emotion and affect can be seen as the product of an originating event or episode such as violent conflict 'in the past'. Emotions of various kinds come to be experienced and understood as something caused by and attached to this event. According to one kind of account, this emotion then persists continuously after the event into the present, where it is always ready to be given expression again; as, for example, in Freud's thinking about melancholy as persistent loss. Another kind of account sees the emotional and affective response to the event becoming overlaid by subsequent emotional experience and development, such that it becomes progressively distanced in time while retaining potential to be reconnected to the present. This can be seen in the phenomenon of 'return' to, and re-experiencing of, a disturbing event which has not been psychically 'absorbed' or 'digested' at the time of its occurrence but remains in the unconscious as a 'trace' – what Roper calls 'emotional residues' – capable of 'animating later recollections'.[104] Eva Hoffman, writing of the 'the transmission of loss across generations' after the Holocaust, describes a form of knowledge that is 'not a memory' but 'states of feeling conveyed by survivors to their offspring'.[105] 'What we children of survivors knew ... were the emotional sequelae of our elders' experiences';[106] 'affective messages' communicated 'by some means', such that 'children speak of being permeated by sensations of panic and deadliness, of shame and guilt', conveying an 'imperative to perform impossible psychic tasks' of rescue and reparation.[107]

Even if temporally located 'in the past', then, emotions are durational and involve complex relations between past, present, and future. Their temporality may be fluid rather than fixed once and for all, and characterised in various ways; as longevity, but also as capacities for recurrence, re-emergence, ebb and flow, repetition. Further complications stem from the mutability of affect and emotion, and what Bourke calls its 'fluctuations in intensity over time'.[108] One emotion or affective state may also transform into another – such as sadness into anger, or anger into guilt – and these may condense together into compound formations like those found in Derry/ Londonderry after the Bloody Sunday shootings.[109] This points to the way that emotion and affect can be considered according to a second kind of temporality, as produced and expressed, lived and handled in the context of circumstances and concerns of a present moment. Much of the work on memory and subjectivity undertaken within oral history and life-history analysis has emphasised the making of new meanings, namings, and interpretations of experience, including states of feeling, that subjects produce retrospectively, possibly many years later. Making sense of past events in new ways may transform what is felt about them now, as Nicola King argues in her take on Freud's concept of *Nachträglichkeit*, translated as 'afterwardsness'.[110] The oral historian Alistair Thomson captures the dynamics of temporality within the ordinary life course, and the way life transitions associated with the process of ageing and looking back over time may trigger a re-evaluation of feelings long attached to past events, in his phrase 'experience never ends'.[111]

Work on the history of emotions is also opening up the significance of futurity in constituting feelings in the present. In her work on the history of love, Claire Langhamer understands emotional life in Britain during the Second World War in terms of a temporal break in those 'normal' patterns and expectations of courtship, engagement, and marriage that traditionally gave meaning and value to sexual attractions as well as criteria for evaluating and choosing sexual partners and behaviours, founded on the projection and planning of a shared trajectory of life in the future. Amid the fears and uncertainties of wartime, permeated by the 'feeling you might be gone tomorrow', confidence in any imaginable future was shattered.[112] This produced a new emotional ethos of 'living for the moment' and fostered desire for short-term relationships and hasty marriages grounded on immediate gratification rather than long-term commitment; for, as one female Mass-Observer remarked in 1942, when a 'man's mind is so uncertain of its future he cannot in fairness to himself or another undertake a tie of permanence ... the only thing to do so long as the war continues is to live for the present only, and evade ties so deep that their destruction would destroy as well one's stability'.[113] Such considerations of futurity open up further questions, about how subjective composure organised within a short-term temporal horizon of this kind is interpreted and evaluated subsequently as one looks back having 'cross[ed] into a new temporal space' of the postwar with its 'radical reorientation of the present'.[114]

CONCLUSION

I have argued in this article that historical approaches to the phenomena of feeling and emotion, especially those concerned with war and conflict, open up new perspectives on emotional life that move beyond the frame of trauma and avoid some of its difficulties. These approaches offer a number of productive concepts for understanding the social dynamics and temporalities of lived experience and memory and its representation during and after the Troubles, and suggest new kinds of orientation towards, for example, the storytelling and life history projects and archives that have flourished during the peace process. As well as informing what it is that such projects explore, by seeing their work as a production of emotional histories richer use could be made of the stories they elicit and collect, as sources for investigating structures of feeling and the meanings that are being made and remade of emotional life over a fifty-year period since the onset of the conflict.[115] With a new horizon of the future now opened up by the UK's 'Brexit' vote to leave the European Union, posing the threat of a restored 'hard border' in Ireland that reawakens emotions 'of the past', historical approaches to the social dynamics and afterlife of emotion and feeling in memory offer tools for understanding the present that are more specific, flexible, multifaceted, and complex than those offered by Caruthian trauma theory.

This is not to advocate 'history' at the expense of 'psychology', and I want to end by arguing for the retention of a psychoanalytic dimension to the investigation of emotional histories, rooted in the object-relations tradition. Feelings and emotions are, as the social historian Michael Roper puts it, 'always relational',[116] in that they arise and make themselves felt in relation to others, both real and imagined, and are mediated, in psychoanalytic terms, through internal object relations that figure modes of intersubjectivity and colour with feeling our social and political relationships. For object-relations theorists, recovery from deeply disturbing experience and the nurturing of psychic health depends upon capacities for 'reparation' being mobilised to think about the meanings and emotions attached to internal objects, to undo defensive splitting within the psyche, and to integrate contradictory emotions and conflicting aspects of the self within a less polarised inner world. The work of reparation is strengthened by the 'introjection', or taking in, of such capacities where they are encountered in social life. This, as well as the perception of discrepancies between anticipations derived from the internal world and the complex realities of the external social world, enables 'something new to happen' within both psychic and social reality.[117]

Work by historians of emotion has already begun to explore how concepts and insights from object relations theory may be used in historical interpretation of emotional formations and dynamics; as in my previous thinking about 'reparative remembering' as a means of undoing 'defensive' modes of subjective composure of the self, and in Roper's reading of soldiers' writing as a means to 'get rid of disturbing feelings' or as attempts at 'containing' otherwise 'nameless dread'.[118] There is scope for further work of this kind, to explore how emotional transformations in self and society are brought about after war and conflict, and to illuminate the complex and challenging meanings of 'moving on'.

NOTES

1. Susannah Radstone, 'Trauma Theory: Contexts, Politics, Ethics', *Paragraph* 30.1 (2007), pp.9–29 (10). See Shoshana Felman and Dori Laub, *Testimony: Crises of Witnessing in Literature, Psychoanalysis and History* (London: Routledge, 1992); *Trauma: Explorations in Memory*, ed. by Cathy Caruth (Baltimore: John Hopkins University Press, 1995); Cathy Caruth, *Unclaimed Experience: Trauma, Narrative and History* (Baltimore: John Hopkins University Press, 1996).
2. Radstone, 'Trauma Theory', p.10.
3. Radstone, 'Trauma Theory', p.11. See also Susannah Radstone, 'Screening Trauma: *Forrest Gump*', in *Memory and Methodology*, ed. by Susannah Radstone (Oxford: Berg, 2000), pp.85–90.
4. APA's *Diagnostic and Statistical Manual of Mental Disorders* (DSM III, 1980 and IV, 1994), quoted in Graham Dawson, *Making Peace with the Past? Memory, Trauma and the Irish Troubles* (Manchester: Manchester University Press, 2007), p.63 (hereafter abbreviated as *MPWP*).
5. Radstone, 'Trauma Theory', p.12.
6. Radstone, 'Trauma Theory', p.14.
7. Ruth Leys, *Trauma: A Genealogy* (2000), quoted in Radstone, 'Trauma Theory', p.13. Radstone identifies Judith Herman, *Trauma and Recovery* (New York: Basic Books, 1992) as a key text in this respect.
8. Radstone, 'Trauma Theory', p.15.
9. Caruth, *Unclaimed Experience*, p.4.
10. Caruth, *Trauma*, p.5.
11. Radstone, 'Trauma Theory', p.20.
12. Radstone, 'Trauma Theory', p.17.
13. Radstone, 'Trauma Theory', pp.18–19.
14. Radstone, 'Trauma Theory', p.18.
15. Caroline Garland, 'Introduction: Why Psychoanalysis?', in *Understanding Trauma: A Psychoanalytic Approach*, ed. by Caroline Garland (London: Duckworth, 1998), p.12.
16. Radstone, 'Trauma Theory', pp.13,14.
17. Radstone, 'Trauma Theory', p.22.
18. Radstone, 'Trauma Theory', p.24.
19. Radstone, 'Trauma Theory', p.24.
20. The wider range of debate on trauma in Irish Studies is beyond the scope of this article, but see Dawson, *MPWP*, where the PTSD paradigm is married (uneasily) with an object-relations psychoanalytic approach to trauma; Joseph Valente, 'Ethnonostalgia: *Irish Hunger* and Traumatic Memory', in *Memory Ireland, Volume 3: The Famine and the Troubles*, ed. by Oona Frawley (Syracuse NY: Syracuse University Press, 2014), pp.174–92, who argues that in work on the Irish Famine, the Caruthian dissociation model has been less influential than the Freudian model of repression producing amnesia; Emilie Pine, *The Politics of Irish Memory: Performing Remembrance in Irish Culture* (Basingstoke: Palgrave MacMillan, 2011), where the concept of trauma is detached from its psychological roots and used to

signify cultural constructions of the past in terms of unresolved pain and suffering; and the range of contributions to *The Body in Pain in Irish Literature and Culture*, ed. by Fionnuala Dillane, Naomi McAreavey and Emilie Pine (Basingstoke: Palgrave MacMillan, 2016).

21. Oona Frawley, 'Introduction', *Memory Ireland*, pp.1–14 (7).

22. Frawley, 'Introduction', p.11.

23. Berber Bevernage, *History, Memory, and State-Sponsored Violence: Time and Justice* (New York: Routledge, 2012), pp.65, 4–5; Jennifer Edkins, *Trauma and the Memory of Politics* (Cambridge: Cambridge University Press, 2003).

24. Stefanie Lehner, 'The Irreversible and the Irrevocable: Encircling Trauma in Contemporary Northern Irish Literature', in Frawley, *Memory Ireland*, pp.272–92 (273).

25. Lehner, 'The Irreversible', pp.277, 291.

26. Fionna Barber, 'At Vision's Edge: Post-conflict Memory and Art Practice in Northern Ireland', in Frawley, *Memory Ireland*, pp.232–46.

27. Dawson, *MPWP*, p.62.

28. Chris Gilligan, 'Traumatised by Peace? A Critique of Five Assumptions in the Theory and Practice of Conflict-related Trauma Policy in Northern Ireland', *Policy and Politics* 34.2 (2006), 325–45.

29. See Fabrice Mourlon, 'Assessing the Achievements of Assistance to the Victims of the Conflict in Northern Ireland', in *Ireland and Victims*, ed. by Lesley Lelourec and Grainne O'Keefe Vigneron (Bern: Peter Lang, 2012), pp.189–208; and Dawson, *MPWP*, pp.233–37.

30. Gilligan, p.329.

31. Gilligan, p.327.

32. Gilligan, pp.326, 336.

33. Quoted in Gilligan, p.329.

34. Gilligan, p.327.

35. Gilligan, pp.330–31.

36. Brandon Hamber, *Transforming Societies after Political Violence* (Dordrecht: Springer, 2009), pp.79–80; Brandon Hamber, *Dealing with Painful Memories and Violent Pasts* (Berlin: Berghof, 2015), p.8. < http://image.berghof-foundation.org/fileadmin/ redaktion/Publications/Handbook/Dialogue_Chapters/ dialogue11_hamber_lead.pdf >. Accessed 22 January 2016.

37. Hamber, *Transforming Societies*, p.77; Hamber, *Dealing with Painful Memories*, p.8.

38. Hamber, *Dealing with Painful Memories*, p.4.

39. Gilligan, p.330.

40. Hamber, *Dealing with Painful Memories*, p.4.

41. Hamber, *Transforming Societies*, p.21.

42. Gilligan, 'Traumatised by Peace?', p.328.

43. Hamber, *Dealing with Painful Memories*, p.4.

44. Hamber, *Dealing with Painful Memories*, p.4.

45. Hamber, *Dealing with Painful Memories*, p.3. See Hamber, *Transforming Societies*, pp.19–25.

46. Hamber, *Dealing with Painful Memories*, p.5.

47. Gilligan, p.330.

48. Hamber, *Dealing with Painful Memories*, p.13. See Hamber, *Transforming Societies*, p.85.

49. Hamber, *Transforming Societies*, pp.65–74.

50. Grainne Kelly, *'Storytelling' Audit: An Audit of Personal Story, Narrative and Testimony Initiatives Related to the Conflict in and about Northern Ireland* (Belfast: Healing Through Remembering, 2005), p.3.

51. Cahal McLaughlin, *Recording Memories from Political Violence: A Film-maker's Journey* (Bristol: Intellect, 2010), p.17.
52. McLaughlin, *Recording Memories*, p.21.
53. *Report of the Consultative Group on the Past* (Belfast: Consultative Group on the Past, 2009), p.100.
54. See Dawson, *MPWP*, p.315; Hamber, *Transforming Societies*, pp.75–91.
55. House of Commons Northern Ireland Affairs Committee, *Ways of Dealing with Northern Ireland's Past. Interim Report – Victims and Survivors, Tenth Report of Session 2004–05. Volume II: Oral and written evidence* (London: Stationery Office, 2005), Evidence Ev 141, Q654. < http://cain.ulst.ac.uk/victims/docs/british_gov/ni_affairs_ctte_hc/vol_2_060405.pdf.> Accessed 26 July 2016.
56. Hamber, *Transforming Societies*, p.88.
57. Marie Breen Smyth, *Truth Recovery and Justice after Conflict* (New York: Routledge, 2007), p.81.
58. Hamber, *Transforming Societies*, p.93.
59. Hamber, *Transforming Societies*, p.88.
60. Stephen Frosh, *The Politics of Psychoanalysis* (Basingstoke: MacMillan, 1987), p.119. See also Michael Rustin, *The Good Society and the Inner World: Psychoanalysis, Politics and Culture* (London: Verso, 1991).
61. Graham Dawson, *Soldier Heroes: British Adventure, Empire and the Imagining of Masculinities* (London: Routledge, 1994), p.30. See pp.27–52.
62. Quoted in Radstone, 'Trauma Theory', p.17.
63. TRC Commissioner Wendy Orr, quoted in Hamber, *Transforming Societies*, p.46. See also pp.37, 80, 96, 103, 193. For another example of the use of object relations psychoanalysis in post-apartheid South Africa, see Pumla Gobodo-Madikizela, 'Psychological Repair: The Intersubjective Dialogue of Remorse and Forgiveness in the Aftermath of Gross Human Rights Violations', *Journal of the American Psychoanalytic Association* 63.6 (2015), 1085–1123.
64. The key texts are Raymond Williams, *The Long Revolution* (Harmondsworth: Pelican, 1965), pp.57–88; Raymond Williams, *Marxism and Literature* (Oxford: Oxford University Press, 1977), pp.128–35; Raymond Williams, *Politics and Letters* (London: Verso, 1979), pp.156–74.
65. Williams, *Marxism and Literature*, p.132.
66. Williams, *Marxism and Literature*, p.132.
67. Williams, *Long Revolution*, pp.63, 64.
68. Williams, *Long Revolution*, p.65.
69. Williams, *Marxism and Literature*, pp.133–34
70. Williams, *Marxism and Literature*, pp.131,134.
71. Jennifer Harding and E. Deirdre Pribram, 'The Power of Feeling: Locating Emotions in Culture', *European Journal of Cultural Studies* 5.4 (2002), 407–26 (p.417)
72. Jennifer Harding and E. Deirdre Pribram, 'Losing Our Cool? Following Williams and Grossberg on Emotions', *Cultural Studies* 18.6 (2004), 863–83 (pp.870–1).
73. Harding and Pribram, 'Power of Feeling', p.417.
74. Harding and Pribram, 'Power of Feeling', p.418.
75. Williams, *Long Revolution*, p.65.
76. Joanna Bourke, *Fear: A Cultural History* (London: Virago, 2005), p.289. See also Barbara H. Rosenwein, 'Worrying about Emotions in History', *American Historical Review* 107.3 (2002), 821–45 (pp.834–37).
77. Bourke, *Fear*, pp.200–8.
78. Michael Roper, *The Secret Battle: Emotional Survival in the Great War* (Manchester: Manchester University Press, 2009), pp.252–3.

79. Bourke, *Fear*, p.354, quoting Sara Ahmed, *The Cultural Politics of Emotion* (New York: Routledge, 2004).
80. Rosenwein, 'Worrying about Emotions', pp.837–38.
81. Bourke, *Fear*, p.287.
82. Bourke, *Fear*, p.75.
83. Claire Langhamer, *The English in Love: The Intimate Story of an Emotional Revolution* (Oxford: Oxford University Press, 2013), p.8.
84. Rosenwein, 'Worrying about Emotions', pp.841, 842.
85. Rosenwein, 'Worrying about Emotions', p.842.
86. Rosenwein, 'Worrying about Emotions', pp.842–45.
87. Rosenwein, 'Worrying about Emotions', p.842.
88. Roper, *Secret Battle*, pp.161, 162, 178.
89. Roper, *Secret Battle*, pp.88, 33.
90. Langhamer, *English in Love*, p.19.
91. Rosenwein, 'Worrying about Emotions', p.839 note 68; Roper, *Secret Battle*, p.188.
92. Bourke, *Fear*, p. 353.
93. Lucy Noakes, 'Gender, Grief, and Bereavement in Second World War Britain', *Journal of War and Culture Studies* 8.1 (2015), 72–85 (p.79).
94. Noakes, 'Gender, Grief and Bereavement', pp.77, 74.
95. Bourke, *Fear*, p.353. See pp.33, 365–66.
96. Dawson, *MPWP*, p.62; Bourke, *Fear*, pp.59–61, 226.
97. Bourke, *Fear*, pp.228–32.
98. Bourke, *Fear*, p.355; Ahmed, *Cultural Politics of Emotion*.
99. Bourke, *Fear*, p.354.
100. Bourke, *Fear*, p.353.
101. Bourke, *Fear*, pp.375, 380.
102. Bourke, *Fear*, p.382.
103. This section draws on Graham Dawson, 'Memory, 'Post-Conflict' Temporalities and the Afterlife of Emotion in Conflict Transformation after the Irish Troubles', in *Irish Studies and the Dynamics of Memory*, ed. by Marguérite Corporaal, Christopher Cusack, and Ruud van den Beuken (Oxford: Peter Lang, 2017), pp.257–96.
104. Roper, *Secret Battle*, pp. 243–66 (247, 254).
105. Eva Hoffman, 'The Long Afterlife of Loss', in *Memory: Histories, Theories, Debates*, ed. by Susannah Radstone and Bill Schwarz (New York: Fordham University Press, 2010), pp.406–15 (406, 407, 409).
106. Hoffman, 'Long Afterlife', p.407.
107. Hoffman, 'Long Afterlife', pp.408, 409.
108. Bourke, *Fear*, p.150.
109. Dawson, *MPWP*, pp. 139–41.
110. Nicola King, *Memory, Narrative, Identity: Remembering the Self* (Edinburgh: Edinburgh University Press, 2000).
111. Alistair Thomson, 'Experience Never Ends: Migrant Memories, Unsettled Identities and Historical Change', in *Crossroads of History: Experience, Memory, Orality*, Proceedings of the XIth International Oral History Conference (Istanbul, 2000), pp.1081–7.
112. Langhamer, *English in Love*, pp.165–69 (quoting a 23-year-old female Mass Observer, p.167).
113. 28-year-old female Mass Observer, quoted in Langhamer, *English in Love*, p.169.
114. Rebecca Bryant, 'History's Remainders: On Time and Objects after Conflict in Cyprus', *American Ethnologist* 41.4 (2014), 681–97 (p.683).

115. See, for example, Sara Dybris McQuaid, 'Passive Archives or Storages for Action? Storytelling Projects in Northern Ireland', *Irish Political Studies* (2016). DOI:10.1080/07907184.2015.1126929.
116. Roper, *Secret Battle*, p.24.
117. J.R. Greenberg and S.A. Mitchell, *Object Relations in Psychoanalytic Theory* (Cambridge, Mass.: Harvard University Press, 1983), p.134.
118. Dawson, *MPWP*, pp.77, 311–12; Roper, *Secret Battle*, pp.68, 250.

Stefanie Lehner

'Parallel Games' and Queer Memories: Performing LGBT Testimonies in Northern Ireland[1]

In *Trouble*, the recent performed queer archive (with video installations), written by Shannon Yee and produced, designed, and directed by Niall Rea (the latter, with Anna Newell), Northern Irish actor Jimmy Kerr delivers a short monologue from a video screen, explaining to the audience the difficulty of living in Northern Ireland as a gay man:

> Staying in Northern Ireland ... there is a sort of trauma that stays with you, someone in a battering relationship or poisonous relationship with alcohol, you know you should break away from it but you keep returning to it. That's a problem. There's a cognitive dissonance there for gay people. You want to be part of a family, you want to be part of a church, you want to be part of society but if they know you as you really are, they won't accept you. But you really want to be accepted. So you play a parallel game in your life.[2]

Trouble, as apparent in its promotion poster (*Figure 1*), uses for its 'o' the symbol of a 'pink triangle, rewind button' to indicate its intention of recovering 'the experiences of a generation of individuals from the LGBT [Lesbian, Gay, Bisexual, and Transgender] community that realised their sexuality while growing up during the Troubles in Northern Ireland'.[3] Based on forty-six interviews, it documents 'individual's private stories of cultural identity, sexuality and coming out, religion, feminism, sectarianism, racism, conversion therapy, paramilitaries, politics, the normalization of violence and the effects of the Troubles on the psyche' against the larger historical, political backdrop of the Northern Irish conflict.[4] As such, it delineates a complex matrix of exclusions – but also a desire for inclusion – that define and regulate expressions of identity and sexuality in

Irish University Review 47.1 (2017): 103–118
DOI: 10.3366/iur.2017.0259
© Edinburgh University Press
www.euppublishing.com/iur

Northern Ireland, as suggested by the speaker above. His desire to belong to structures that oppress and discriminate against him force this man to 'play a parallel game': for him, this is a necessary strategy of survival in an extremely homophobic society.[5] While the concept of playing a 'game' gestures here towards the rules, roles, and regulatory practices that define and confine expressions of identity (including gender and sexuality), it foregrounds at the same time their construction; the performative nature of all identities. The notion of parallelism suggests the incompatibility of ethno-nationalism with LGBT issues in a deeply divided society such as Northern Ireland. The incommensurability between sectarian and queer politics is also addressed in Niall Rea's *Divided, Radical and Gorgeous (D.R.A.G.)*, which explores the personal experiences of a Belfast drag queen in the form of a testimonial monologue that recounts her relationship with a closeted 'freedom fighter'. Furthermore, queer identities are used by both productions as an 'analogous' lens to deconstruct and disrupt sectarian divisions of difference. The notion of playing a 'parallel game' can, thus, be read as a meta-theatrical commentary that emphasises that while these plays, based on personal memories of the Troubles, are products of their socio-historical reality, they also provide an alternative, transformative realm, in which it is possible to rethink the conditions of the present through uncovering silenced and neglected voices and experiences of the past. Both plays do so by 'queering' memories of the Troubles that may otherwise be filtered through an ethno-nationalist lens. While in Northern Ireland, collective memory has congealed into two mutually exclusive versions of history (namely, Protestant/unionist/loyalist and Catholic/nationalist/republican), 'queer memory', as David Cregan suggests, 'is transformative in seeking to destabilise any particular version of the past. It offers a self-reflective and socially challenging voice in the midst of memory formation, queering marginalized memory as well as memory of the dominant.'[6]

This essay explores how the notion of 'parallel games' works to queer memory in two productions of Northern Ireland's first publicly funded gay theatre company, TheatreofplucK, led by artistic director Niall Rea.[7] Both plays have seen different versions as part of their development: *Trouble* saw its first incarnation in an invitation-only workshop at the Metropolitan Arts Centre (MAC) in Belfast in the summer of 2013,[8] while there have been three iterations of *D.R.A.G.* to date: Rea initially worked with Gordon Crawford (who performs as the Belfast drag queen Trudy Scrumptious), who played in the first two versions in 2012, and was joined by Paul C. Boyd, who took over the role in 2012. This essay focuses on the world premiere of *Trouble* at the MAC in November 2015 as part of OUTBURST Queer Arts

Figure 1. Poster of TheatreofplucK's *Trouble* (2015).

Festival, and the last, recorded version of *D.R.A.G.* at The Belfast Barge as part of the Belfast Pride Festival in July/August 2012. As post-conflict memory works, based on the testimonies of the interviewees, as in the case of *Trouble*, or autobiographical memories of both director and actors, as in the case of *D.R.A.G.*, and conceived, developed, and produced after the 1998 Belfast Agreement, both plays directly engage with contemporary debates about how to deal with the legacy of the past in Northern Ireland. In publicly performing and thus giving voice to previously silenced and hidden stories of LGBT people during the conflict, both productions address the call of the 2014 Stormont House Agreement, that resulted from the series of negotiations between Dr Richard Haass and Professor Meghan O'Sullivan in Autumn 2013, for the establishment of 'an Oral History Archive to provide a central place for people from all backgrounds (and from throughout the UK and Ireland) to share experiences and narratives related to the Troubles.'[9] This endeavour promises plurality by including disparate and incommensurable stories; yet, there is also a danger within any archival project that certain experiences, voices, and stories find more representation and greater valorisation than others. Given the reluctance of certain groups, such as former police officers, to participate in such storytelling activities, and the high profile of other voices and stories, it seems difficult for such an archive to present proportionally who was affected by the Troubles in equal measure.[10]

In *Archive Fever*, Jacques Derrida points to the etymology of the term 'archive', which 'names at once the *commencement* and the *commandment*': that is, archives denote origins as much as they are products of authority, control, and power.[11] As Ed Madden puts it, 'they produce as much as they record and preserve'.[12] As the promised multiplicity of stories will commence new understandings of the past, present, as well as the future, and thereby contribute to the 'fresh start' envisioned by the 1998 Agreement, the archival impulse displayed in its wake is, as Colin Graham notes, at the same time, suggestive of a desire 'to cram all that glistens with the not-so-gold of the Troubles into a memory bank of material culture and traumatic non-recall.'[13] In this regard, the establishment of an oral history archive seems a necessary step for 'moving on' from the legacy of the past; for moving beyond the trauma and residual sectarian legacies of the Troubles. In other words, the past is viewed through an educative prism and is closely connected to a progressive and purposive morality that was perhaps most succinctly captured in the decision to use Margaret Fairless Barber's words as an epigraph to the 2009 Report of the Consultative Group on the Past in Northern Ireland: 'To look backward for a while is to refresh the eye, to restore it, and to render it more fit for its prime function of looking forward'.[14] Given the effective institutionalisation of ethno-nationalist understandings of the conflict,[15] the political imperative, then, seems to be double-edged: in one respect it must entail, if not a suppression, then at least a muting, of memories that stand outwith the ethnic paradigm; and, in another, it ought to facilitate the implicit valorising of narratives that support a progressivist vision of contemporary Northern Irish society.

Both *D.R.A.G.* and *Trouble* disturb such a progressivist understanding of 'moving on': instead of memories being harnessed to the ethno-nationalist template established by the Belfast Agreement, the plays 'move' memory work in different directions at the same time, giving rise to a diverse set of emotions. This movement, in other words, parallels the Agreement's filtration of experience and belief into ethnicised modalities. The plays thus resonate with Michael Rothberg's concept of 'multidirectional memory', which is based on a malleable, pluralist understanding of memory, considering it 'as subject to ongoing negotiation, cross-referencing, and borrowing: as productive and not privative'.[16] Whereas the focus of Rothberg's model is on the articulation and performance of traumatic memories across transnational and intercultural contexts, the testimonies performed in both TheatreofplucK productions are 'multidirectional' insofar as they rupture the dominant perception of Northern Ireland as a 'place apart' – 'a recalcitrantly regressive place somehow separate from the modern progressive world':[17] for by focusing on the memories of LGBT people, they challenge (ethno and hetero)normative understandings of victimisation, oppression, and isolation while, at the same time, recovering 'new forms of solidarity and new visions of justice'.[18] In this way, the productions could also be said to initiate 'parallel games' with their audiences: the past is dis/uncovered not just in terms of regionality, sectarianism, and violence, but also in its containment of alternative forms of communality and togetherness.

This creates not so much 'moving memories' in the sense of simply becoming emotionally involved through sympathy or empathy in identifying individually with the characters; instead, the use of memories in both productions produces quasi-Brechtian *Verfremdungseffekte* that emphatically unsettle the spectators to make them adopt 'an attitude of inquiry and criticism' towards accepted and prescriptive readings of Troubles memories as well as contemporaneous approaches to dealing with the past along those lines.[19] In line with several post-conflict theatre performances by companies such as Kabosh, Tinderbox, Big Telly, and Prime Cut, both *D.R.A.G.* and *Trouble* do so by harnessing experimental theatre techniques, such as the use of verbatim, improvisation, multi-media, and audience involvement, if to different extents. For instance, whereas *Trouble* is predominantly inspired by verbatim theatre, in the style of American playwrights Anna Deavere Smith and Eve Ensler, whereby actors seek to carefully replicate the natural cadences, enunciation, silences, and emotions of the original voice recordings,[20] *D.R.A.G.* uses detailed autobiographical interviews with the performers to inspire games of improvisation. Both productions construct a bricolage of the different memories and testimonials, repeatedly challenging audience experience and expectation by creating parallel sensations of estrangement, exclusion, and isolation as well as connectedness, inclusion, and integration.

D.R.A.G. and *Trouble* self-consciously draw attention to their status as 'games' that ask for audience participation but also their awareness of what Al Head calls 'the "Foolish" insight' that 'all the conventional ways of being are "only a game" and that the "masks" that we play can be picked up or put down at will.'[21] Head suggests this as a queer strategy 'to help us in our analyses of the dominant society and the way it "creates" stereotypes of gender and sexuality' and other forms of identity, and, we might add, history; as such, it plays a crucial role in TheatreofplucK's queer dramaturgy.

Rea opens both productions with a short spiel introducing the spectators to what he calls 'the rules of game'.[22] For *D.R.A.G.*, he asks each of them to write a queer 'devotion' on a small piece of black paper before entering the actual performance space, which they then place on the stage, itself already covered with hundreds of other identical pieces of paper. The significance of these papers is twofold: on the one hand, handwritten notes with directorial comments, often based on the autobiographical interviews held before each rehearsal with the actors, were used for the improvisations that shaped and developed the direction of *D.R.A.G.*, and were also included in the final productions, which use the pieces of paper, apparently randomly picked up from the floor of the stage, to introduce different scenes, subjects, and topics of the life of the main character 'P'. On the other hand, by offering a personalised 'devotion', which was often a private memory, wish, or just a thought or a comment,[23] the audience engaged through these papers in what Rea conceived of as a 'community ritual', resonant of the rag trees that dot the Irish landscape.[24] As Rea explains, this 'ritual' was intended to offer each spectator 'a kind of direct and personal queer connection to the onstage world; temporally disconnected from the "straight" outside world', yet thereby suggesting their parallelism.[25]

D.R.A.G. itself opens with the performer, initially covered by these papers, rising naked, vulnerable, and bruised from this heap; as Rea notes: 'The performer here was born from the audiences['] own engagement, queerly energised'.[26] This, I want to suggest, is a truly queering and thus destabilising energy that creates intimacy at the same time as discomfort, drawing the audience in as much as keeping them at bay. Given that the performance uses the same black papers to mark its scenes, with each seemingly randomly selected paper shown to a camera so that its inscription is projected to the black back wall of the stage, there is an anxiety amongst the audience that their own personal 'devotions' will be revealed.[27] At the same time, their 'queer confessional' creates what Rea calls a 'public bond'[28] with the performer, which is compounded by what a reviewer describes as 'the cramped, claustrophobic surroundings of the Belfast Barge [where] the seating arrangements bring the audience challengingly close to Paul C. Boyd's tormented, stripped down presence.'[29]

Rea's thrust staging replicates the space dynamics of drag clubs, evoking both a dressing room as well as a nightclub stage. The white cubic set provides the audience with a sort of proscenium frame, which – together with the use of the camera, installed next to a vanity mirror, and projecting onto the back wall – raises awareness of the dynamics and power of the spectator's gaze. This visual play with intimacy and exposure parallels the use of the papers and the way in which 'P' immediately distances himself from his own 'confessions' by asserting that 'This is not a biography/ It has fuck all to do with me/ It's just a bunch of stories that relate to each other – don't try to read anything deep or meaningful into any of this ... I am not gonna be sharing any of my innermost secrets – or confessing any sins.'[30] Yet, he immediately appeals to (and thereby exposes) our desire as spectators to witness 'Some dark, dirty sins that you will be shocked by.... Some horrifying sins that make you feel so much more superior to me', while he puts on a *'balaclava as a confessional – kneels'*.[31] The repeated emphasis on 'sins' together with the symbolism of the balaclava, a 'hyperbolic symbol of terror'[32] typically used by Northern Irish paramilitaries, speaks to the specific context of the Northern Irish Troubles in which the perceived 'sin' of homosexuality (by both unionism/loyalism, if to a larger extent, as well as nationalism/ republicanism) could, when disclosed, easily lead to homophobic hate crimes and killings, as addressed in both *D.R.A.G.* and *Trouble.*[33]

The implication of the audience as potential voyeurs and consumers not only of his personal 'sins' but also 'your sins ... our sins' confronts them with their collusion in Northern Ireland's 'surveillance culture', which, as Kathryn Conrad argues, while helping in the post-conflict context to make issues, such as sectarian hate-crimes, visible and bring them into the civic realm, still 'impinges on privacy and bodily integrity as much as or more than the surveillance employed during the conflict.'[34] This becomes evident in the following scene where we watch the performer carefully putting on make-up, slowly transforming him into 'her', thereby 'highlighting the process of creating 'roles' of any type, whether theatrical or social.'[35] Here, again, the intimacy of the moment is abruptly ruptured when the performer *'threatens [the] audience'* with a gun, exclaiming 'Freaks' in reaction to the perceived intrusion of his personal space by the public gaze of the spectators. The confrontation and shock is somewhat deflated when he playfully *'winks at one cute man in front row'*. Both scenes work to 'queer' these paradigmatic symbols of hyper-masculine paramilitary sectarian identities through their subversive handling by a drag queen.[36] However, both times these symbols are also used to expose the collusion of the audience with processes of voyeurism, making us, evocative of Seamus Heaney's description in 'Punishment', complicit in 'cast[ing] the stones of silence'.[37] This complicity is brought to the fore in the Brechtian interlude *'An Ode to Our Silence'* in which Boyd stands directly in front of the camera so that his 'accusatory face' is magnified onto the back wall, while recounting the crimes of what Rea describes as 'the serial killer of prejudice and bigotry within all humanity'.[38] The last stanza directly addresses the present audience, thereby implicating them, as by-standers, in allowing violence against any kind of 'other' to continue to happen: 'There is a serial killer loose in this town – he is killing people who go to strange experimental theatre shows in tiny venues.'[39]

Comparable to Frank McGuinness' queer dramaturgy in *Carthaginians*, which offered Rea an important inspiration, *D.R.A.G.* repeatedly engages its audience with painful memories of the Troubles as well as their contemporary resonances. Yet, its use of both 'camp aesthetic and a campy drag-queen' unsettles our reaction, creating laughter in the face of distress, as apparent in the audience reaction to the last stanza of the 'Ode' above. As Cregan argues, 'These contradictory characteristics of camp allow it to function as a performative praxis in the queer project of unsettling what has become the normative approach to either histories, ideologies, or subjectivities.... In its queerness, camp has the capacity to hold together what otherwise might be considered antithetical: the authentic and the theatrical.'[40] As such, it provides not just a sense of 'identity and togetherness, fun and wit', but, as Richard Dyer suggests, camp must be also seen as form of 'self-mockery' (or even 'self-hating').[41] This becomes apparent in the exaggerated parody of different types of gays that the performer depicts in a more and more frantic dance around the small stage set. This scene becomes something of a 'play-within-a-play', a 'parallel game' to the stage reality, self-consciously foregrounding these different 'types' as 'roles' in a way in which we recognise what Sontag calls 'the metaphor of life as theatre.'[42] At the end, the performer collapses on the heap of papers, expressing the 'need write all this down –/ How we got here – got to be all these different people. Tell it the way it was – [...] all the false turns and dead ends / All the abuse ... and the laughs too'.[43] Such an alternative historiography can be provided by a queer archive, to which Rea's *D.R.A.G.* seeks to contribute.

The pile of papers is intended to allude here to the many other untold stories that together show a potential to suggest 'how things might start to be'.[44] In this, *D.R.A.G.* evokes Derrida's claim that the archive must involve 'a question of the future, the question of the future itself, the question of a response, of a promise and of a responsibility for tomorrow.'[45] Yet, in the play itself, the process of memory-mapping an alternative queer future is forestalled by P's reminiscences of the breakup of her relationship with her 'beautiful closeted freedom fighter'. While this liaison between a drag queen and a hyper-masculine terrorist could be read as 'a sexualized metaphor for reaching across sectarian division of difference',[46] his parting letter emphasises the apparent inhospitality of consociational Northern Irish politics with a queer agenda in his new role as peacemaker-politician:

Dear P
I've been doing a lot of reading in here.
I wanted to sort out in my head what happened and where we
    fitted....
I think you are brave in your skirt
Looking for something different – some other way of being...
But we're fighting with our words now
Taking it up to that place on the hill
You're stronger than I am
You don't need to follow the rules I do
Sure maybe sometime in the future....[47]

This incongruity is emphasised by the fact that in Rea's play, it is this closeted gay lover who is imagined to be the killer of Darren Bradshaw, a police constable killed by the Irish National Liberation Army (INLA) in May 1997. *D.R.A.G.* prepones the event so that the closeted killer can become part of the Agreement's early release of prisoners scheme, effectively turning him from paramilitary to peacemaker – in effect, echoing the failure of the anti-discrimination legislation contained in section seventy-five of the 1998 Northern Ireland Act to inaugurate substantive changes in the political culture.[48] At the time, the killing was justified by a member of the political wing, the Irish Republican Socialist Party, who was also gay, in the following terms: 'I have no problem with the attack.... He put on a police uniform and became part of a state which oppresses nationalists. His sexuality was irrelevant'.[49] Yet, the murder happened in the leading gay club venue at the time, the Parliament (which is now Villa), which Bradshaw was known to frequent. At the time of the shooting, he had been suspended and his personal firearm had been taken away. The event caused a shock amongst the LGBT community in Northern Ireland, shattering the conception of gay bars as safe and neutral spaces.

Notably, Bradshaw's murder also marks the crucial turning point in Yee's *Trouble*, emphasising their intertextuality. Like *D.R.A.G.*, *Trouble* opens with Rea briefing the audience about its 'rules', which involve staying on the white lines on the floor and following the instructions of the 'Pluckers', a group of ushers who will direct the spectators to the different parts of the performance, the latter offering audience participation in a dance, which Rea suggests will be fun, thereby self-consciously setting us up for an unexpected ending. The set of the longer first part consists of a transparent cubic room, which is created out of scratched perspex – visually recalling an interrogation cell, as well as the iconic photograph of the 'Soldier Behind Shield, Northern Ireland' (1973) by Philip Jones Griffiths,[50] thereby immediately situating the piece in a Troubles memorial context. On each of the four sides of this cube three video screens are installed: on the main screen, the edited verbatim testimonies of over forty-six LGBT people are performed by a high-profile cast of Northern Irish performers, including, amongst many others, Paul Boyd, Marie Jones, and Carol Moore, and these are juxtaposed on the other screens with images of the past, specifically the Troubles but also 'gay life' from magazines such as *Gay Times* or *Spare Rib*, and repeatedly a stone wall, in grey or rainbow colour, as an iconic reminder of LGBT history.

The audience is divided out between these four sides and asked to stand very closely together on the white lines, resonating with the spatial dynamics of the seating arrangements for *D.R.A.G.* The feed opens on all monitors with a moving torch song version of 'Dance Yourself Dizzy' by Ross Anderson, set up to evoke what Rea describes as a 'community spirit', which foreshadows what is yet to come.[51] The screens then jump into different feeds, so that each side is listening to a different set of memories while the acoustics enable an overhearing of fragments of those other stories. In his review, Chris McCormack describes this as a 'rush of repressed histories, released at once, threatening an overload.'[52] The spatial acoustics and visual stimuli, with the flickering images on the monitors mantled on the translucent cube, in which the figure of an almost naked man (Andrew Stanford) sits still on chair with a table, telephone, and microphone, indeed have an overwhelming and almost disorientating effect on the spectator, whose focus and attention shifts from the different screens and their stories to those of the other sides and the inside of the cube, trying to individually make sense of these sensations.

The testimonies on all sides are organised in a rough chronological order, addressing topics, issues, and experiences of religion; education; therapy; isolation; sectarian violence; organisations, such as Northern Ireland Gay Rights Association (NIGRA), Cara-Friend, and the Rainbow Project; queer clubs and discos; as well as HIV and AIDS. Together, these testimonies tentatively trace what Yee describes as a 'journey' from 'violence, loneliness, fear, isolation and the unspoken' to 'a place of community, acceptance, friendship and confidence (for some, a salvation).'[53] I suggest 'tentatively' because these stories refuse to be channelled into a clear and progressive trajectory that would provide a safe and stable memory. This movement has a spatial parallel in the way in which Belfast emerges in these memories from its traditional conception as a place of sectarian divisions as a possible space for alternative forms of togetherness, specifically through the reopened dance clubs in the 1980s. As one man (performed by Gordon Mahn) recalls:

> With it [the clubs] was a whole other culture, those on the periphery of society. You did get the punks, you got skinheads, you got the gays, you got the lesbians, the androgynous-y whatevers, all thrown into this mismash one Saturday night at the Delta. It was really alternative. And alternative cultures just grew from that, it was really really exciting. That was part of the reason you went to the Plaza or the Delta was to meet people from the other side, from everywhere, from all over Belfast, which was quite exciting.[54]

An *'older, Belfast'* female voice (Katie Tumelty) confirms:

> I say the gay community was doing cross community then. They had the common the nominator [sic] was their sexuality. And as long as they were accepted for who they were didn't matter about religion. Everybody was there and everybody was welcomed. Didn't matter what tribe you came from. Even in the heart of the troubles, and I mean the <u>heart</u> of the trouble [sic] is, there wasn't one tri-colour, not one union jack, nothing was brought into the gay community. That space.

That 'queer' space and its promise of alternative communality beyond sectarian politics is, however, brutally shattered by the killing of Bradshaw that is addressed in the live performance of the exposed man who has sat the whole time inside the cube, which ends the installation part. As he slowly and carefully dresses himself in the uniform of an RUC officer, he recounts his experiences of homophobia in the police force and his encounter with the 'very vulnerable' young officer, Bradshaw, stating: 'I just thought that if the [police] had looked after Darren better, the Parliament wouldn't have been the only place he felt he could go that he was safe. That changed my life. His death impacted on me deeply. Because I felt we, the organization all the way to the top, and I had failed him.'[55] The scene ends in blackout in which the audience is led over to another part of the room and asked to keep between two white lines on the floor that create a circle. As the ushers turn into dancers, the lights and soundtrack transform the scene into a disco, with the crowded surrounding audience transmuted into the present spectators, fellow clubbers, part of the club community. As suggested by Rea at the beginning, several members of the audience (some more cautiously than others) start to move to the rhythm and interact with the performance in this way. Suddenly, we notice actor Stanford on stage, his white shirt illuminated by a pink beam, and at first timidly, then more confidently, he joins in the dance – before he is killed by an invisible member of the crowd, the gunshot reverberating through the space. While a white spotlight freezes his paralyzed body, the disturbed audience is ushered out by the Pluckers, with (at the performance I watched) several spectators being severely shocked and traumatized, some (almost) crying and comforting each other. The unexpected recreation of Bradshaw's murder creates parallel sensations of threat, isolation, and rupture - as well as connectedness and communality. Thus, *Trouble* reproduces a 'moving memory', which, true to its multidirectional dynamics, does not endorse a progressivist vision to suggest how far we have 'moved on'. Instead, the choice to conclude this testimonial work, which also evoked many redemptive memories, with this moment works to remind the audience of the current political dispensation in Northern Ireland – notably, the situation where, just prior to this premiere, the currently largest party in the Northern Irish Assembly, the Democratic Unionist Party (DUP), vetoed a proposal for legislating same-sex marriage. When the installation part of *Trouble* transferred to Belfast City Hall in December to celebrate the tenth anniversary since the UK's first civil partnership ceremony there – namely of Shannon Yee and her partner[56] – it, arguably, managed to parallel this trauma with a more hopeful memory.

The endings of both productions aim to inspire a form of social activism in raising awareness of the challenge LGBT memories bring to the present political situation. Where the conclusion of *Trouble* alerts us to the continuous inability of ethno-nationalist politics to redress LGBT justice, *D.R.A.G.* closes with Boyd's powerful rendition of a 'Punk Torch Song', dressed in a bejeweled balaclava that he then rips off – an image that was used in slightly modified form as the promotion poster:

> We're not invisible now
> We're here to be counted
> You'll not be pushed to the ground
> If you're lost
> You'll be found
> Do you hear me?
> I won't forget who you are
> Just hold your head up
> I'll be the freak that's unique
> Be the Queer without fear
> Can't you see me?[57]

As addressed here, both works trouble the invisibility, voicelessness, victimization, and oppression of the LGBT community in Northern Ireland. In performing previously silenced stories, the works under consideration unveil the parallel existence of hidden and marginalised memories within the ethnically structured polity and hetero-normative political culture of post-conflict Northern Ireland. Furthermore, in so doing, both problematise archival projects that, in an unintended way, may recycle the parallelism of exclusion and liminality. As such, the productions work to emphasise an archival and memorial responsibility to creating as well as commencing a different future. As Derrida reminds us: 'as much as and more than a thing of the past, before such a thing, the archive should call into question the coming of the future'.[58]

NOTES

1. I would like to express my deep gratitude to Niall Rea and TheatreofplucK for their kind support of this research by making scripts, recordings, photographs, and other information available to me and for permission to use this material for this article. I am also very grateful to Cillian McGrattan for invaluable feedback on an earlier draft of this paper.

2. Shannon Yee, unpublished script of *Trouble*, October 2015.

3. Shannon Yee, 'Gay & Troubled?' synopsis, Shannonyee Blog 22 July 2011, shannonyee.wordpress.com/category/tr/ (accessed 23 May 2016).

4. Yee, 'Gay & Troubled?' (2011).

5. '*parallel, n., adj., and adv.*' OED Online. Oxford University Press, June 2016. Web: www.oed.com.queens.ezp1.qub.ac.uk/search?searchType=dictionary&q=parallel&_searchBtn=Search (accessed 18 July 2016).

6. David Cregan, 'Remembering to Forget: Queer Memory and the New Ireland,' in *Memory Ireland*, ed. by Oona Frawley (Syracuse: Syracuse University Press, 2010), pp.184–94 (p.193).

7. TheatreofplucK, originally known as 'Pluck', was formed by Irish director/designer Niall Rea and American performers Karl Schappell, Robin Patchefsky, and Jon Stark in 1998 in Philadelphia. As noted on the company's website, 'The name Pluck was chosen to honour the memory of Christopher Hawks who had lived with Rea and Schappell, but who died from AIDS shortly before the company was formed. Hawks would have undoubtedly been a core company member, and his catchphrase of "oh pluck!" when someone did or said something special or out of the ordinary or brave seemed to embody the ethos of our attitude to performance.' After spending some time in Europe, Rea returned to Belfast in 2004, where the company changed its name to TheatreofplucK. In 2008, it was awarded a small grants award from the Arts Council of Northern Ireland making it the first publicly funded queer theatre company in Ireland. TheatreofplucK aims to produce 'quality theatre for everyone, but with a queer slant', engaging with 'issues of Lesbian, Gay, Bisexual and Transgender identities in Ireland.' To date, it has produced seven original full productions, details of which are on the website (see www.theatreofpluck.com/archive).

8. For a detailed discussion of this workshop version, see Fiona Coffey, 'Blurring Boundaries and Collapsing Genres with Shannon Yee: Immersive Theatre, Pastiche, and Radical Openness in the North', in *Radical Contemporary Theatre Practices by*

Women in Ireland, ed. by Miriam Haughton and Maria Kurdi (Dublin: Carysfort Press, 2015), 135–50.

9. *The Stormont House Agreement* (December 2014), available at www.gov.uk/government/uploads/system/uploads/attachment_data/file/390672/Stormont_House_Agreement.pdf (accessed 3 April 2015).

10. See Cillian McGrattan, 'The Stormont House Agreement and the New Politics of Storytelling in Northern Ireland', *Parliamentary Affairs* (2015), 1–19.

11. Jacques Derrida, 'Archive Fever: A Freudian Impression', trans. by Eric Prenowitz, *diacritics* 25.2 (1995), 9–63 (p.9).

12. Ed Madden, 'Queering Ireland, In the Archives', *Irish University Review* 43.1 (2013), 184–221 (p.185).

13. *The Agreement: Agreement Reached in the Multi-party Negotiations (Belfast/Good Friday Agreement)*, 'Declaration of Support', Paragraph 2, available at: www.gov.uk/government/uploads/system/uploads/attachment_data/file/136652/agreement.pdf (accessed 5 June 2016); Colin Graham, 'Every Passer-by a Culprit?', *Third Text* 19.5 (2005), 567–80 (pp.567–8).

14. *Report of the Consultative Group on the Past* (23 January 2009), 4; available at http://cain.ulst.ac.uk/victims/docs/consultative_group/cgp_230109_report.pdf (accessed 1 May 2016).

15. See Robin Wilson, *The Northern Ireland Experience of Conflict and Agreement: A Model for Export?* (Manchester: Manchester University Press, 2010).

16. Michael Rothberg, *Multidirectional Memory: Remembering the Holocaust in the Age of Decolonization* (Stanford CA: Stanford University Press, 2009), p.3.

17. Eamonn Hughes, 'Introduction: Northern Ireland – Border Country', in *Culture and Politics in Northern Ireland 1960–1990*, ed. by Eamonn Hughes (Milton Keynes: Open University Press, 1991), p.1; see also George Boyle's chapter in that collection, 'Northern Ireland: a Place Apart?', 13–26.

18. Rothberg, *Multidirectional Memory*, p.5.

19. Berthold Brecht, 'Short Description of a New Technique of Acting which Produces an Alienation Effect [1940]', in *Brecht on Theatre*, ed. and trans. by John Willett (London: Methuen, 1964), pp.136–147 (p.136). Dominick LaCapra's concept of 'emphatic unsettlement' is also gestured to here, see LaCapra, *Writing History, Writing Trauma* (Baltimore: The Johns Hopkins University Press, 2001), p.78.

20. See Fiona Coffrey, 'Blurring Boundaries', p.140n.

21. Al Head, 'The Queer Fool,' *Sexualities* 15.1 (2012), 3–10 (p.9).

22. Niall Rea, unpublished interview with author, 13 July 2016.

23. See 'Appendix IIIc: Secret Queer Devotions left by the audience on the stage at the start of the show (all iterations)', in Niall Rea, *Queer Identity in Performance in Northern Ireland: Dissemination through Live Performance, with Attention to its Post-Conflict Context*. PhD Thesis. Queen's University, Belfast, 2016, 343–50.

24. Rag trees in Ireland are often hawthorn trees, close to holy wells or other symbolic geographical landmarks, which are covered in scraps of fabric, ribbon, or clothing, representative of wishes, dreams, hopes or problems that are believed will be fulfilled or overcome as the rag disintegrates.

25. Rea, *Queer Identity*, p.200.

26. Rea, *Queer Identity*, p.201.

27. In the post-show discussion at the Courtyard Theatre, Newtownabbey, on 6 August 2012, one audience member emphasised that he felt 'terrified' putting his piece of paper on stage but then became 'curious as to how they would be used'. See Rea, 'Appendix II: Transcripts of Post Show Discussions', in *Queer Identity*, p.314.

28. Rea, *Queer Identity*, p.202.

29. Jane Coyle, review of *Divided, Radical, And Gorgeous*, *Irish Theatre Magazine* (2012). Previously available at: www.irishtheatremagazine.ie/Reviews/Current/D-R-A-G----Divided--Radical-and-Gorgeous (website closed down in 2014). The review is reproduced in 'Appendix V' in Rea, *Queer Identity*, pp.422–24.

30. Niall Rea, 'Appendix I – Annotated Performance Script of *Divided, Radical, And Gorgeous* – Third Iteration', in Rea, *Queer Identity*, 264–81 (p.265). [In the following abbreviated as Script of *D.R.A.G.*].

31. Rea, *Queer Identity*, p.265.

32. Joseph Pugliese, 'Biotypologies of Terror', *Cultural Studies Review* 14.2 (2008), 49–66 (p.61).

33. For a detailed exploration of homophobia in Northern Ireland, see Marian Duggan, *Queering Conflict: Examining Lesbian and Gay Experiences of Homophobia and Northern Ireland* (Farnham: Ashgate, 2012).

34. Kathryn Conrad, '"Nothing to Hide … Nothing to Fear": Discriminatory Surveillance and Queer Visibility in Great Britain and Northern Ireland', in *Ashgate Research Companion to Queer Theory*, ed. by Noreen Giffney and Michael O'Rourke (Farnham: Ashgate, 2009), 329–46, (p.342).

35. David Cregan, *Frank McGuinness's Dramaturgy of Difference and the Irish Theatre*, (New York: Peter Lang, 2011), p.141

36. See Caitriona O'Reilly, 'Politics, Pride and Performance: TheatreofplucK's Devised Queer Dramaturgies in Northern Ireland,' in *Devised Performance in Irish Theatre: Histories and Contemporary Practice*, ed. by Siobhan O'Gorman and Charlotte McIvor (Dublin: Carysfort Press, 2015), 243–59 (p.254).

37. Seamus Heaney, *North* (London: Faber and Faber, 1975), p.38.

38. Rea, *Queer Identity*, p.155.

39. Rea, Script of *D.R.A.G.*, p.272.

40. Cregan, *Frank McGuinness's Dramaturgy*, p.127.

41. Richard Dyer, 'It's Being So Camp As Keeps Us Going', in *Camp: Queer Aesthetics and the Performing Subject*, ed. by Fabio Cleto (Ann Arbor, MI: University of Michigan Press, 1999), p.110.

42. Susan Sontag, 'Notes on "Camp"', in *Camp*, p.56.

43. Rea, Script of *D.R.A.G.*, p.279.

44. Rea, Script of *D.R.A.G.*, p.279.

45. Derrida, 'Archive Fever', p.27.

46. Cregan, *Frank McGuinness's Dramaturgy*, p.140.

47. Rea, Script of *D.R.A.G.*, p.279.

48. See also Stefanie Lehner, 'Post-Conflict Masculinities: Filative Reconciliation in *Five Minutes of Heaven* and David Park's *The Truth Commissioner*', in *Irish Masculinities: Reflections on Literature and Culture*, ed. by Caroline Magennis and Raymond Mullen (Dublin: Irish Academic Press, 2011), pp.65–76.

49. Cited in David McKittrick, Seamus Kelters, Brian Feeney, Chris Thornton, and David McVea, *Lost Lives: The Stories of the Men, Women and Children Who Died as a Result of the Northern Ireland Troubles* (Edinburgh: Mainstream, 2012), p.1407.

50. Exhibited in *Northern Ireland: 30 Years of Photography* by Belfast Exposed (in partnership with the MAC), 10 May–7 July 2013. Photograph available on Maxim Surin, 'Northern Ireland: 30 Years of Photography. Belfast Exposed', Blog: www.maximsurin.info/blog/northern-ireland-30-years-of-photography-bx (accessed 23 July 2016).

51. Rea, unpublished interview with author.

52. Chris McCormack, review of *Trouble*, *Exeunt*, 16 November 2016: http://exeuntmagazine.com/reviews/trouble/ (accessed 20 November 2016).

53. Yee, unpublished script of *Trouble*.

54. Yee, unpublished script of *Trouble*.
55. Yee, unpublished script of *Trouble*.
56. BBC News, 'Gay weddings' first for Belfast', 19 December 2005, www.news.bbc.co.uk/1/hi/northern_ireland/4540226.stm (accessed 20 July 2016).
57. Rea, Script of *D.R.A.G.*, p.281.
58. Derrida, 'Archive Fever', p.26.

Úna Kavanagh and Louise Lowe

The Work of Anu: The Audience is Present

By placing the audience at the very centre of our practice in order to create autonomous exchanges, we have created a new kind of hybrid theatrical model of performance.[1] Working in real environments and slipping between the artificial and the real, we are interested in the changing nature of contemporary cultural thinking. Our multi-disciplinary aesthetic represents the independent and the experimental. We make performances which are outcomes of a devising process, usually made off-site and very often in a socially charged, political, or community context over a long period of time. Our work is derived from historical events, physical space, and ethnographical sources. Each production contains multi-narrative strands, whereby audiences become participants within the environment, seeing the show through a lens of *now-then-now*. Using a variety of methodologies, we explore how these can be transmitted without using narrative, without making up fictions, and using as few instructions as possible. We place our findings in non-traditional sites and use immersive engagement to create shared intimacies between audience and place and audience and performer.

We aim to challenge theatrical conventions by blurring the lines between theatre, visual art, and dance. We curate each production as part of a series of works, created around central themes or provocations. Frequently these works operate as inquiries, forensically examining unremembered casualties of our state and then framing and re-framing forgotten histories that have been doubly disavowed by national politics and by time. Our studio enquiry, led by multi-discipline teams, forensically builds to spatial immersion and finally to direct communion and engagement with audience. As much as possible we try to avoid exposition, believing that its absence opens up a kaleidoscope of myriad possibilities. Deploying (on top of this), a cubist dramaturgy – by exposing multiple surfaces and states simultaneously – we invite audiences to create their own

Irish University Review 47.1 (2017): 119–125
DOI: 10.3366/iur.2017.0260
© Edinburgh University Press
www.euppublishing.com/iur

multi-fractured narratives, becoming auteurs of their own instinctive experience.

THE MONTO CYCLE

Our first major series of work, The Monto Cycle (2010–2014), positioned us inside a north-inner city community over four consecutive years. Our street-facing studio invited (and indeed enticed) collaboration from our surrounding neighbours throughout the time we were there. From its inception, we knew that the series would take four years to complete, culminating with a two-day international symposium,[2] inviting leading academic and audience response. The tetralogy (presented as part of Dublin Theatre Festival 2010–2014) sequentially explored the quarter mile area and history of Foley Street through four critical regenerations. Through these durational works, micro-histories of the area were further distilled into highly personal encounters with those who had been erased and who were intent on rewriting themselves back into the present.

Immortalised in popular folk songs and in the Nighttown chapter of James Joyce's *Ulysses*, the first of this series, *World's End Lane* was an intimate one-to-one exploration of the notorious Monto area in the north inner city in the 1920s. This was once the largest and most prolific red light district in Europe. Told in multiple tenses through the eyes of five pivotal real-life characters, audiences of three were divided and taken on a rotating journey where they got to experience the area as a punter, tourist, and complicit worker.

Following on from *World's End Lane*, *Laundry* was performed as part of the Dublin Theatre Festival 2011 and once again picked up the female history in this area. In an Ireland whose collective consciousness was reeling from the exposition of the Magdalen Laundry institutions (as well as other residential institutions for children), the issues of naming and witnessing was at the heart of the performance. We wanted to explore, through the female body, how traumatic memory could be transmitted.

The third regeneration of the area was captured in the *Boys of Foley Street* (2012; see cover image), which was set in the 1970/80s when the community was undergoing a period of immense change. These seismic events included the demolition of tenement housing, the impact and rise of heroin, the Dublin / Monaghan bombings, the Concerned Parents Against Drugs movement, and ultimately captured a community imploding in on itself.

Finally *Vardo* ('*The Business of Hope*') was performed for the 2014 Dublin Theatre Festival and explored invisible communities who live and work there in the present day.

2016

Brian Singleton asserts that 'The political power of ANU's performative acts, stand as a direct challenge to the nation's desire to remember the past through an act of forgetting'.[3] The 2016 centenary of the 1916 Easter Rising presented us with the opportunity to challenge the canon of male-hero-led history. To explore our state in microcosm, not sterilised or neutralised, or simplified into pageantry, but distilled into charged encounters that pulled gravitationally towards the fault line of the 1916 Rising. Throughout the year, we presented 6,302 performances in thirty-two locations, with nineteen co-presenters across ten productions.

At the centre of this programme was a major triptych of work that looked at acts of rebellion and how they shifted cultural identity at home and abroad. This triptych embraced a radical year-long interrogation that blurred reality to create a complex, volatile, and richly textured series of works.

Over the past 100 years, there have been punctuated moments of rebellion and incitement that have shifted the optic of how the role of the Irish revolutionary has been perceived both from inside and out. The 1916 Rising is normally spoken of in the exclusively masculine sense. Historical accounts of the week tend to describe conflict almost solely in terms of male participation as combatants – thus reinforcing the myth of the rebellion as an exclusively male preserve. Set in 1916, 1966, and 1996 respectively, with a sharp focus on the female body, we began our exploration with a projected look into the future, starting with a key production, *Sunder*, in collaboration with the National Museum of Ireland, National Archives, and Dublin Theatre Festival. This was followed by a second production, *On Corporation Street*, commissioned as part of Culture Ireland's 'I am Ireland'[4] strand and co-commissioned by HOME Manchester, to mark the twentieth anniversary of the Manchester Arndale shopping centre bombing. The final part of the triptych was a highly charged co-production, *These Rooms*, with CoisCéim dance theatre, exploring through the optic of the 1966 commemoration, the catastrophic North King Street massacre. This Arts Council 1916 project was performed as part of Dublin Theatre Festival at Sean O'Casey's birthplace on Dorset Street.

Together these productions ask the questions: who are we and why are we? Each part of the trilogy reveals the interpenetration and overlap of space, place, and culture, creating an evolving work of historical and contemporary detail. Throughout, we cultivated a new language and ecology, moving between art forms and between the realms of the real and symbolic, the material and the metaphorical, the perceived and the remembered. We wanted to animate multiple forensic layers of each event to explore the creative potential of time and space and of memory and forgetting. Commemoration is often viewed as offering one version of nationhood and national sovereignty. In fact, the act of commemoration is in itself a discourse in time and space, fragmented and positioned between the *now-then-now*. In itself, this is often a paradox, offering complex questions rather than answers. At pivotal points throughout each production, time and place collided, allowing moments of contemporary life to interrupt, contradict, and indeed eclipse the historical, creating new spaces to invent imagined futures.

Beginning our exploration, *Sunder* focussed on the situations that rebels and civilians found themselves in 100 years ago. We used the geography of Moore Street itself to inform a series of visceral installations, propelling audiences through alternating tenses. From the tragic killing of teenager Brigid O'Kane and the picking up of pieces of her skull as mementos in the charge from the GPO, to the silent meals, the forgotten child commandant, and the men of the *'death or glory'* squad, each space presented another story and another set of circumstances which collectively built, creating dreamlike landscapes, capturing conversations and fragments of the final hours, revealing the events of Moore Street as never before.

Audiences began their journey speaking to a disembodied voice asking for them by name on a mobile phone. Their ensuing conversation with a live actor centred around the question: *'How do you choose to engage?'* Throughout this performance (as in all our work) audiences were invited and encouraged to break the rules, smash through the fourth wall – to move around, follow and track performers, and mould the action. They were implicated as opposed to removed; addressed as opposed to ignored. This unleashed a dynamic meaning-making process. Performed in such close spatial proximity, this means that they were invited into the discourse and offered autonomy throughout. What made *Sunder* all the more immersive is that it was *not* happening in a carefully constructed, controlled environment. It collided with real life. The performance (to which the audience is central) happened in the full public view of Moore Street, enveloped by real life in real time.

2016 also marked the twentieth anniversary of the bombing of Manchester by the provisional IRA. This bomb, the largest ever detonated in mainland Britain, devastated the city centre, and injured 212 people. Commissioned by HOME Manchester and supported by Culture Ireland (I Am Ireland Programme), *On Corporation Street* responded to this seismic event. A pivotal moment that transformed the shape of the city, we were invited to respond by staging a take-over of their building, transforming our three public civil inquiries into a shape-shifting spectacle that sprawled across

HOME, occupying and cross-pollinating their theatres, cinemas, and galleries.

These Rooms, a response to the 1916 North King Street civilian massacre, was awarded an ART: 2016 commission and formed part of the Arts Council's programme 'Ireland 2016'. It was co-commissioned by 14–18 NOW: WW1 Centenary Art Commissions in the UK, and also by the National Museum of Ireland and the National Archives. Combining eye witness testimonies from thirty-eight female voices, with newly released findings of the government inquiry which followed the massacre, *These Rooms* investigated questions of dignity, belonging, and dispossession in a fearless, intimate, and embodied physical performance. Set on the fiftieth anniversary of the Rising, the production explores the female body as a post-trauma political site. Their physical bodies betray them. The women are within and watching at the same time, confronting themselves though the point of view of the 1966 commemoration and, ultimately, each other.

NOW-THEN-NOW

This kind of immersive, site-specific / responsive work is no longer an alternative or fringe genre but symptomatic of increasing diversity in art forms. Our work extends the debate beyond interaction between performance and space, beyond how the past is propelled into our present. Ultimately memory is physiologically active and present in the visceral experience of our audiences. By creating conditions through which audience and performer collaboratively engage in a shared kinaesthetic state, we ultimately aim to produce sensory-rich experiences where years of history can fold, clash, interact, contradict, and tell their own story in their own way.

We strive to make work that is immediately relevant. We are not interested in recreating events which may have happened in the past. Characters emanate from the site in their past, present, and future states as *now-then-now* collide. Pierre Nora reminds us that the purpose of sites of memory is 'to stop time, to block the work of forgetting', and share 'a will to remember',[5] not just in the physicality of the performers who create and make kinaesthetic memory in their bodies, but also with our one-on-one scored experiences. This holding of a physical being, an audience member, is an inclusion of embodied cohesion. Watching performers deal with situations and tasks in real time (and often within the real world) is a big part of what makes our work engaging. Very often it is negotiated as it unfolds in the moment, being discovered and made by the performers and viewer at the same time, not as an enactment of something but an inhabitation of real time and space.

Embedded within each of the works are multiple points of direct (and often physical) contact between character and audience, a spatial suspension within time and space of the real and artifice. This taking, then holding and letting go, becomes a catalyst for reflection in the moment. The audience is invited to exercise their free will. The communion becomes a situation wherein actual and representational blur; a gesture and aspiration to fuse art and life and the choice to create a new dual reality. We endeavour not just to depict these moments, but to actualise them, with authenticity and respect. Critically, the work of art lies not in representing philosophical concepts but in embodying them together with the audience whereby, in the present tense, they together become another.

Audiences frequently return to performances for a second or third time. Sometimes they return to experience different strands of narratives, sometimes to view alternative perspectives. Redeploying their agency, they also come back to change the choices that they made in their first experience and to re-engage with a moment. They embrace being agents of change and construct new narratives and memories. In *World's End Lane* (2010), an audience member who had stolen a Virgin Mary bottle of Meth for a drug addicted prostitute came back a second time to re-enact that same moment and to make the choice not to steal for her. She wanted not to be complicit in the woman's addiction but to make a moral decision to abstain and perhaps help her in the long run. That audience member now has two embodied memories of one moment creating a dual-dimensional layered memory.

The particulars of each performance might fade, but the semblance of the experience will remain in the audience's sense memory. The greater the sense of agency was within the encounter, the stronger the physical memory of the encounter in the body of the audience. Thus memory becomes physiologically embodied in each viewer, and only through the recalling of all the senses, can it then be remembered or shared. In the communion of this moment, past and present, performer, audience and archive collide. The space (active), acts as a threshold through which the living are able to make contact with those who have gone before. The audience is present.

NOTES

1. Anu Productions, founded in 2009, has changed the Irish theatre landscape and helped to shape an artistic commemorative agenda in which the past is engaged with as a dynamic and challenging space. Anu creates immersive and site-specific productions that strive to reimagine and remake everything that was radical and alive about the past in the present.

2. *Now Then Now: Witnessing Future History*, symposium, Dublin, 8 October 2014. Supported by Dublin City Council, Dublin Theatre Festival and CREATE National Agency for Collaborative Arts Practice.
3. Brian Singleton, 'ANU Productions' Monto Cycle: Performative Encounters and Acts of Memory', Lecture delivered at *Memory, Space and New Technologies* symposium, June 2015. Available as part of the Irish Memory Studies Network MemoryCloud: http://irishmemorystudies.com/index.php/memory-cloud/#singleton.
4. See http://www.cultureireland.ie/iamireland/
5. Pierre Nora, quoted at http://wayback.archive.it.org/6473/20160819144829/ https://tspace.library.utoronto.ca/citd/holtorf/2.6.html

Claire Lynch

'Everything not saved will be lost': Videogames, Violence, and Memory in Contemporary Irish Fiction

This is an essay about Irish boys who die. Boys who play at dying and boys who play at killing. Boys who kill other boys, and boys who kill themselves. In Paul Murray's *Skippy Dies* (2010), Eimear McBride's *A Girl is a Half-Formed Thing* (2013), and Rob Doyle's *Here Are the Young Men* (2014), boys die as a result of illness, overdose, and even murder. In all three novels, boys' bodies are portrayed as vulnerable; invaded by tumours, manipulated by abusers, and destroyed by drugs. Small wonder then that these boys are also shown retreating from the physical world, finding solace, distraction and even digital immortality through the videogames they play.[1] Unlike the fragile human body, a videogame avatar can survive multiple virtual deaths. In a videogame, kicks, punches, bullet wounds, even decapitations, can all be undone, the virtual body resurrected and the game re-played. These immortal virtual bodies operate in an alternate moral arena in which the player's joy is frequently tied up with inflicting symbolic violence.

> See this fella he does that. See this fella he kicks him. See now. Hit. That button. Go on. Now. Now. Now. A back flip. Isn't it mad? Isn't it brilliant. I say. It is.... Bash him hard into the floor. You saying left one right one that's it now and more forward get the hang. I. Hours of it. Hours of fun.... It's stupid game. It is. It is. Is it not life and death.[2]

The unnamed boy in *A Girl is a Half-Formed Thing* is giddy with pleasure as his on-screen double punches, kicks, and pins his opponent, punctuating McBride's prose with strikes on the keyboard and jerks of a joystick. His enjoyment becomes an obsession and the more he plays the better he gets. Better at kicking, better at hitting, better at killing in those endless 'Hours of fun'. For the boy's mother,

Irish University Review 47.1 (2017): 126–142
DOI: 10.3366/iur.2017.0261
© Edinburgh University Press
www.euppublishing.com/iur

however, these are lost hours, unproductive and morally questionable. The computer, as she sees it, is for 'further education' and futuristic work done by enigmatic 'analysts in rows in shirts'.[3] While certainly not in the way his mother had imagined, the computer in this novel is, unquestionably, a site of learning and, consequently, a repository of memory. At the very least, a successful videogame player must remember how they have played before in order to do better next time. Remembering strategies, locations, and keypad combinations allows the player to progress further in a game each time he or she plays. But there is something more than this simplistic cycle of recall and repetition which concerns me here, namely, that videogames alter the way we experience a virtual past. Conventional analyses of videogames make a distinction between the human player operating the computer and the onscreen character who represents him or her within the game, the avatar. The avatar and the player have a complex relationship which varies according to several factors, including, the type of game played, the environment and context in which the game is played, and the experience and skill of the person playing. In the three Irish novels discussed here, fictional characters are depicted playing both real and imagined videogames featuring a number of avatar perspectives. In the earlier videogames, such as those referenced in *A Girl is a Half-Formed Thing,* players view a side-on, cartoonish avatar, limited to the frame of the screen and the physical movements of hand-to-hand combat. By contrast, in *Here Are the Young Men,* characters are portrayed playing contemporary first-person shooter games in which the photorealistic action is seen as if through their own eyes. *Skippy Dies* features a quest-style game in which an elf-like protagonist stands in as the player's digital other. Notably, in all of these novels, players suspend their disbelief so far as to over-identify with their avatars, jeopardising their sense of self in the process. Such a blurring of player and avatar raises several questions about how memory is experienced, articulated, and mediated. Do an avatar's actions subsequently become a player's memories? Does playing videogames alter memory or shape the way a player interacts with the past? And perhaps most crucially, when an avatar stabs, punches, or shoots an opponent, does the player remember that act of violence as a witness or a collaborator?

LEVEL 1: BASH HIM HARD INTO THE FLOOR

Necessarily a relatively recent phenomenon, videogames are often represented in literary fiction as a form of allegory or mythology. Tropes of fantasy, science-fiction, and horror may enter an otherwise realistic narrative via characters' games consoles without jarring genre conventions. Equally, when characters play videogames in novels their actions permit thematic and structural experiments, inviting the author to explore non-linear time, alternative lives, and unreliable memory. While the games played in novels are in themselves rich in interpretive potential, the player-characters are revealed to us uniquely unguarded during the act of gameplay. More conscious than in a dream, less censored than in a conversation, a character's behaviours and motivations are clarified or distorted as they manipulate an avatar. In Rob Doyle's debut novel *Here Are the Young Men* (2014), Kearney, a crude and increasingly unstable eighteen-year-old, is highly influenced by videogames, not only playing well-known titles but also designing his own games. Riffing on the cliches of well-known videogames and real-world violent contexts he imagines the game *Provos!*

> Ye have to start shootin loads of Proddy fuckers in the street in front of their families and everything. Then ye have to plant bombs in shopping centres and all, and shoot yer way out if the RUC get wind of ye. And when yer coming to the end of the game, it switches over to England, ye have to start taking the war to the Brits . . . the last fuckin mission is ye have to assassinate the queen.[4]

Later in the novel, Kearney's notebook reveals a longer list of fantasy videogames, including: '*Sexkrime* where you play a rapist in a squalid inner-city high-rise.... Alcoholocaust, merging autobiography and zombie-slaughter, an atmospheric first-person shooter set in Dublin'.[5] There is parody here but the imagined videogames are also plausible, allowing Doyle to test the limits of censure and disapproval. If produced, these games would surely draw media outrage; imagining them within a novel, however, is apparently legitimised. Their function in the narrative is clear, providing a shortcut to the mind of the repellant character. Kearney's imagined videogames are deliberately disturbing, even without the sensory stimulus that an actual game would involve. In a literal sense, there is nothing to see here, the game must be conjured in the reader's imagination. Indeed, this is exactly what Kearney does throughout the novel. When not playing videogames he projects the violence from games onto real life; on the bus to school, for instance, 'he slaughters everyone onboard . . . as gunfire tears through the upper deck, blasting out windows, ripping children in half amidst howls of terror'.[6] These imagined acts of violence on the one hand, and simulated acts of violence in videogames on the other, gradually move closer and closer together in the novel, culminating in deadly consequences.

Violent videogames and debates about their influence on young people have existed for as long as home computers have been commercially available. Reactions to the 1976 game *Death Race* capture the tone of the early commentary. Inspired by the dystopian American film of the same name, the game depicted:

> a cross-country road race where contestants run down and kill pedestrians for points. People in wheelchairs are the most valuable prey, earning the contestants a hundred points, elderly people seventy points, and adolescents only 30.[7]

Condemned in the US, the National Safety Council described the game as 'sick and morbid' leading to televised discussions on the psychological impact of videogames on young people.[8] While the premise for the game is undeniably disturbing, in our own age of increasingly realistic computer generated images, it is almost inconceivable that this game could be interpreted as so morally threatening. Limited by early computer graphics, the simple geometric white shapes on a black background which constitute *Death Race* look more like a remedial cross-stitch sampler than a scene of mindless violence. This early period of videogaming, described as the 'Atari Era', was characterised by games featuring 'Abstract Violence', 'considered to be "violent" because they portrayed smaller blips destroying larger blips'.[9] As the moral panic surrounding *Death Race* demonstrates, it is not *seeing* or even *playing* violence that threatens harmful real-world consequences but *imagining* it. With limited visual stimulus, the gamer must project meaning onto these basic symbols, either using memories of images from the related film, or from his or her own imagination. In simple terms, the violence is in the gamer not the game. Yet as Clive Thompson observes, the paradoxical argument 'that games either brainwash us into violence or are harmless fantasies'[10] persists, fuelling a relentless media 'preoccupation with the assumed dangers of videogames'.[11] Those who argue that videogames can 'brainwash' see violent games as leading to desensitisation, even an altered morality. Such concerns are not so much with what the player imagines during gameplay, but what they might remember, consciously or otherwise, afterwards. In this reading of videogames, playing creates a false memory in which violence experienced or perpetrated by the avatar is, in effect, experienced or perpetrated by the player.

In many ways, videogames are all about memory; the game and console remember the player's progress, the player remembers what their avatar should do next and what not to do again, their muscles remember the precise combination of thumbs on buttons, eyes on pixels. This concept, an aspect of 'digital memory', is considered in this essay across two contexts: the machine and the mind. In the first instance, digital memory is understood here as both the generation and preservation of data. In the broadest sense, everything we create and store using computers can be understood as contributing to the phenomenon of digital memory. Secondly, digital memory is read as a new manifestation of human memory in response to the digital age. How has the ubiquity of digital technology begun to change what, where, and how we remember? These two aspects frequently intersect resulting in artefacts of digital memory such as:

> Online mementos, photographs taken with digital cameras or camera phones, memorial web pages, digital shrines, text messages, digital archives (institutional and personal), online museums, online conference message boards, virtual candles, souvenirs and memorabilia traded on eBay, social networking and alumni websites, digital television news broadcasts of major events ... blogs, digital storytelling, passwords, computer games based on past wars, fan sites and digital scrapbooks.[12]

As this list suggests, manifestations of digital memory can be unsettlingly broad, encompassing 'the ordinary and mundane as well as the traumatic and newsworthy.'[13] While the examples cited here are all characteristic of the last few decades, they are also, of course, just the latest versions of long-established human habits. Since humans produce more data than their brains can store they are compelled to find alternative ways to preserve and transmit memory. Early civilisations acknowledged the frailty of human memory by creating objects and, later, texts as alternatives sites of memory using stone tablets, written manuscripts, and then printed books. To some extent the development of digital memory is a continuation of this and part of the ongoing drive for immortality by 'outsourcing the contents of our minds to ever more durable, compact, and portable objects'.[14] For Abby Smith Rumsey, the current age of digital memory is simply the latest example of 'information inflation', a tipping-point at which we risk becoming overwhelmed by our own ingenuity.[15] The perceived threats surrounding digital memory are typically shaped around three factors: scale, pace, and fragility. Certainly, the rate at which digital data is generated, and, therefore, the volume that needs to be stored is beyond lay imagining. More significant, however, is the gap between the perceived durability of digital memory and the reality of its impermanence. As Rumsey warns, 'Digital memory is ubiquitous yet unimaginably fragile, limitless in scope yet inherently unstable.'[16] In practical terms, digital memory is reliant on storage formats and devices which rapidly become obsolete. Equally, all manifestations of digital memory, including the now pervasive social networks, blogs, and computer games, require a reliable power source and stable internet connection to function. We ignore the precarity of the digital, perhaps because we cannot comprehend the consequences of it failing us.

LEVEL 2: IT'S STUPID GAME.

Paul Murray's *Skippy Dies* (2010) is set in a present-day Irish school, where boys huddle 'around the Nintendo'[17] warmed by their 'digital hearth'.[18] For the boys who board in the elite Dublin boys' school in which the novel is set, videogames provide both private solace and communal bonding, adding domestic familiarity to the institutional setting. As Bernadette Flynn contends, the focus of the domestic gaze, once trained on the fireplace, then the radio, then the television, is now drawn to the games console.[19] By their nature, videogames are narratives of conflict and contest and these ideas are reflected in the multiple battlefields of *Skippy Dies*. From the classrooms and corridors of the school, through the virtual worlds of their videogames, and finally to the massacres of the First World War discussed in their history lessons, the boys are surrounded by real and symbolic acts of violence. History teacher Howard's efforts to draw Skippy and his classmates towards the alternative narrative of Irish soldiers in the First World War stands in direct challenge to the mesmerising warmth of the screen. For the contemporary Irish schoolboys in this novel, videogames offer a legitimised space to fight, standing in for the wars of previous generations. Yet they are also a place of sanctuary; a way to keep the digital home fires burning. Textbook history and acts of remembrance are perceived by the schoolboys as the equivalent of 'Atari era' games, black and white and, frankly, boring.

> They live in a continuous sugar-rushed present, in which remembering is a chore left to computers, like tidying your room is a chore left for the Third World maid. If the war briefly caught their imagination, it was only as another arena of violence and gore, no different from their DVDs and video games.[20]

If World War I fails to catch the imagination of the class, teacher Howard is absorbed to the point of obsession. In the very act of teaching this topic, he draws attention to the First World War's status as 'marginalised to such an extent that it is characterised by a combination of forgetfulness and embarrassment' in the history of both the Free State and the Republic.[21] Indeed, it is precisely this absence of memory that Howard hopes to correct. Initially at least, the teacher's efforts to help the boys access material sites of remembrance are comically thwarted. An impromptu school trip is undermined when the National Museum admits to having nothing related to the War on display and the Memorial Gardens at Islandbridge are anti-climactic, positioned 'between a scrap merchant's and a mental institution'.[22] Nevertheless, the boys' very presence in the 'isolated and rarely visited' yet 'beautiful and symbolic gardens' is significant, precisely because the location forms 'part of Ireland's numerous inactive geographies of memory.'[23] Standing together in the gardens the boys receive a lesson in memory, coming to understand that 'representations of the past are coloured by the views of the rememberer'.[24] If the relatively distant past of World War I is inaccessible and irrelevant, the recent death of their classmate Skippy remains visceral. United in communal grief, the boys stand in the memorial park, transformed into ghostly avatars of their ancestors:

> in their grey uniforms for all the world like an incorporeal platoon, materialised out of the winter clouds to scour the bare park for someone who has not forgotten them.[25]

For history teacher Howard at least, the parallels between the generations of young Irishmen are self-evident, not least in their shared appetites for 'violence and gore'. The contemporary boys revel in the simulated violence of their screens, just as their ancestors were incited to 'play up, play up and play the game!' This jingoistic convergence of playing a game and fighting a war is disturbing, not least because it seems to target a particular kind of boyish naivety; as if trench warfare were really no more than a game of rugby union that has got a little out of hand.[26] The experiences diverge, inevitably, at the point of consequences; playing at war is not the same as fighting in one.

And yet, as suggested by the controversies over violent videogames, if your brain and body experience the rush of adrenaline, your finger pulls the trigger, your eyes see the consequences of your actions, is this not, on some level, an experience stored as a memory? Each time the virtual experience is repeated and recalled, the more compelling the memory becomes, yet also, the further it strays from the original version. As Rumsey explains:

> During recollection, a memory is opened up like a book or computer file, gets reworked, then receded and stored in a slightly modified way.... Recall is literally a rebuilding process, executed chemically, and new perceptions are incorporated into the old.[27]

Memory is iterative but also cumulative, each act of recall building on the last. In the way that previous generations marvelled at 'labour-saving devices', our own age may be defined by 'memory outsourcing' machines, devices which paradoxically save us time while consuming it all. One might assume that outsourcing our mundane memories, phone numbers, directions, and dates, say, to our devices, creates space for more complex and emotionally sustaining memories. If only the human brain were this compliant. Memories, however spontaneous they may seem, are, in fact, 'constructions mediated by means of complex psychical and mental processes.'[28] The use of digital technology has not changed how we remember but it has affected what we expect to remember. We have abandoned all kinds of memory-work, safe in the knowledge we can easily find the information online. Having a so-called 'good memory' in the digital age is 'less a question of remembering and more a matter of [knowing] where to look.'[29] In his essay on 'Digitising Historical Consciousness', Claudio Fogu imagines a fictional videogame, 'Holocaust II', as the source of a thought experiment. As Fogu argues, the playing of such a game, based in historical reality and experienced through immersive gameplay, 'would surely provide virtual memories of something perceived as real.'[30] 'Virtual memories', Fogu hypothesises, are likely to be created by gameplay, rather than via other media such as film and television, because of the distinguishing element of 'action'.[31] The player of a videogame does more than witness, he or she participates, their 'work' is 'a mixture of the physical and the mental.'[32] Whereas an audience in a theatre observes a drama unfold from their seats, the videogame player must take to the virtual stage, improvising, reacting to co-actors, using the props, and responding to the changing scenery. This analogy might be taken even further since, for all the ingenuity and reflexivity required of a videogame player, the action is necessarily pre-scripted by the game's designers. Far from being spontaneous or deviant then, violent acts in videogames are, inevitably, pre-programmed. As Cameron Loyd Grey explains:

> The player may bomb a corporate headquarters and thus release some of his suppressed rage in a virtual environment, but he is following a script much more than he is an active creator of his own adventure.[33]

In this reading, acts of gratuitous virtual violence are seen as displacement activities, an acceptable means of releasing frustration or dissipating anger. The act itself, throwing a person from the top of a high-rise block, driving into pedestrians on the pavement, shooting police officers in their car, is permitted, even prescribed, within the rules of the game. Since the actions are scripted, the player's moral culpability is arguably ameliorated. Rather than viewing violent games as dangerously suggestive, this reading attempts to disassociate the act of virtual violence from its real life equivalent. In this interpretation, a player on a killing spree in *Grand Theft Auto* can no more be seen as preparing to do the same in real life than a chess player can be accused of rehearsing high treason. As Skippy's compulsion to complete *Hopeland* demonstrates, the act of gameplay is more significant than the game itself. His playing is purposeful; at the very least, playing videogames occupies long hours of adolescent boredom. At most, absorption in the game serves to delay the return of traumatic memory. As Fogu argues, 'gaming is a matter of role-playing, simulation, immersion, and interaction, not representation.'[34] Any acts of virtual violence Skippy perpetrates within *Hopeland* are permitted, required even, by the internal logic of the game world. Indeed, just like the young soldiers the schoolboys learn about, distanced from the political motivations and consequences of war, videogame players simply do what is required of them.

LEVEL 3: HOURS OF FUN

In his review of *A Girl is a Half-Formed Thing*, James Wood describes McBride's 'blazingly daring' novel as set in 'an Ireland shorn of dates and obvious historical specificity', only conceding that the presence of a Walkman hints at the 1980s.[35] But what about the computer? Are computers and games consoles really so ubiquitous as to have become invisible to readers? Contrary to Wood's sense that it is a timeless narrative, the arrival of the first computer in this Irish home dates McBride's novel precisely.[36] Unquestionably, the arrival of the new computer fractures the already strained family structure, annexing the son/brother to his bedroom and away from the communal domestic spaces. When the mother complains of her evenings 'sitting down here on my own'[37] while her children are upstairs playing videogames, she highlights the way in which computers change how and where we spend our time. That *A Girl is a Half-Formed Thing* is set at the early stage of a co-dependent relationship with computers is significant. All computers are a memorial to both past and future, a reminder of the fissure between what was and what will be possible (so that here the technology which seems thrillingly futuristic to McBride's characters is already quaint to her readers). For the son/brother character a clear distinction is made between the way he spends his time in the Before Computer epoch, and after it. While the mother continues to insist that playing games on a computer is a waste of 'God's good fruits', its impact cannot be undone.[38]

If playing videogames is a waste of time, the way they disrupt time is all the more subversive. In part as a reflection of this, all of the novels considered here operate within unconventional narrative timeframes. Murray's novel starts with the death of his protagonist on the front cover, subsequently working back from the denouement. Doyle's novel is a retrospective account of a summer made up from the multiple perspectives of suicidal, drug-fuelled, and lovesick teenagers. McBride's novel is notoriously experimental in structure and form, toying with childhood recollections and counter-nostalgia. Although in different ways, they might all be thought of as novels of memory, that is, texts which face up to the clash between chronological history and memory as circuitous and associative. In these novels, memory rushes in at pace, coming in unbidden flashes before being slowed down, repeated and editorialised for private comfort or sanitised for public consumption. In part this is a consequence of the young protagonists and their unwavering absorption in their own experiences. The intensity with which the young characters experience time is consequently translated to the reader via highly recursive and immersive narrative structures. If these novels all rely on memory it is precisely because they understand it to be capricious. The instability of memory means that it is already a subversion of the traditional historical narrative 'commonly understood as the unfolding of events in broadly linear fashion' within a 'cause and-effect structure'.[39] Crucially, these novels reject such a limited and limiting structure by engaging with both remembering and forgetting. Information, data if you prefer, must be rationalised and filtered, connections made and extraneous details rejected. Remembering, in other words, is also a question of forgetting since

> any attempt to save memory always entails loss and forgetting as well as additions and supplements. We save our pasts only *as* something else: something different, something less than, something more than.[40]

Videogames are employed by these novelists precisely because they portray a temporary forgetfulness of the real world and the dual memory landscapes of life within and beyond the game.

LEVEL 4: NOW. NOW. NOW.

Throughout Murray's novel, Skippy plays a fictional videogame, *Hopeland*. Structurally, the videogame serves as a simultaneous plot strand, character and avatar progressing through multiple temporal levels. As the avatar incrementally overcomes trials, moving towards the final salvation of the inevitable princess, in his off-screen life,

Skippy's quest for the beautiful but troubled Lori stands in obvious parallel. Skippy spends hours each day over a period of several months playing the game so that his sense of real time is disrupted by the time spent within the game. Whether in the game or out of it Skippy must fight, search, overcome. That said, when gripping tightly to the controller of his Nintendo, Skippy is able to enact the kind of heroism not possible in his real life. Physically connected to the game through his hands on the buttons and his eyes on the screen, Skippy becomes cut off from the real world as 'the circuit of affection and logic that passes from computer to player and back closes onto itself'.[41] Skippy is fully absorbed in the game, not because he is unusually susceptible but because of the digital's unique 'ability to make us forget the medium, and thus achieve an immersive effect of presence (immediacy)'.[42] While Skippy's game play is clearly an act of escapism, it might more accurately be thought of as virtual embodiment since Skippy 'becomes' Djed, the avatar of *Hopeland* as he plays. While Murray describes the landscape and aesthetic of *Hopeland* in some detail, we only really 'see' Djed when Skippy adopts his form at the Halloween Hop, wearing 'his runners, fitted out with tiny wings' and 'crepe-paper hunting hat'.[43] Skippy's embodiment of his videogame avatar speaks to the comfort he finds hiding behind and within him. Equally, in his schoolyard fight with bullying sociopath Carl, Skippy imagines enacting Djed's onscreen moves. His inner voice offering advice learnt from the game, 'every Demon has a weak spot',[44] Skippy frantically tries to remember: 'the forward roll and jab, the spinning kick, the tiger throw'.[45] Just as Skippy's Halloween costume transports Djed's capacity for adventure from the computer screen to the school hall, during the real fight, his movements echo what Taylor calls the 'embodied experience of fighting in computer games' and the 'duality of presence' of the self in and out of the game.[46] In the act of playing, that is, the player becomes unreal, a work of fiction, their cyber-body 'a confluence of machine and flesh'.[47]

Just as Skippy brings his avatar out from the screen, the brother in *A Girl is a Half-Formed Thing,* attempts to move the virtual violence from the screen to his own body saying: 'I think I'd like to kick like that. I practise it when there's no one in. I hiya'd the clothes line and it broke'.[48] While the emulation of videogame violence may seem childish it is, in many ways, an appropriate response to the immersive experience. To play successfully, to win, the player must collaborate with the computer, learning to think and behave in the way the computer demands. The pleasure of play, one might argue, depends upon the player melding with the computer, sharing its thought processes. As the adult brother and sister share videogames in

McBride's novel, they return to childhood play and the sibling alliance which has protected them from their mother. Their regeneration as playmates also marks a further shift in the novel's complex timeframe. As the Girl gets older and more independent of the controlling family unit, her brother's brain tumour makes him younger, a little boy again and eventually, a baby in nappies needing to be spoon-fed. The videogames they play are a component of this narrative, creating an imagined other, the man he is never to become; a man who might use computers for work in contrast to the boy who only uses them for play and fantasy.

> Mad lust of it you get for computer games go blip across a screen. That's your eighteenth birthday gift improve your mind with. . .. The new love take up all your time. Eating sweets and Jupiter Landing. Come on and have a go. No. I don't want to. It's killing all your brain cells. So?[49]

The videogames aren't killing his brain cells but they are dying all the same. *Jupiter Landing*, one of the early videogames available on the Commodore 64 computer, challenges players to probe the planet's surface, carefully navigating the folds and valleys of the dark landscape, not unlike the surgeons who concede in their efforts to root out the invading tumours in the boy's brain. The destruction of his brain, caused both by the tumour and the various operations which fail to remove it, result in a hardware memory fault; the brain is simply unable to process memory as it once did. Somewhat more conventionally, Skippy's initial failure to recall and comprehend that he has suffered sexual abuse is represented by Murray as a suppressed trauma. The abuser's attempts to erase Skippy's memory by giving him drugs are ultimately unsuccessful, not least because it is in a drug-fuelled fugue that Skippy's memory returns as he finally completes his videogame. So while McBride's boy endures a memory tragically destroyed, Skippy's memory is shown painfully emerging. Skippy's reconnection with his suppressed memories of being abused illustrates memory's capacity to create a circular sense of time when he re-experiences the abuse as a flashback. The boy, by contrast, remembers less and less, fading away as he loses all sense of time. For both boys, the attacks on their memory induce a state of hopelessness and understandably so. As Rumsey makes clear:

> Our memories are not just an accumulation of data points about the past. They are the very fabric of the self, woven of our experiences, endowing us with time, place, personality, and identity in the world.[50]

LEVEL 5: IS IT NOT LIFE AND DEATH

Here Are the Young Men is a coming of age novel in which the children have no desire to grow up. Kearney's obsession with violent imagery and media increases as the novel progresses so that, as other characters' thoughts turn to college, he is absorbed further and further into the screen. Simply put, playing at death so relentlessly finally overloads Kearney's brain until he is unable to make the distinction between the virtual and the real. His real-life murder of two homeless men marks the transfer of videogame violence to his own body, although he continues to think of his actions as 'like a game'.[51] Kearney is a proficient gamer because he has repeated virtual actions over and over, learning from the game and then re-writing history by forcing the avatar to do what is required. As Doyle's novel suggests, however, failure to distinguish between appropriate behaviour within and beyond the game is potentially destructive. Kearney's obsessive gameplay alters him, creating a faux-traumatic past as a result of the virtual violence he repeatedly witnesses and enthusiastically perpetrates. Playing violent videogames gives Kearney a sense of invincibility because his avatar provides him with licence to inflict harm without being hurt in return. His reckless disregard for the lives of others is a further symptom of his perceived immunity against the kind of violence he enacts both digitally and physically. More than this, Kearney's desire to kill, on screen and on the streets, is a perverse form of self-preservation, a quest for immortality, or, more precisely a deferral of his own death.

In the end, Kearney's violence is meted back to him; when his friends discover his actions they conspire to kill him. His death is suitably gruesome, after drinking a concoction heavily-spiked with illegal drugs, Kearney appears to dance into a fire, his organs shut down, his body is mutilated.

> Kearney's entire face was charred black, with pink globs dripping over the singed, smoking mass of flesh. His hair was still ablaze. One of his eyes had burst in the heat, but the other gazed up at the night and all its stars.[52]

The dramatic end of Kearney's life is presented as a case of tragic inevitability. His friends take his life with an apparent moral impunity; murdering for the collective good, their act of violence presumably preventing many more. *Here Are the Young Men* begins as a novel fixed in the memories of a life-changing summer, the post-school bridge between youth and adulthood. What transpires is a series of tragedies and disillusionments. Whereas mainstream narratives of youthful summers stand upon nostalgic foundations, Doyle's novel is populated by characters desperately trying to forget. Understandably, these young men want to forget their knowledge of Kearney's crimes, as well as their contribution to his death. One of the challenges of living in the digital age explicated by this novel is precisely this conflict between the solace of forgetting and the reverence, even mania, 'for capturing, storing, retrieving and ordering' memories.[53] It is hugely significant that when Kearney poisons and beats to death homeless men he simultaneously makes a video of the event on his smartphone. Rather than thinking of this footage as incriminating evidence, Kearney's warped pleasure is found, not only in the act of violence itself, but also in the capacity to watch and re-watch it onscreen. The digital memory of his crime, the 'recording, retrieving, stockpiling, archiving, backing-up and saving' of a murder captures the extent to which 'information loss' has become 'one of our greatest fears of this century.'[54] Fiction creates a space for exploring these ideas in extremis, so that even digital memories we might assume to be unconscionable are preserved. Is this novel a morality tale then? Certainly Doyle extends the question of influential videogame violence to dystopian proportions, but this is surely for the purposes of provocation rather than social commentary. *Here Are the Young Men* is certainly not a technophobic novel but it is cognisant of the ways videogames might prompt trauma as well as catharsis.

GAME OVER?

While Kearney is alone in his direct adoption of ludic violence, all of the player-characters considered here are lost in some way to the games they play. Their immersion in the world of the game and confluence with the onscreen avatar is a rejection, or at least a deferral, of reality. As Djed, Skippy performs a masculine authority and physical autonomy denied him in real life as a victim of sexual abuse. The brother in *A Girl is a Half-Formed Thing* kicks and punches against the weakness of his physical body through the jagged pixels of his onscreen others. Both look to videogame avatars for an alternate body, a stronger, braver, more invincible shape. Kearney, in Doyle's *Here Are the Young Men*, takes this to its horrifying extreme, irrevocably forgetting the difference between a game and reality when he pushes a boy to his death in, of all places, the Garden of Remembrance.[55] Digital memory is not immortal either. Quite apart from the fragile infrastructures of storage and power discussed above, computers are vulnerable to viruses, leading to 'a loss of memory and a digital amnesia that makes digital memory just as fallible and unstable as human memory.'[56] While the threats to digital memory are well-worn topics in the fields of computer and information sciences and, increasingly, digital humanities, much is to be done to expand these topics into the full range of memory studies scholarship. The so-called 'turn to memory' with its associated emphasis on trauma and 'oral history's quest to retrieve the memories of groups whose histories had previously been neglected'[57] has much to contribute here, not least in regard to the tensions between individual and collective memory in the digital context. In the novels discussed here, the family, schools and the church, are complicit in the boys' fates, yet rarely called to account. After all, it is far easier to confer blame on the abstract category of the 'media' or the experienced scapegoat that is violent videogames than any of these venerated institutions. With diseased brains unable to remember or drugged brains able to remember all too clearly, all three boys die. Whatever acts of violence they have played at, imagined, or committed via their avatars, their physical bodies remain vulnerable to attack. Importantly, and in contrast to reality, in a videogame, death is an invitation to simply try again; the more the avatar dies, 'the better the player becomes.'[58] For both real and fictional gamers, the onscreen epitaph 'Game Over' is not an end at all, but rather a prompt to memory, an invitation to try again, to do better. In a videogame at least, 'one dies so that one may live.'[59]

NOTES

1. The term videogame is used throughout this essay, rather than the more recent coinage 'digital game', to indicate the full historical range of computer games referred to in the novels under discussion. While digital games are now played via a range of devices, including most recently the smartphone, videogames are typically associated with consoles such as the Nintendo Xbox or Sony PlayStation. The essay's title is drawn from the Nintendo's quit screen, with its (unintentionally) profound warning to players: 'Everything not saved will be lost'.
2. Eimear McBride, *A Girl is a Half-Formed Thing* (London: Faber & Faber, 2013), p.91.
3. McBride, p.80.
4. Rob Doyle, *Here Are the Young Men* (London: Bloomsbury, 2014), pp.8–9.
5. Doyle, pp.34–5.
6. Doyle, p.25.
7. Faltin Karlsen, *A World of Excesses: Online Games and Excessive Playing* (London: Ashgate, 2013), p.4.
8. Karlsen, p.5.
9. Steven J. Kirsh, *Children, Adolescents, and Media Violence: A Critical Look at the Research* (Thousand Oaks: Sage Publications, 2006), p. 229.
10. Lucien King, ed., *Game On: The History and Culture of Videogames* (London: Laurence King Publishing, 2002), p.24.
11. Jesper Juul, *Half-Real: Video Games Between Real Rules and Fictional Worlds* (London: MIT Press, 2005), p.21.
12. Joanne Garde-Hansen, Andrew Hoskins, and Anna Reading, eds., *Save As. . .Digital Memories* (Basingstoke: Palgrave, 2009), p.1.
13. Garde-Hansen et al, *Save As*, p.4.
14. Abby Smith Rumsey, *When We Are No More: How Digital Memory is Shaping Our Future* (Bloomsbury: London, 2016), p.3.
15. Rumsey, p.4.

16. Rumsey, p.4.
17. Paul Murray, *Skippy Dies* (London: Penguin, 2010), p.25.
18. Bernadette Flynn, 'Geography of the Digital Hearth', *Information, Communication & Society* 6.4 (2003), 551–76.
19. Flynn, p.561.
20. Murray, p.541.
21. John Morrissey, 'Ireland's Great War: Representation, Public Space and the Place of Dissonant Heritages', *Journal of the Galway Archaeological and Historical Society*, 58 (2006), 98–113 (p.100).
22. Murray, p.552.
23. Morrissey, p.103.
24. Susannah Radstone, 'Reconceiving Binaries: The Limits of Memory', *History Workshop Journal* 59 (2005), 134–50 (p.135).
25. Murray, p. 557.
26. This apparently irresistible conflation is sustained through the old cliche of the battle of Waterloo being won on the playing fields of Eton and the compelling story of the Dublin Pals signing up and training for war at Lansdowne Road.
27. Rumsey, p.114.
28. Radstone, p.135.
29. Andrew Hoskins, 'The Mediatisation of Memory', in Garde-Hansen et al., 27–43 (p.29).
30. Claudio Fogu, 'Digitalizing Historical Consciousness' in *History and Theory* 48.2, (2009), 103–12 (p.105).
31. See Alexander R. Galloway, *Gaming: Essays on Algorithmic Culture* (Minneapolis, MN: University of Minnesota Press, 2006).
32. Sarah Cameron Loyd Grey, 'Dead Time: Aporias and Critical Videogaming', *Symplokē*, 17.1–2 (2009), 231–46 (p.241).
33. Cameron Loyd Grey, p.243.
34. Fogu, p.118.
35. James Wood, 'Useless Prayers: Eimear McBride's *A Girl Is a Half-Formed Thing*', *New Yorker*, 29 September 2014. http://www.newyorker.com/magazine/2014/09/29/useless-prayers.
36. The computer in McBride's novel seems to be the Commodore 64, a hugely popular early home computer, selling over 17 million machines between 1982–1993. For more on the early years of Home Computing see Centre for Computing History http://www.computinghistory.org.uk/det/1336/commodore-64 (accessed 10/06/16).
37. McBride, p.104.
38. McBride, p.105. As the Girl responds, 'I don't think commodores were hanging on the tree Mammy'.
39. Radstone, p.138.
40. Garde-Hansen et al, p.19.
41. Aden Evens, 'The Logic of Digital Gaming', *Mechademia* 6.1 (2011), 260–9 (p.266).
42. Fogu, p.105.
43. Murray, p.164.
44. Murray, p.358.
45. Murray, p.359.
46. T. L. Taylor, *Play Between Worlds: Exploring Online Game Culture,* (London: MIT Press, 2009), p.109.
47. Jonathan Boulter, 'Virtual Bodies, or Cyborgs are People Too', in Nate Garrelts, ed., *Digital Gameplay: Essays on the Nexus of Game and Gamer* (Jefferson, NC: McFarland & Co., 2005), p.53.
48. McBride, p.94.

49. McBride, p.80.
50. Rumsey, p.131.
51. Doyle, p.254.
52. Doyle, p.293.
53. Garde-Hansen et al, p.5.
54. Garde-Hansen et al, p.5.
55. Kearney commits this murder in the garden famously dedicated to 'all those who gave their lives in the cause of Irish freedom'. This Garden of Remembrance, located in Parnell Square in the centre of Dublin is not to be confused with the Irish National War Memorial Gardens visited by the schoolboys in *Skippy Dies*. The latter, dedicated to the memory of those killed in the the 1914–18 war, stands geographically and symbolically on the capital's outskirts.
56. Garde-Hansen et al, p.13.
57. Radstone, p.138.
58. Gary Westfahl, 'Zen and the Art of Mario Maintenance: Cycles of Death and Rebirth in Video Games and Children's Subliterature, in *Immortal Engines: Life Extension and Immortality in Science Fiction and Fantasy*, ed. by George Slusser, Gary Westfahl and Eric S. Rabkin (Athens, GA: University of Georgia Press, 1996), p.213.
59. Jeffrey Douglas, 'Wooden Reels and the Maintenance of Virtual Life: Gaming and the Death Drive in a Digital Age', *ESC* 37.1 (March 2011), p.86.

Fionnuala Dillane

Breaking Memory Modes: Anne Enright's and Tana French's Silent Interruptions

In the landscape we survey, silences are spaces either beyond words or conventionally delimited as left out of what we talk about. Topographically, they are there whether or not they come to the surface; and their re-emergence into our line of sight can occasion a reiteration of the interdiction on talking about them or the end of the interdiction itself ....Critically, therefore, we cannot accept the commonplace view that silence is the space of forgetting and speech the realm of remembrance. Instead, we offer the following definition of silence. Silence ... is a socially constructed space in which and about which subjects and words normally used in everyday life are not spoken.

(Jay Winter, 'Thinking About Silence', 2010)[1]

'Remembering *is* an ethical act, has ethical value in and of itself' asserts Susan Sontag in her influential exploration of the representation of atrocity, the value of witnessing and of recording, *Regarding the Pain of Others* (2003).[2] She nonetheless asks us to consider, 'Perhaps too much value is assigned to memory, not enough to thinking'.[3] One of Sontag's concerns is that the act of contemplating and remembering what others have suffered is limited to experiencing emotion only; the wider political context that produced or continues to produce such history that hurts[4] is left out of the picture, never fully considered. The politics of remembering is overridden by the pathos of remembering. In more recent philosophical works, Judith Butler takes up the challenging politics of empathic identification with individual suffering.[5] Like Sontag, she attends to how modes of representation determine, provoke, or produce feeling for the other, but provides a sustained and more expansive critique of the ethics of this process. She moves beyond the photograph and image to interrogate how

Irish University Review 47.1 (2017): 143–164
DOI: 10.3366/iur.2017.0262
© Edinburgh University Press
www.euppublishing.com/iur

language and a more broadly-conceived understanding of frames (including genre as frame), determine whose pain is acknowledged, whose ignored or 'forgotten'. An underlying claim in these works is that affective recognition too readily stands as the justification for action and reaction, suppressing or pushing to the margins the claims of alterity that, following Levinas, it is suggested, should form the basis of our obligations to each other.[6] Marianne Hirsch likewise emphasises a need for critical distance, the core understanding that 'though it could have been me, it was decidedly not me'.[7] Such realizations positively work against the danger of homogenising the experience of pain and flattening historical difference, a potential problem of overly portable and repeatable representational frames and tropes that feature, for instance, in popular transnational memory genres such as memoirs, trauma narratives, or detective fiction.

Butler draws attention to the frames that are used to contain, make comprehensible, or regulate what constitutes the recognisable while gesturing, crucially, to the unknown that lies outside our representational modes and means. The significance of attending to processes of framing:

> [t]o call the frame into question is to show that the frame never quite contained the scene it was meant to limn, that something was already outside, which made the very sense of the inside possible, recognizable …. Something exceeds the frame that troubles our sense of reality; in other words, something occurs that does not conform to our established understanding of things.[8]

This essay is concerned with how the 'established understanding of things' is shaken by frame ruptures. These ruptures constitute instances of aesthetic dissensus in a specifically Irish context though the processes described are not unique to this country, turning as they do on transnational genres. It will look at two twenty-first century fictions, Anne Enright's *The Gathering* (2007) and Tana French's *The Secret Place* (2014), both recognisable memory modes, the trauma novel and the crime novel, both time-obsessed, retrospective, and future-oriented genres that have dominated Irish literary culture in the past two decades.[9] Characteristically, trauma narratives and crime fiction offer some type of redemption through the interlinked processes of remembrance, articulation, and recorded speech. Both modes seek to address wrongs of the past from a position in the present that will enable better futures. Enright and French operate purposefully within the familiar codes of their respective genres to a degree that draws attention to the processes of emotional and cognitive recognition that give such codified works their emotional power: repetitive, affective, recognisable framing patterns. Both authors, however, also deploy what I call, following Hirsch, an aesthetics of interruption: this is an affective, political resistance to the gratifying dispensations that characterise most memory modes and that feature in closure-driven detective fictions in particular. Hirsch draws our attention to more overtly activist, visible, real-world versions of aesthetic resistance in her accounts of this concept. Amongst her examples is US writer Grace Paley's political, literary, performative activism. Paley's practice of 'embodied politics and aesthetics of interruption, disruption and surprise',[10] involved the reorientation of public and private boundaries with confrontational transgressions of the architectures of containment that forge such boundaries, such as participation in dramatic anti-war protests at the Pentagon in the 1980s.[11]

The interruptive aesthetics of Enright and French are obviously more circumscribed, individual, localised, and less overt and transformative in their penetration of the public sphere when considered in the context of Paley's collective, collaborative resistance work. And in many ways, both novels examined here are perfectly compliant and emotionally consoling rather than resistant. Each text, in different ways, demonstrates the value of recuperative memory work. In the case of *The Gathering*, the traumatised first person narrator, who witnesses her grandmother's landlord abuse her younger brother, finds a way forward into narrative and coherence; in *The Secret Place*, a murder case is resolved and the rationale for committing the crime, explained. Hirsch's concept, however – the provocative reorientation of space by means of aesthetic rupture or confrontation, interruption rather than interpretation – illuminates the processes by which both novelists exceed genre parameters to make us think about frames and what exceeds both the frame and its contained, comprehensible narrative. The aesthetic interruptions in both texts, I will argue, force us to think about the silences that obtain around community collusion in criminal actions and unrelenting structural oppression, those 'large numbers of punctual acts of non-action', to borrow a phrase from Paul Ricoeur's sceptical interrogation of 'forgetting' that produce, facilitate, and sustain asymmetrical relations of power.[12] The operative codes of these recognisable memory modes, in these works by Enright and French, are sporadically scrambled to force consideration of the insufficiency of memory modes' pathos-oriented focus on the individual. Their interruptive acts draw attention to the not-yet-written, the not-yet-said, so the representational issues at stake are not a simple matter of direct showing or telling. Rather, both narratives attempt the paradoxical act of conveying silence. Their interruptive aesthetics turn on the tension between what is articulated and what is not by producing a sense of untethered affect rather than defined emotional responses to individual suffering, what Brian Massumi calls the 'capture and closure of affect'.[13] Enright is particularly drawn to this challenging, dynamic, affective aesthetic. 'I realise that I am actually moving towards being all interested in irresolute states; the emotions that happen before things become clear, so all these unsettled, unresolved things', she explained in an interview with Hedwig Schwall in 2008, the year after the publication of *The Gathering*, 'I like the restless before it is arrested by words. I am interested in all the disturbance that goes before that, in that, sort of, agitation, of not knowing, or nearly knowing'.[14]

Memory, willed or felt, is always first and foremost individual; as Ricoeur reminds us, it is the 'subject' who remembers, 'memory is a model of mineness, of private possession, for all the experiences of the subject'.[15] *The Gathering* reinforces the subjective reality of the processes of memory-making. The narrative is deliberately and over-determinedly fixed on the individual voice, reflecting both the obsessive pathology of trauma while at the same time demonstrating by the very partial presence of a wider social context in which abuse of the narrator's brother Liam took place (and the possible abuse of generations of the narrator's family), the persistent failure to find a language or a social political will to address wider questions of culpability.[16] The confronting omission of a substantial social realist landscape to match Enright's rich and graphic psychological portrait of her central character is thus striking and deeply pointed. Published in 2007, *The Gathering* is written in the wake of a series of media revelations about the systemic abuse of children in State-supported, Church-run institutions that resulted in the 1999 Commission to Inquire into Child Abuse and a State apology that acknowledged 'our collective failure to intervene' to detect the pain of victims and 'come to their rescue'.[17] The decision to write about violent sexual abuse that takes place within the domestic space, in the context of a wider state-sanctioned breaking of the silence on institutional abuse, serves to draw attention to the gaps that remain in the national debate. Specifically, we are alerted to the continuing silences or so-called collective forgetting that 'allowed' by omission and that failed to intervene so that criminals such as the sexual abuser landlord in this novel, Lamb Nugent, was unchecked in his destruction of individual minds and bodies over two and maybe even three generations of Veronica's family. The inadequacies of the terms in which the wider social, political and legal bodies acted on the then Taoiseach's words because of restrictions imposed on the Commission (the obligation to not name accused abusers, specific orders or victims in the final report) following a lawsuit brought by the Christian Brothers, meant that even in this context newly open to acknowledging suffering so long suppressed and occluded, silences still prevailed. The purposefully shadowed suggestion that Liam's abuse within his grandmother's home is linked to the institutionalisation of their uncle Brendan in a psychiatric hospital is indicative of this continued murkiness and wilful reluctance to acknowledge the continued gaps in the narrative. Such omissions are egregious and persistent at the domestic level, partial and inadequate at the Inquiry level,[18] and compounded by revelations of behind-closed-doors deals between Church bodies and the State that hampered the effectiveness of the Inquiry's Redress Board. *The Gathering*, then, tellingly, provides a forceful and vivid account of individual suffering and confronting aporia when it comes to situating that suffering in a wider interpretative context.

Enright's disruption is a structured omission; French's a provoking insertion. French constructs a police procedural around a cold case: the hitherto unsolved murder of a teenage boy in the grounds of a girl's school that confidently, compactly moves to swift resolution through the processes of memory gathering (oral testimonies; text, phone and video records) over the space of one day of intense investigation. However, one of the two main narrative frames in the novel includes an entirely inexplicable and apparently irrational, extraneous dimension: the display of psychokinetic powers that defy comprehension and challenge our complacent confidence in cogent conclusions that typically feature in this most codified of genres.

As in all of French's Dublin Murder Squad novels to date,[19] in *The Secret Place* the explicit links between perverse acts of violence and socially-conscripted gender roles feature centrally. The mechanism of plot reinforces French's broader understanding of what she argues is the disturbing appeal of crime fiction for women: as a woman, she writes,

> You're socialised to have an emotional response, to be frightened; basically, you're socialised towards fear. I think that applies to both crime writing and crime reading – the majority of crime readers are women. Reading and writing becomes a way of trying to understand the incomprehensible. Because in crime writing, usually evil is exposed and punished.[20]

In *The Secret Place* the insufficiency of the detective story as retributive memory mode, offering some sense of justice or order, resolution, or consolation, is made particularly stark as French emphasises the endemic and unquestioned social structures that produce such gender-specific fears. The novel makes clear that men, women, teenage boys, and girls are all damaged by hyper-sexualised, aggressive cultures of gender containment. There is nothing new in this. However, French's bizarre disruptive intervention into the realist frame of her police procedural, so confronting to her readers that one critic suggested it seems to belong in another book,[21] is a provocative challenge to think about containment and the complacency and obedience it produces.

GENRE, TIME, AND MEMORY'S MODES

Time and memory, of course, are key to detective fiction and central to its insistent progressive modernity. Formal and thematic elements that constitute the genre are time-inflected or time-bound. These include psychological suspense; causality; agency; and the 'complex double narrative', as Laura Marcus puts it, where the 'absent' story (the crime) is reconstructed in the narrated present ('the investigation').[22] The flourishing crime fiction scene in Ireland in the past twenty years or so has been indexed to the accelerated developments of industry, urban centres, and capital expansion – a mirroring of the development of the genre in nineteenth-century Britain and the early twentieth-century United States.[23] Along with these so regularly argued-for links with incipient and advanced modernity, detective fiction is dependent on looking back, on memory, on the recounting and repeating of narrative perspectives until the plot takes shape, cause and effect are clarified, and the story coheres around a climactic revelation. The crime is investigated based on the gathering of individual recollections for the most part that play out at two levels: (1) what the eye-witnesses have seen, recall, and recount; (2) what the detective figure, acting as the agent or container of memory, draws together. The detective's function is to gather relevant detail for the purpose of trial and retribution to restore and/or safeguard communal order, however temporary or fragile. The 'truth claims' of the narrative belong to a specific order of authenticity – the accumulation of evidence, proof, confession – and crucially, these claims always involve testimony based on memory.

Trauma narratives, implicated as they are in distressed psychological states, are more layered temporally, more marked by chronological instability and unreliable narrators. Here is Robert Garratt's useful definition:

> Most novels about trauma employ conventional narrative strategies, points of view, linear story lines. A trauma novel, by contrast, employs a narrative strategy in which a reconstruction of events through memories, flashbacks, dreams and hauntings is as important as the events themselves. In a trauma novel, both subject and method become central: in addition to developing

trauma as an element of the story and part of its dramatic action, it depicts the process by which a person *encounters and comes to know a traumatic event or moment that has previously proved inaccessible*. In doing so, the trauma novel stakes its claim as a literary hybrid, a work that balances narration and narrative, a story that both describes an external violent action and portrays the mind's attempt to remember it.[24]

As Garratt's own study argues, in the Irish context, such trauma narratives, concerned as they are with alternate, suppressed, secret histories, go on to re-present such narratives, re-centred, even if temporarily, surfaced, even if incompletely. Evidently the act of narration constitutes an unsilencing. Formally, stylistically, thematically such narratives, including *The Gathering*, bear the scars of difficult rebirth: they are fragmented, partial, temporally dislocated, and disorienting. Nonetheless, most ultimately offer a sense-making and emotional re-construction so that the reader, at least, if not the often still traumatized narrators or character, 'comes to know', as Garret puts it. Garratt's book, the only one to date that focuses exclusively on Irish trauma fiction,[25] analyses novels by John McGahern, Jennifer Johnston, William Trevor, Seamus Deane, Patrick McCabe, and Sebastian Barry mostly from the late twentieth and early twenty-first centuries. Even the most chronically unstable of these narratives, Barry's *The Secret Scripture*, with its traumatised central speaker, a 100 or so-year-old woman, institutionalised in a psychiatric hospital since the birth of her illegitimate child, has her narrative contextualised by an alternative witness: a local priest fills in the gaps in her history. His narrative, as well as the woman's, are mediated further by the doctor treating her. The doctor's measured, interpretative, objective prose is alert to the contradictions and instabilities in the primary witness and underscores the misogynistic bias of the counter narrative offered by the priest. The doctor is our mediating intelligence and rationalising decoder: his role is to frame, to help us to comprehend, and in this instance, revealed in an emotional climax as the long-lost son of the central character, to make us feel even more.[26]

Griselda Pollock has repeatedly drawn attention to this contradiction at the heart of the trauma narrative, the fact that articulation at all is a form of structuring, what she calls in a potent phrase, 'the relief of a signification'.[27] Both Enright and French, in contrast, make us think about non-signification. In what is ultimately a purposefully incongruous aesthetic strategy, both novelists imply that though we more fully remember *individual* traumatic events or uncover and redress *individual* crimes, silences surround the social and political structures that facilitate exclusion and suppression, that police what can be spoken, and that determine how we frame remembering and act on injustice in wider national contexts. The crucial point is that these are not histories or contexts that are forgotten or in need of remembrance, rather, using the terms outlined in Jay Winter's epigraph to this essay, these stories, these facts, are there, in the topography, but are subject to socially-constructed silences. A language to comprehend or to put these narratives in a frame has yet to be found, and perhaps may never be found. I am not speaking about the difficult processes of recovering trauma then, or the articulation of occluded histories. Such histories are not lost, as John Banville observed with reference to the collusion between families, the State, and the Catholic Church in a striking response piece to the publication of the Commission to Inquire into Child Abuse, the 2009 Ryan Report: 'Everyone knew'. This short, sharp sentence that opens his article is both hard hitting and belated. He continues,

> Surely the systematic cruelty visited upon hundreds of thousands of children incarcerated in state institutions in this country from 1914 to 2000, the period covered by the inquiry, but particularly from 1930 until 1990, would have been prevented if enough right-thinking people had been aware of what was going on? Well, no. Because everyone knew.[28]

Both Enright and French, I suggest, have produced works that leave the wider social picture purposefully blank as a way of provoking us to attend to what 'everyone knows' but no one talks about, with a specific emphasis in both texts on abusive cultures *outside* of the institutions investigated by both the Commission to Inquire into Child Abuse and the 2004 Commission of Investigation into the Catholic Archdiocese of Dublin. When characters in their novels attempt to find a language to address what 'everyone knows', it erupts through the realist frame of the text in the form of the supernatural or the grotesque, and, crucially, moves back outside the realist frame again. We are left to continue the work of connecting, of filling in gaps, of considering the relationship between individual suffering recounted in these novels and the wider, still blurred, cultures of silence and collusion.

'We knew, and did not know. That is our shame today', Banville's piece concludes. In these words he echoes Enright's narrator, Veronica, who identifies shame as the overwhelming response to the emergence of individual stories of suffering, which we are left to presume are the narratives that emerged over the public airwaves, penetrating every private space, in the late 1990s: 'a whole fucking country – drowning in shame', she sarcastically observes (168). And she claims her own share of that shame in response to the continuous revelations of abuse that trigger her own memory of her family's abuser, Nugent: 'Over the next twenty years, the world around us changed and I remembered Mr Nugent. But I would never have made that shift on my own – if I hadn't been listening to the radio, and reading the paper, and hearing about what went on in schools and churches and in people's homes. *It* went on slap-bang in front of me and I did not realise *it*. And for *this*, I am very sorry too' (173, my emphasis). The use of the untethered referents 'it' and 'this' in these final two sentences are particularly revealing instances of the confused and confusing elision of guilt: it is made deliberately unclear if Veronica is sorry for not intervening on behalf of her brother or for her part in sustaining a wider culture of silence and fear. The grammatical blurring plays out at the level of the sentence the confusion that remains in wider, as yet unwritten, narratives about how such communities of collusion were constituted. Though of course, an individual sense of shame, such as Banville's or the fictional Veronica's, is no doubt typical, genuine, and heartfelt, shame as a response more broadly, is insufficient and problematic for its affecting indulgence that in fact reinforces the 'then/now', progressive, moving-on binary, which fails to attend to wider motivating impulses of both abusers and those who knew but did not speak.[29] As Sara Ahmed has so persuasively explicated in her influential study of the cultural politics of emotion:

> National shame can be a mechanism for reconciliation as self-reconciliation, in which the "wrong" that is committed provides the grounds for claiming a national identity, for restoring a pride that is threatened in the moment of recognition, and then regained in the capacity to bear witness. Those who witness the past injury through feeling "national shame" are aligned with each other as "well-meaning individuals": if you feel shame, you're "in" the nation, a nation that means well and therefore reproduces the nation as ideal.[30]

As Gerardine Meaney warns us, narratives of national progress are 'dependent on the suppression of the evidence of the persistence of structures of conformity, domination and exclusion at the heart of Irish society and culture'.[31] Both of the works, here, I suggest, challenge the exculpatory tendencies of affective memory modes that are premised on such emotional consensus. The disturbing and baffling genre interruptions that feature in both narratives signal a wariness of such empathic identification as a substitute for more difficult considerations about the structural conditions that produce and continue to reproduce inequity and discrimination.

151

THE GATHERING: 'A MILLION FLAKES OF SKIN'

Enright's novel is the first-person narrative of a middle-aged, middle-class, ostensibly successful Dublin woman, Veronica Hegarty. The narrator is enduring a breakdown apparently triggered by the death by suicide of her brother, who was the victim of sexual abuse, perpetrated by Nugent, a long-term acquaintance of their grandmother, Ada, and likely witnessed by the narrator. Veronica's first-person narrative, however, is shadowed throughout by an unspoken, frustratingly vague context that gestures towards but by definition cannot yet articulate or clarify how such abuses were allowed to occur. Veronica's painfully fierce sense of anger, confusion, and loss drives her 'need to bear witness to an uncertain event' which she feels 'roaring' inside of her (1). This need to speak is counterbalanced by the other Irish obsession, 'Don't tell Mammy'. The phrase, repeated with sarcasm and seriousness throughout the narrative, becomes totemic of the insistence on silence, which is reinforced at the level of form by Enright's implied but disarticulated wider social context.

Veronica's partial recovery of her memory and her efforts to find a voice, return to the world, and begin to heal, are central to most readings of the novel. We, as readers, as Liam Harte puts it, 'partake of the protagonist's gruelling struggle to make sense'.[32] But the sharing and sense-making are blocked when we consider what is outside the domestic frames and individual stories of suffering and grief. Harte and Meaney, for instance, move beyond this focus on the central traumatised narrator to indicate how the complicated stylistics of the text recharge the narrative's wider political meaning. Both critics make persuasive cases for how Veronica's story is indicative of larger narratives of abuse, repression, and crime, but crucially note that these larger narratives are ones for which we have yet to account. In the absence of that wider picture, both still focus on Veronica.[33] This critical consensus around the centrality of Veronica, even in these accounts most attentive to the wider context, is entirely understandable, and not just because a narrative that strives to convey a sense of the wounded body and mind are obviously made compelling by being focalised through the eyes and voice of the woman who is wounded. There is the additional sense that with no frames to contain the extent of the physical and sexual abuse perpetrated within family homes as well as in Catholic institutions, with no language to explicate both the levels of violence and widespread acceptance of such violence, we can only attend to the individual voice. An unsettling claustrophobia results: the entire narrative comprises one perspective: Veronica's struggle to find a reason for her brother's suicide, the drive to identify the 'seeds' of his destruction (13). And of course it is impossible to nominate a point of origin in a tangled history of abuse that is so deeply rooted in the wider, still chronically unarticulated, social matrix. To make this point, the narrative circles in repetitive loops around what is presented from the outset as an imagined history, that overtly fictionalised background to the relationship between her grandmother, Ada, and the abuser, Nugent. It is a made-up story, a made-up Ada and Nugent, 'reassembled; click clack' (14) that lurches from Veronica's over-blown romance fiction mode – 'This is all my romance of course' (21) – to explicit sexual and biological naturalism: Nugent thinking of the 'swell of his glans easing out from its sack of skin' at the sight of Ada (18); Ada, pictured by Nugent, as 'laughing at him – standing there like a gobdaw with a lump in his pants' (20). The jagged vacillation functions, amongst other things, to convey Veronica's own uneasy sense of the processes of framing, reinforced in her continual self-consciousness about the act of writing; it signals too Enright's interruption of her own framing act.

From the opening chapter we are alerted to Veronica's self-reflexive understanding of writing as an assertive act of comprehension: 'I wait for the kind of sense that dawn makes, when you have not slept ... I write it down, I lay them out in nice sentences, all my clean white bones' (1). Yet the fictional biography of the dead Ada and Nugent, these made-up memories that so provoke many of Enright's readers, is deliberately perverse, overblown, and garish to demonstrate its substitutive quality for actual knowledge, actual history, real confrontation.[34]

Following theorists of trauma, critics such as Harte extend the suffering body of Veronica to the wider social collective: the social body under scrutiny, he writes, like Veronica, 'is one heavily obscured by cultural amnesia, concealment and denial' and through her 'tormented and amnesiac central protagonist' Harte suggests, 'Enright addresses the prodigious array of psychic, somatic and cultural ramifications of hidden child sexual abuse in modern Ireland'.[35] Yet the social body, it must be reiterated, is not present at all except as a series of repressed shadowy inferences to what is beyond the frame, to recall Butler. The abuser, Nugent, is aligned with the Church through brief references to his devotion to mass and the rosary and his friendship with legion of Mary founder, Frank Duff, who sought to rescue prostitutes from the streets of Dublin as part of his religious remit. The implication is that Ada, Veronica's grandmother and apparent original target of Nugent's obsessive love or lust, was such a 'rescued' prostitute, set up by the increasingly affluent Nugent in her house in Broadstone, and restricted exclusively to his services. That nexus of Church, money, sex, power, and hypocrisy is suggested in this deliberately shady and never fully unpacked arrangement. Veronica's mother, the only link to past and present, and potential holder of such secret arrangements is 'forgetfulness itself' (3) and so no help to us; her grandfather, Charlie, and her 'Daddy', tellingly unnamed and so stereotypically representative – he is a violent alcoholic, an Irish speaker, a lecturer, who grew up in 'the West' (42) – remain chronically ineffective and on the margins of the story. Enright's broader invitation is to consider the silences, the nature of such arrangements, the collusions that permitted them without mediating or categorising or explaining them to us. In striking contrast to Veronica's occluded story and Liam's secret history of abuse that slowly, painfully emerge, these arrangements stay secret and hidden. Memory may rescue the individual narrative from silence but the wider emotional community stays outside the frame, except for striking ruptures that remind us, uncomfortably, of what we do not yet comprehend.

State, Church, and Family are implicitly indicted in the sections of the novel that skirt around the confinement of Ada's son, Veronica's uncle Brendan, in a psychiatric institution, St Ita's in Portrane, north county Dublin.[36] But unlike Barry's *The Secret Scripture*, for instance, where the life in such institutions is described and made core to the present action, we only get an abandoned and empty St Ita's in *The Gathering*'s 'present' or the child Veronica's partial descriptions of the landscape surrounding the building in her recollections from her past. Veronica recounts her childhood journeys to the hospital in detail, and gives a clear sense of the surroundings, but 'I don't remember the hospital' she tells us, 'At a guess, Ada did not take us inside' (115). Her return journey as an adult slips uncontrollably between detailed recollection of the wider landscape and significant gaps: 'The little bridge is still there, and the railway line, slicing north. After which there is sudden slack in my mental map and the road unravels in front of me' (158). Mirroring the difficulty of holding the topography in place, Veronica struggles to link her own trauma to Brendan's and beyond. In the absence of terms with which to describe the collusion of state, church, and community that resulted in the abandonment of intelligent but inexplicably damaged boys such as Brendan (we are told he had a brilliant brain for maths), Enright's narrator reaches for an extreme analogue in her adult exploration with her sister Kitty of the grounds of the deserted St Ita's. Veronica explains that the building is now signed 'Handicap Services' and that 'the lunatics have quite naturally turned to dust ... the lunatics are just a residue of skin in these rooms; scratched off, or hacked off, or maybe just shed: a million flakes of skin, a softness under the floorboards, a quality of light' (159). Pressing on with the reach to historical trauma analogues, she adds: 'We pass a courtyard with a high chimney and low boiler house, all in extravagant, industrial red brick. There are curious round windows on the boiler house, with the Star of David, dividing the panes. "Jesus" says Kitty, thinking, as I am thinking for a second, that they are burning mental patients in there just to keep the radiators hot' (159). They move from this imagined holocaust to the graveyard by the sea (the sea in which Liam drowned across the water with stones in his pockets), where the residents of St Ita's hospital, unnamed, are buried under one cross. Veronica asks: 'I wonder how many people were slung into the dirt of this field and realise, too late that the place is boiling with corpses, the ground is knit out of their tangled bones' (160), keeping the heat of her extended Holocaust metaphor, its original implication in religious sacrifice by fire, to the fore.

The Holocaust analogy is deliberately extreme: its recognisable fullness and horror stand in diametric opposition to the blanks in the Irish context. It also inevitably draws attention to questions of scale, and the irrelevance and impossibility of scale when it comes to thinking beyond the recuperation of individual narratives. As dust, scales of skin, tangles of bones, these bodies in their irreversible annihilation, in their permanent silence, amass outside the frame of what we know and can contain. They are beyond individualisation and in this constitute a powerful 'otherness' that stands in direct confrontation with memory modes' singular recuperations. The final irruption in the novel, then, is not of the shadowy but crucially real Liam, who though haunting the narrative throughout is never figured as anything other than a troubled but actual person. Rather, Brendan, who is never given a voice of his own in the text, is produced in the end as a grotesque concentration, a clumped tangle of victims of this generationally-embedded culture of silence. Tellingly not allowed to speak, even in Veronica's imagined past, and with no one to speak for him, all deaf to his presence, he surfaces as a surreal rip in the psychological realism of the narrative:

> My uncle Brendan, in knee socks and short pants. He stands in the hall outside the twins' room, the room where baby Stevie died, and his middle-aged head is full to bursting with all the things he has to tell Ada, that she will not hear him say. Brendan's bones are mixed with other people's bones; so there is a turmoil of souls muttering and whining under his clothes, they would come out in a roar, were he to unbutton his fly; if he opened his mouth they would slop out over his teeth. Brendan has no rest from them, the souls of the forgotten who must always be crawling and bulging and whining in there; he reaches to

scratch under his collar and handfuls come loose. The only places clear of them are his unlikeable blue eyes, so Brendan just stares as I reach for the light switch, and his shirt heaves, and his ears leak the mad and inconvenient dead (216).

The mad and inconvenient dead, arrestingly unincorporated here, are, all the same, now in the frame as an interruption in Veronica's own story of healing. Yet they are more than this. Their muteness mirrors the other muteness that remains the striking 'other' of the text: the dumb and silent communities of collusion. The eyes of Brendan are clear – everyone sees what is going on – but his mouth is stuffed shut and his ears are blocked. The partial picture of the socially, historically real is thus entirely appropriate. The fully realised presence of a social landscape would suggest a type of integrated understanding of self and society, fundamental to the structures of feeling that Raymond Williams identifies in the nineteenth-century realist novel that, this twenty-first century Irish novel implies, is false and dangerous, since the cultures of evasion, exclusion, and suppression endure.[37]

THE SECRET PLACE: 'WE JUST DIDN'T KNOW HOW TO GET TO IT'

In French's more systematic police procedural the aesthetic disruption is more overt. In the compressed space of less than twenty-four hours her two detectives from the Dublin Murder Squad relentlessly push to its conclusion what was an unresolved closed case: the person who murdered a teenage boy from an affluent family on the grounds of a girl's private school in south Dublin confesses to the first-person narrator detective Stephen Moran and his senior partner, Antoinette Conway. The perpetrator is cornered by a series of interviews that rely heavily on memory and technology. Mobile phone records and phone videos provide the crucial evidence, a commonplace trope of detective fiction that since its emergence in the nineteenth-century has foregrounded the truth-revealing, memory capturing tools of industrial modernity. What remains unresolved, however, is more significant, though it is almost entirely unremarked upon in the novel, and is all the more disruptive for that: these are the bizarre displays of psychokinetic powers amongst the tightly-knit group of teenage girls, Selena, Holly, Julia, and Rebecca, who are suspects in the murder inquiry.

Instances of levitating objects and flickering and exploding lightbulbs irrupt through the smooth surface of rational realism that dominates the text. The psychokinesis that is described as a power exercised only by these four girls, closely bonded in friendship and at the heart of the narrative (one of whom is the murderer, the other, a daughter of another of French's Dublin murder squad detectives), symbolically expresses the intensity of their teenage friendship. But it is also presented as literally true as verified by a peer group: a rival girl gang in the school is present when lightbulbs explode, for instance, and so confirm the 'reality' of these happenings. The witnessing gang package and dismiss the psychokinetic events as yet more evidence of their rivals' witch-like weirdness (237). In this important way, in this instance of external but unprocessed verification, the psychokinesis is of a different order of experience to the apparent manifestation of the ghost of Chris, the murdered schoolboy, haunting the girls' school. The ghost is supposedly seen by numerous boarders in the school but is categorically dismissed by the rational detectives and no-nonsense headmistress as the imaginings of suggestible young girls in heightened states of emotion and collective trauma post-murder. Significantly, the detectives and the headmistress do not witness or even hear about the psychokinetic events so they remain secret, signalling on one level a coded communication, impervious to outside forces, that denotes a closed group, a common strategy in French's work to create the circumscribed communities needed for puzzle-driven mystery narratives.[38]

On another level, however, because no rationalising intelligence is brought to bear on the happenings, they simply stand as inexplicable interruptions to the smooth forward momentum of the text. As such, this element in French's work is entirely without precedent and is quite distinct from the uncanny doubling of victim and investigator in *The Likeness* and the surreal estrangements of *Broken Harbour*. John Teel observes of such works that French creates 'a unique blend of the police procedural with the gothic, a mode that always hovers on the edge of the irrational and unexplainable'.[39] The crucial difference between these hybrid narratives and *The Secret Place* is that the doubling of *The Likeness*, for instance, is fundamental to the unfolding of the plot, sustained as part of the narrative's uneasy suspense, and ultimately addressed and explained by the conclusion. Similarly, the unsettling tensions of *Broken Harbour* are explicated by the mediating detectives as a consequence of the psychological breakdown of one of the central characters, though the chilling effects linger and his mental collapse provokes his wife's murderous acts. In direct contrast to French's characteristic blending of gothic and police procedural elements, *The Secret Place* provides a striking separation of realist procedural and these random, unnecessary eruptions. Our efforts at interpretation are deliberately challenged by these interruptions, and they defy comprehension to the end, a refusal to the reader that does not feature in her other work, even in the open-ended *In the Woods*, where a secondary plot that features the apparent kidnapping of two children in the 1980s goes unresolved; it is a dissatisfying conclusion but an unfortunate part of the daily fabric of life. Psychokinesis is not part of the daily fabric of life, the fabric of detective fiction, or the fabric of this memory-driven story. These actions are extraneous to the resolution of the crime, featuring only in the mostly focalised flashback chapters that provide the back story to the murder and that alternate with those narrated by the first-person detective, Stephen, who provides the cohering intelligence. A braided, shifting, but strictly patterned temporality that is typical of the detective mode is created by these double narrative strands but the disconcertingly unexplained psychokinetic occurrences obtrude as an affront to the procedural modernity of both the detective's narration and the patient, detailed filling in of memory gaps in the case history through witness recollection. In this way they figure as interruption only in marked contrast to French's other work – and so we have to ask, why?

Their newly discovered abilities confound the four girls who recount individual instances of the bizarre happenings, which include the flickering of electric lights when the girls are threatened or experience anger. Struggling to explicate the unfathomable, Selena situates the experiences as indicative of their latent power: 'It's not for anything. It's just there. Like, it was there all along; we just didn't know how to get to it. Till now' (186). The reason-defying events may be read as testifying to the power of the collective, the female collective in these telling illustrations, to alter reality and the laws of physics. But the fact that these so-called powers are ultimately so banal and redundant is core to their interruptive status and to their utter pointlessness as a form of collective will. The power of exploding lightbulbs and levitating pens, fascinating to some no doubt, and signifying potential that we do not yet understand or control, is bathetic in the face of an endemic culture of gender discrimination and manipulation, body regulation, and sexual aggression that persists throughout not just this novel but all of French's murder squad series. What we are left with is a sense of potential alterity misshaped, misunderstood.

This narrative, like all of French's work, continuously points to the destructive dynamics of a culture that repeatedly circumscribes behaviour according to strictly limited and regulated gender roles.[40] It is inscribed from the opening paragraphs of this novel where the four fifteen-year friends gather in a playground, eating ice-cream. Not children, not yet adults, their conversation is suffused with sexually explicit language and jokes, 'traffic noises and guys' shouts seep over the hedge', penetrating the innocent frame of the playground: Julia describes the sticky mess of ice cream that gets stuck in her hair as like 'a blow-job she gave to someone with bad aim' (1). From the first page, French frames all their actions in terms of gender and sex. The second narrative, the first-person account of detective Stephen Moran, provides another iteration of the claustrophobic gendered codes of the private school context, exposing an even more explicitly aggressive sexism operating in the Dublin Murder Squad room that entirely shapes the working practices of all its detectives and, in particular, those of Antoinette Conway. Conway suffers constant, corrosive bullying and linguistic abuse for once challenging a colleague for groping her. Throughout the novel, her own language is scored with the verbal violence she endures every day: in exchanges with male colleagues or when impressing her authority on interviewees, she is, in Moran's words, inner-city 'Rough', but her aggressive edge is clearly established as a response her environment. In their first conversation – that follows a goading from one of her other colleagues that she seal a confession in her current case by giving the interviewee a 'good kick in the nads' (16) – she explains that during their initial investigation she got 'fuck-all' out of Holly, the 'snotty little bitch' (17). In distinct contrast, on the phone to a female colleague immediately after these exchanges, the expletives and edge are entirely toned down (17–18). Moran is aware of the price of aligning himself with this unpopular because atypical, 'unfeminine' woman: 'slaggings from the butch boys, the sniggers rising when I found the gimp mask on my desk. The paperwork and the witnesses that took just that bit too long to reach us; the squad pints we only heard about the next morning' (496). Nothing changes. Gender violence cuts across all classes, all age groups and all contexts; it is not a singular traumatic 'event' or happening, but a continuous, insidious, pervasive aggression. The unrelenting forceful assertion of male power is perverse and crippling: fatal for Chris, the murdered schoolboy, in this narrative, it creates victims of all. The expression of interruptive resistance to its power in the form of individual and collective interference with the laws of physics and probability are purposefully anti-climactic, unharnessed and ultimately, therefore, pointless. The reader is confronted with the suggestion that there is no possibility of resistance. There is nothing, yet, outside the frame.

DISRUPTIVE ACTS OF DISOBEDIENCE

Enright and French give us novels with significantly different levels of affective intensity and aesthetic experimentation, yet that similarly insist that the remembering that is so central to memory modes is not enough: we need to continue to think. They force us to think about what still remains unsaid and to provoke us to consider 'spaces either beyond words or conventionally delimited as left out of what we talk about'.[41] There is no overt didactic instruction here. These narratives do not ascribe to a view of storytelling as a type of 'moral technology'.[42] Rather, Enright and French convey a sceptical questioning of memory acts that focus on the value of individual recollection, or the recuperation and recovery for the record of singular, suppressed events as enough in and of themselves in their production of empathic recognition. To this end, both novelists challenge the feeling reader with purposefully alienating narrative techniques and tropes that buckle and block interpretative strategies. Their works produce striking moments of reader confrontation not flattering collusion or consensus.

Genre is crucial to this version of an aesthetics of interruption. Genre is of course a type of architecture of containment that is reliant on memory. It is, to use John Frow's useful formulation, an 'anticipatory structure',[43] that is codified and that codifies. Its affective aesthetic derives from its iterative dimensions and the spectator's or reader's memory of these repetitive features. And it is precisely these iterative features that, as Jacques Derrida puts it in 'The Law of Genre', inevitably and irrevocably contextualise deviations or interruptions. 'As soon as the word "genre" is sounded', he observes, archly, 'as soon as it is heard, as soon as one attempts to conceive it, a limit is drawn. And when a limit is established, norms and interdictions are not far behind. "Do", "Do not" says genre'.[44] Enright and French draw on the norms and interdictions of genre, what can and cannot be done at the level of form and content, to point up what is outside the limits of our memory modes, what is still not attended to or not yet sayable. In such ways, they leverage and disown at once genre's anticipatory functions – emphasising the memory-restoring capacities of the modes and their scepticism about that restoration as an end-point.

These aesthetic interruptions are not the defamiliarisations that feature in Patrick McCabe's gothic trauma narratives, for instance, or Anu's confronting onsite theatrical productions; aesthetics of estrangement are part of the fabric and purpose of these latter works. The difference between these modes and those analysed here is that we expect such disorientation from McCabe and Anu from the outset: it is part of the inventive and often exhilarating codification of these performative modes and is replicated across their works. *The Gathering* and *The Secret Place* operate as specific realist memory modes but also foreground their codified structures of containment, their law of genre, with disruptive acts of disobedience. This is not a question of genre subversion or hybridization, as Edna Longley, for instance, has argued of the 'Troubles Elegy' in Northern Ireland as a new memory mode.[45] The whole point is the realisation that there is no frame that is yet sufficient or, perhaps, permitted or recognised. Their works offer instances of disobedience, not, as Derrida would have it, a new law of genre. The fact that both Enright and French go on in their subsequent works to operate more fully inside more stable, recognisable genres, (Enright's stylistically and thematically more conventional *The Forgotten Waltz*; French's most straightforwardly procedural *The Trespassers*) signals the fact that the art of interruption cannot be replicated, so it cannot become codified, or it would no longer function as interruption.[46] These then, in the words of Marianne Hirsch, 'are small resistances, little resistances',[47] localised, non-repeatable, so 'small', but nonetheless powerful and indicative of what we have yet to do.

NOTES

1. Jay Winter, 'Thinking about Silence', in Efrat Ben Ze-ev, Ruth Ginio and Jay Winter, eds, *Shadows of War: A Social History of Silence in the Twentieth Century* (Cambridge: Cambridge University Press, 2010), 3–31 (p.4).
2. Susan Sontag, *Regarding the Pain of Others* (New York: Picador, 2003), p.115.
3. Sontag, p.115.
4. The expression derives from Fredric Jameson's more pointed assertion: 'History is what hurts'. See Fredric Jameson, *The Political Unconscious: Narrative as a Socially Symbolic Act* (London: Methuen, 1981), p.102.
5. See Judith Butler, *Precarious Life: Powers of Mourning and Violence* (London: Verso, 2004) and *Frames of War: When is Life Grievable?* (London: Verso, 2009).
6. 'The relationship with the other', Levinas writes in *Time and the Other*, 'is not an idyllic and harmonious relationship of communion or sympathy, through which we put ourselves in the other's place; we recognise the other as resembling us, but exterior to us... The other's entire being is constituted by its exteriority, or rather its alterity'. Reprinted in *The Levinas Reader*, ed. by Sean Hand (Oxford: Blackwell, 1994), p.43.
7. Marianne Hirsch, 'Connective Histories in Vulnerable Times', *PMLA* 129.3 (2014), 330–48, (p.339).
8. Butler, *Frames of War*, p.10.
9. Anne Enright, *The Gathering* (London: Vintage, 2008); Tana French, *The Secret Place* (Dublin: Hachette, 2014). On the upsurge in crime fiction, see Declan Burke, ed., *Down These Green Streets: Irish Crime Writing in the 21ˢᵗ Century* (Dublin: Liberties Press, 2011) and Elizabeth Mannion, ed., *The Contemporary Irish Detective Novel* (Basingstoke: Palgrave Macmillan, 2016); on the pervasiveness of the trauma narrative, see Robert F. Garratt, *Trauma and History in the Irish Novel* (Basingstoke: Palgrave Macmillan, 2011). The memoir completes the triad of dominant memory modes over the past two decades. See, for instance, Emilie Pine, *The Politics of Irish Memory: Performing Remembrance in Contemporary Irish Culture* (Basingstoke: Palgrave Macmillan, 2010), Chapter 2, 'The Remembered Self: Irish Memoir, Past and Present selves', 52–77; Stephen Regan, 'Autobiography and Memoir in Modern Ireland', *BELLS*, 1.9 (2009), 151–70, available at http://doi.fil.bg.ac.rs/pdf/journals/bells/2009/bells-2009-1-9.pdf
10. Marianne Hirsch, '"What We Need Right Now Is to Imagine the Real": Grace Paley Writing against War', *PMLA*, 124.5 (October 2009), 1768–77 (p.1769).
11. Hirsch, '"What We Need", p.1771.

12. Paul Ricoeur, *Memory, History, Forgetting*, trans. by Kathleen Blamey and David Pellauer (Chicago: University of Chicago Press, 2006), p.502.

13. As Brian Massumi puts it 'Formed, qualified, situated perceptions and cognitions fulfilling functions of actual connection or blockages are the capture and closure of affect. Emotion is the most intense (most contracted) expression of that *capture*', see Brian Massumi, *Parables for the Virtual: Movement, Affect, Sensation* (Durham NC and London: Duke University Press, 2002), p.35. For a critique of aspects of affect theory, and Massumi's work, see Ruth Leys, 'The Affective Turn: A Critique', *Critical Inquiry* 37 (Spring 2011), 434–72.

14. 'Muscular Metaphors in Anne Enright: An Interview with Hedwig Schwall', *The European English Messenger* 17.1 (2008), 16–22 (p.17).

15. Ricoeur, p.97, p.96.

16. Stef Craps, amongst others, has urged for the need to move beyond accounts of individual trauma to attend to the wider contexts: 'Refusing to move from the individual psyche to the social situation can only have damaging consequences. A narrow focus on individual psychology ignores and leaves unquestioned the conditions that enabled the traumatic abuse. Indeed, the individualization of social suffering encourages the idea that recovery from the traumas affecting the members of marginalized groups is basically a matter of the individual gaining linguistic control over his or her pain.' See Stef Craps, 'Wor(l)ds of Grief: Traumatic Memory and Literary Witnessing in Cross-cultural Perspective', *Textual Practice* 24.1 (2010), 51–68 (p.55).

17. The apology was made by Taoiseach Bertie Ahern on 11 May 1999, and repeated again by Taoiseach Brian Cowan in his response in June 2009 to the publication of the Commission's report. http://www.taoiseach.gov.ie/eng/News/Archives/2009/Taoiseach's_Speeches_2009/Dail_Debate_on_the_Report_of_the_Commission_of_Inquiry_into_Child_Abuse11_June_2009,_Speech_by_An_Taoiseach,_Mr_Brian_Cowen_TD.html. The ground-breaking work by documentary maker, producer, and writer Mary Raftery, such as *States of Fear* (RTE, 1999), as well as Louis Lentin's *Dear Daughter* (1996) brought individual stories into the wider national debate further fuelled by individual testimonies on talk radio shows in particular.

18. See, for instance, the resignation letter of the first Chair of the Inquiry, Mary Laffoy, in the wake of concerns about government support for an independent inquiry, available at http://www.irishtimes.com/news/justice-mary-laffoy-s-letter-of-resignation-1.373996.

19. French has written five other novels in her Dublin Murder Squad series: *In The Woods* (2007); *The Likeness* (2008); *Faithful Place* (2010); *Broken Harbour* (2012); and *The Trespasser* (2016).

20. Tana French, in 'Paper Tiger: An Interview with Tana French', by Claire Coughlan, in Burke, ed., *Down These Green Streets*, 335–44 (p.335).

21. A review in *The Guardian* for instance is not alone in being unconvinced by what the reviewer with withering understatement calls 'the supernatural touches' in the novel. 'The ghost-spotting' of the murdered teenage boy, she suggests 'works because, in this milieu of hysterical and attention-seeking schoolgirls, it is entirely explicable, but other elements belong in a different sort of novel', Laura Wilson, review of Tana French, *The Secret Place*, *The Guardian*, 6 September 2014, available at https:// www.theguardian.com/books/2014/sep/06/the-secret-place-tana-french-review. So confronting are these 'other elements', and so dismissed as extraneous, they are not even named by the reviewer.

22. Laura Marcus, 'Detection and Literary Fiction', *Crime Fiction*, ed. by Martin Priestman (Cambridge: Cambridge University Press, 2003), 245–67 (p.245).

23. On this explanation for the newly flourishing crime fiction scene, see Burke; Mannion; and the special edition of the journal *Clues* on Tana French's work, *Clues: a Journal of Detection* 32.1 (Spring 2014).

24. Robert Garratt, *Trauma and History in the Irish Novel* (Basingstoke: Palgrave Macmillan, 2011), p.5 (my emphasis). For an argument that draws out the connections between trauma narratives and detective fiction, see Shirley Peterson, 'Voicing the Unspeakable: Tana French's Dublin Murder Squad', in Mannion, ed., *The Contemporary Irish Detective Novel*, 107–20. I do not share Peterson's view of the so-called traumatising effects of the Celtic Tiger in *The Secret Place*, that 'nurtured in the Celtic Tiger years' this 'generation' of teenagers seems 'unhinged from its heritage' (p.115). The structural inequities depicted are more embedded, endemic, and cross-generational, I suggest.

25. Vital work that is more conceptually suggestive, more thematically varied, and less tied to monumental event-based traumas as Garratt is in his birth-of-the-nation focus continues in this area, see for example, Claire Bracken, 'Queer Intersections and Nomadic Routes: Anne Enright's *The Pleasure of Eliza Lynch*', *Canadian Journal of Irish Studies* 35.1 (2010), 109–127; Susan Cahill, *Irish Literature in the Celtic Tiger Years: Gender, Bodies, Memory* (New York and London: Continuum, 2011); Liam Harte, 'Mourning Remains Unresolved: Trauma and Survival in Anne Enright's *The Gathering*', *Lit: Literature, Interpretation, Theory* 21 (2010), 187–204. Gerardine Meaney, 'Waking the Dead: Antigone, Ismene and Anne Enright's Narrator in Mourning', in *Anne Enright*, ed. by Claire Bracken and Susan Cahill (Dublin: Irish Academic Press, 2011), 145–64; Anne Mulhall, '"Now the Blood is in the Room": The Spectral Feminine in the Work of Anne Enright', Bracken and Cahill, eds, 67–86; Maria Mulvany, 'Haunting, Trauma and Time in Contemporary Irish Historical Fiction', unpublished Ph.D. dissertation, UCD, 2016, and recent comparative studies such as Biata Piatek *History, Memory, Trauma in Contemporary British and Irish Fiction* (New York: Columbia University Press, 2014).

26. Sebastian Barry, *The Secret Scripture* (London: Faber and Faber, 2008).

27. Griselda Pollock, 'Art/Trauma/Representation', *Parallax* 15.1 (2009), 40–54 (p.41).

28. John Banville, 'A Century of Looking the Other Way', *New York Times*, 23 May 2009, p.21 available at http://www.nytimes.com/2009/05/23/opinion/23banville.html. Carol Dell'Amico footnotes this Banville article in 'Anne Enright's *The Gathering*: Trauma, Testimony, Memory', *New Hibernia Review* 14.3. (Autumn 2010), 59–73, (p.74, n.21). Dell'Amico cites Banville's suggestion that Irish people were in thrall to the authority of the Catholic Church and shaped too by the Protestant doctrine of the elect, that is, if children were sent to industrial schools and reformatories and so on, they must have been destined for it, deserving it, and therefore not our concern to interfere. Such generalised explanations are obviously insufficient.

29. Those who experience violence and abuse, of course, cannot be made to also carry the burden of speaking out, even presuming the memory of such traumatic injury is available to them.

30. Sara Ahmed, *The Cultural Politics of Emotion* (New York: Routledge, 2004), p.109.

31. Gerardine Meaney, 'Race, Sex and Nation', *Irish Review* 35 (2007), p.46.

32. Harte, p.192

33. See Harte, p.189. Gerardine Meaney's account of the narrator in mourning provides an illuminating and ultimately hopeful explanation of how Veronica retains her 'attachment to life' and offers the possibility of recovery, see Meaney, 'Waking the Dead', p.147, p.161. Dell'Amico suggests that Veronica may be seen as a 'conduit' through which Enright 'refers to a host of national lapses' specifically focussing on the superficial Celtic Tiger success of Veronica and her husband Tom, but Veronica remains the focus of attention in this account. See Dell'Amico, p.64. See also Dennell

Downum, 'Learning to Live: Memory and the Celtic Tiger in novels by Roddy Doyle, Anne Enright and Tana French', *New Hibernian Review* 19.3 (Autumn 2015), 76–92 (p.77).

34. See for example, the hostile response to its Booker prize success in 2007 in the *New Statesman* where an editorial dismissed the novel as 'pornographic' suggesting 'in the end there is only so much to be learned about fumbling, priapic landlords and the stale smell of liquor. For a book that leads with the heart or the brain, rather than the penis. Try one of the others on the short list instead', Editorial, *New Statesman* 37.115 (22 October 2007), p.7.

35. Harte, p.188. Dell'Amico, Downum, Meaney, and Harte all point towards the disconnection between the particularised and sustained narrative of suffering of Veronica and her family and the implied wider social context. Downum attempts to overcome the relentless focus on the individual that is typical of trauma narratives citing Jan Assman's claim 'the remembering self is the locus in which society is inscribed' to suggest Veronica's experience is indexical and representative. See Downum, p.77, n.6.

36. St Ita is known as the foster mother of the Saints of Ireland; she founded a school for boys and one of her pupils was St Brendan. As always, with Enright, the layers of myth, history, and social specificity are both dense and politically pointed.

37. For Enright's insistence on how the moral, linguistic, and political lacunae of *The Gathering* persist, see her recent essay, 'Antigone in Galway', *London Review of Books* 37.24 (17 December 2015), 11–14, for a powerful exploration of our continued inability to account fairly for both the living and the dead.

38. My thanks to my colleague Prof. Anne Fogarty for this insight.

39. John Teel, 'Blurring the Genre Borderlines: Tana French's Haunted Detectives', *Clues: A Journal of Detection* 32.1 (Spring 2014), 13–21 (p.21).

40. It is important to register that this restrictive coded culture affects all. Men and women are equally victim to gender-based violence in French's work: women kill men and children; men kill women and young girls.

41. Winter, p.4.

42. The phrase is Stephen Pinker's. See Steven Pinker, Interview, 'The Seed Salon: Stephen Pinker and Rebecca Goldsmith,' *Seed* 10 (2004), 44–49 (p.48).

43. John Frow, *Genre* (London: Routledge, 2003), p.104.

44. Jacques Derrida and Avital Ronell, 'The Law of Genre', *Critical Inquiry* 7.1 (1980), 55–81 (p.56).

45. Edna Longley, 'Commemoration, Elegy, Forgetting', *History and Memory in Modern Ireland*, ed. by Ian McBride (Cambridge: Cambridge University Press, 2001), 223–53 (p.253).

46. Anne Enright, *The Forgotten Waltz* (London: Jonathan Cape, 2011); Tana French, *The Trespasser* (Dublin: Hachette, 2016).

47. Marianne Hirsch, 'Mobile Memories', public lecture, Central European University, Budapest, 30 September 2014.

Convened by Charlotte McIvor and Emilie Pine
Participants: Stef Craps, Ghent University;
Astrid Erll, Goethe-University Frankfurt am Main;
Paula McFetridge, Kabosh Productions;
Ann Rigney, Utrecht University;
Dominic Thorpe, artist

Roundtable: Moving Memory

This roundtable brings together a group of academics and artists working throughout Europe to discuss the question of memory in theoretical and artistic contexts at a historical moment highly preoccupied with acts of commemoration and moving memory.

As the convenors of this roundtable, we are working and writing within an Irish context. Hence, we ourselves are in the middle of the Irish State's 'Decade of Centenaries', which marks events from 1912–1922 and the founding of the Irish Free State. At the time of coordinating this roundtable, we have been engaged in the yearlong celebration of the Easter Rising centenary in particular, celebrations that have raised anew debates about scales of commemorative practice in relationship to the representation of militarisation as a primary commemorative mode at state level and the need to animate and centralise marginalised voices, particularly those of women and children. The artists participating in this roundtable from both the Republic and Northern Ireland have engaged centrally with questions of national narratives, minority histories, and scales of remembrance as communal (or performative) acts; the academic participants are, likewise, informed by their work in diverse areas of memory studies, and particularly by their membership of the COST Action Network *In Search of Transcultural Memory in Europe* (2012–16).

What does memory mean to you as a theoretical, artistic or philosophical concept in relationship to its experience (by self or community) and its use value within culture?

Irish University Review 47.1 (2017): 165–196
DOI: 10.3366/iur.2017.0263
© Edinburgh University Press
www.euppublishing.com/iur

Paula McFetridge: Memory is a sensory recollection of a moment, event, feeling – it can remind you of a physical or emotional sensation. It is completely personal and as unique as DNA – each of us can share an experience but recall it with a range of subjective framing devices. It can recall a split second of time or a longer, less detailed period of engagement. Memory alters over time – it can both gain and lose clarity.

Even though memory is personal that does not necessarily mean you own it. There can be a 'real', fully formed memory of something that lives with and in you but do you have the right to share it? Is there a central protagonist that has increased hierarchy regarding ownership and, ultimately, say over what and when, and if ever, it is recalled? Is it even an accurate memory? Are the others who participated in the original ready for it to be shared – how will they feel about your version of events, who manages the fall-out?

As memory is not absolute, it is constantly reassessed and distilled. Therefore it is ideal territory for artistic intervention – through offering alternatives the artist can encourage the viewer to question and reimagine. Art blossoms in doubt. The artist can lead to a new memory being formed and/or stabilise the pre-existing and/or encourage others to add to the memory. Then when the memory is recalled again it is from a different context and with different detail: it's fluid.

Dominic Thorpe: The relationship between memory and art feels fundamental and vast. I find creativity and memory are intrinsically linked and dependent on each other. My memory and creativity feed and respond to each other and can seem to move in tandem while working through artistic process, formulating and interpreting ideas, perhaps similar in some ways to how parts of the body move simultaneously in achieving a particular gesture. While important discourses and practices related to values around collecting and archiving artworks are prominent within the visual arts I find myself often thinking about the importance of artwork residing in each individual's own personal memory. In many ways I can't think of a more potent place.

I find experiences of memory, like the experiencing of artworks as an audience member, rely strongly on creativity and invention. For example I often recall aspects of a performance artwork I have seen, but in a jumbled sequence or format. I can vividly remember certain elements while not recalling others. Sometimes I have images and actions in my mind which feel like memories of a performance I experienced but which didn't actually happen during that particular performance. At times I find I have constructed what seem like solid memories of performances I didn't experience first hand but may have heard about or seen images of. What gets remembered seems most often to connect closely with the personal. While this raises questions about the reliability of memory from an historical accuracy perspective, as an arts practitioner it is a useful opening up of uncertainty, perhaps indicating that both personal memory and engagement with art can be relied upon to never fully remove individual identity.

Ann Rigney: Memory is for me a theoretical concept that helps me as an academic in describing how information is preserved and transformed across time by individuals and by societies. This makes for a potentially very broad field. In practice people approach 'memory studies' from different perspectives and disciplines. Where psychologists study the mental capacity of recall and how this plays out over a person's lifetime, my concern as a literary scholar and cultural historian is with 'cultural memory,' meaning the memory that is carried through media rather than brains, and that involves the transfer of stories across individuals, groups, and generations. How are shared narratives culturally produced and what is their impact on social relations? Scholars working in the social sciences tend to work instead with the term 'collective' memory', which harks back to Halbwachs' pioneering work in the 1920s and emphasizes the social rather than cultural constituents of the sharing of memory.[1] But it's not a matter of either-or. In my view, 'individual,' 'cultural', and 'collective' memory should be seen as complementary rather than as competing terms; they are all useful in asking particular questions under the umbrella term of 'memory studies.'

Astrid Erll: As an academic field, memory studies bases its critical function on an analytical approach to memory. In fact, much of the fundamental research that emerged since the 1980s (e.g. the contributions by Jan and Aleida Assmann in cultural studies, Elizabeth Loftus in psychology, Jeffrey Olick in sociology)[2] was deeply critical of 'memory' and has systematically shown that memories, individual and collective, are volatile constructs. Using detailed case studies, research on collective memory has uncovered how memory is put to political uses, and how memory culture creates foundational stories that make a group's discourse about norms, values and identity plausible. In more recent work, scholars such as Michael Rothberg or Dirk Moses have been investigating how modern societies might conceive of memory in a different, more productive way, for example, how political discourse could break out of the vicious circle of schematized thinking about the 'Other', or how coercive links between identity and memory could be relaxed, dynamised, and pluralised.[3] For today's globalizing world I would envision a memory practice characterized by self-awareness and the will to transcend boundaries (of nationality, ethnicity, class, religion, language etc.), that is, a *reflexive transcultural memory*. Memory studies can contribute to this goal, by studying not only what there *is*, but also by imagining what *could be*: the potentialities of cultural memory.

Ann Rigney: One of the biggest challenges facing cultural memory studies is the fact that the term 'memory' is both a scholarly concept that does analytical work, and an 'everyday' concept that is invoked by actors in the field. In that regard, it is interesting to note the use of 'memory' *tout court* in public debates. 'Memory' is often invoked in an essentialist way to indicate a type of embodied truth that is supposed to be unmediated and 'authentic' as opposed to the 'false' and 'hegemonic' truths that are characteristic of history (Ricoeur has described this dialectic between history and memory very well).[4] The idea that memory is a hotline to lived experience has been used as the basis for claims to recognition on the part of minority groups who have been left out of hegemonic views of history. It has also been appropriated by state institutions eager to mark their affinity with populist sentiment. To be sure, this idea of memory as more authentic than history resonates within cultural memory studies. It too emerged in opposition to the discipline of history and the dominant narratives about the past that the discipline of history was believed to sustain. It involved, and still involves, an intellectual and ethical commitment to understanding narratives produced across a range of communicative and commemorative practices, not just historiography, and linked to this, a commitment to exploring non-hegemonic narratives that had been marginalised in public debates. By now, however, it is time to take a step backwards and build a *critical* memory studies in which we consider more clearly the costs involved in popular evocations of memory as a locus of unquestioned authenticity as well as the cost in the very commitment to a memory conceived in terms of victimhood. Cultural memory studies should remain committed to understanding the power politics at play in the production of collective narratives; but in order to do so we need to develop a *critical* memory studies that is also willing to reflect on its own blind spots and its complicity in sustaining a public discourse about memory and identity that may ultimately be constraining rather than liberating.

Astrid Erll: Yes, it is time to think about how academics could bring their analytical and critical thinking into a dialogue with the broader public. My first impulse as a university teacher is to *teach* about memory. I do think that insight into the processes of cultural remembering and forgetting enables students to see through and critically assess most currently pressing world affairs, from Brexit to ISIS, from Donald Trump to the 'refugee crisis', as well as our inability to halt climate change. Memory studies concepts (such as 'postimperial nostalgia', the 'invention of religious traditions', 'social forgetting' and 'cultural remembering' as well as questions of 'framing' and 'the economy of attention') can help us unlock some of the complexities of these present challenges. At my home university in Frankfurt, we have implemented memory studies modules into two Masters programmes, and my feeling is that students do value this perspective – even if they may have started, say, their Masters in English Literature not expecting this to be a component of their studies. However, the 'home match' of teaching memory studies at their university should not be the only agenda item for memory scholars. They should also seek a sustained dialogue with curators in historical museums, producers of television documentaries, politicians, memory activists, and artists. An important node in this process is postgraduate education. I would like to see more practice-led doctoral research, i.e. dissertations that closely engage with and (self-)critically analyse different kinds of memory practice. This would not only foster a new generation of memory scholars, who can negotiate academic and corporate, political or popular spheres with relative ease, but also (for those who decide against a career in the academic system) be a way of training young actors in memory culture who bring a firm grounding in the theories and methodologies of memory studies to their respective fields.

In the second decade of the twenty-first century, we are in the middle of what feels like endless commemorations, both in terms of centenaries or the recent quartercentary of Shakespeare's birthday. Some commentators have referred to 'commemoration fatigue' emerging from this. Do you agree? When, if ever, does engaging in acts of memory become counter-productive?

Ann Rigney: Commemorations linked to centenaries and anniversaries are fascinating in that they introduce an artificial, calendar-time periodicity into collective memory. Where individual memory is thought of as following biological time, public commemorations follow ten-year and hundred-year cycles that are entirely predictable and absolutely arbitrary. Their popularity since the early nineteenth century,[5] serves as a reminder of the fact that modern collective memory is 'synthetic' in the sense of non-natural: not just because it is shaped through media of all sorts but because it follows a calendar-dictated rhythm that generates intense moments of synchronised remembering against a background of everyday forgetting (anniversaries represent on the temporal axis the equivalent of Pierre Nora's 'sites of memory' on the spatial one). By and large history is *un*predictable (who could have predicted five years ago the current influx of refugees to Europe? Or the Bastille Day terrorist attack in Nice?). But centenaries are 'historic' in the sense of being momentous events that can be planned years in advance. In that regard, they have the distinct characteristic of having already happened before their time has come, so often have they been pre-mediated in all the discussions about what should be done and by whom. By the time a centenary comes around and heads of state have visited memorials and cut ribbons, it may seem like a 'historic' non-event. In the second decade of the twenty-first century, centennial commemorations have indeed become ubiquitous, and it is easy to become cynical and dismiss them as occasions for rehearsing pieties, political grandstanding, feeding euro-hungry museums, and, last but not least, providing employment for academics and a market for academic books.

Paula McFetridge: We cannot under-estimate the role of the commissioner; they control what is commemorated and what might be possible to commemorate – this may explain why the Northern Irish narrative was absent in any truly engaged manner within the 1916 programme in the Republic of Ireland. The fear of the fall-out over-rode recognising the need for the interrogation.

Within a period of heightened commemoration increased resources allow for new possibilities and support an environment where new narratives come to the fore. Within 2016 Kabosh worked with Diversity Challenges to stage a new play by Laurence McKeown entitled *Green & Blue*.[6] Based on stories gathered from serving Royal Ulster Constabulary and An Garda Síochána officers patrolling the border area during the height of the conflict, this exploration of the person behind the uniform gave voice to a silent community. These cross-border voices have not been heard before now. Undoubtedly the societal drive to explore the past laid the foundation for this unique project. A collective climate of questioning and finding a voice encourages the unearthing of others.

Ann Rigney: While their importance needs to be relativised, as I just suggested, commemorations do have a role to play in the slow transformation of dominant narratives – in two ways. Firstly, in being high profile, official ceremonies lift what people know or half-know as individuals into *common* knowledge. A centenary can thus seal and make visible to all a revised narrative whose public recognition may have begun decades earlier in the arts and civil society. If in some contexts it is merely a way of reinforcing dominant narratives, in others it helps crystallize long-term trends into a public, attention-grabbing performance. Like a wedding, a centenary makes it official. It was interesting in this regard to note that the ongoing commemoration of World War One involved not only definitive recognition of Irish participation in the conflict, but also of the other four million colonial troops who served in the European theatres of war. That recognition is still piecemeal, but it nevertheless marks what Yaël Zerubavel calls a 'turning point' in the evolution of the transnational commemorative narrative.[7] The arts played a key role in bringing those colonial voices into circulation, while the centenary's role is one of consolidation; but it is crucial nevertheless. However, and this is my second point, unofficial commemorations may also be linked to contestation. The periodicity of ten years, twenty-five years and the centenary *provides an occasion* for public demonstrations of adherence to a counter-memory and for recalling unfinished business. Thus anniversaries have seen regular commemorations of the 1989 Tiananmen Square massacre that are at the same time calls for more democracy in China. In short: commemorations may be much more than empty gestures and shouldn't be dismissed too easily. Crucially, however, their mobilizing power remains dependent on their relative infrequency; too much and too often indeed generates commemoration fatigue. Structural changes in collective memory cannot happen every day, meaning that the adage that one should choose one's battles applies also in the case of public acts of commemoration.

Paula McFetridge: We need to remember also that people have the right to forget. If we decide to commemorate, then what are we saying about the past within the current context to help us better deal with the future? I always ask myself three questions when deciding what to comment on as an artist:

1. Is it the right time to tell the story?
2. Am I the right person to tell it?
3. Who is it for?

This then determines the form of the event. I do believe commemorations are valuable as both artists and citizens as it can focus the mind, encourage us not to be passive but rather formulate opinions. Even if that means we choose to actively disengage.

It becomes counter-productive if the commemoration says nothing new and doesn't put the past into a new framework, doesn't assist us in looking at the past through a new lens so when the next commemoration comes around that we can distil the past yet further. It is also key that we are acutely aware of when is the right time to commemorate – we have a responsibility when examining memory and asking questions to take care of the human spirit.

I have commemoration fatigue when we say nothing but rather simply state. It is imperative artists are employed to respond to the past and ask difficult questions that the media and politicians can't and/or won't.

Dominic Thorpe: Making artwork at any time which feels personal, honest, rigorous in its questioning and relevant in the here and now can be challenging. During large scale commemorations in particular, artworks can become stuck or swallowed up by the weight of dominant narratives, rendering them somewhat ineffective and even counterproductive in asking new and relevant questions. However, in a demonstration of the strength of the arts in Ireland today there have been many examples of powerful and effective work across all art forms throughout the 2016 commemoration period. Among the best examples I feel are works uncovering previously buried stories, such as those giving recognition to the pivotal role, lives and position of many women at the time of the 1916 rising. I find the most interesting works raise issues still relevant today, often illuminating and unraveling complexities between that which is put aside due to a sense of necessity and that which is grounded in denial.

A factor impacting significantly on engagement with memory during 2016 has been Ireland's ongoing and painful experiences of straining to acknowledge, come to terms with, and respond to, the scale of institutional abuses in Ireland's past.[8] The tsunami of revelations in recent times of systematic perpetration, denial and cover up of abuses, at every level in Irish society, of huge numbers of children and adults in the care of the state over decades has forced us to become more mature and re-evaluate memory from an ethical perspective.

It is important to note national commemorations are not the only valid or relevant context for artworks dealing with memory. Artists are continually excavating the past, marking particular events, moments and people they think important for varied reasons, not only at times of heightened commemoration. Often this can be deemed unwelcome activity. Sometimes the most relevant moment and context to make such work is when it is unwelcome.

Certain modes through which we engage with memory can be counterproductive. For example, when artistic processes of recalling and commemorating serve only to reinforce our capacity for forgetting in ways that are destructive. Focus can become stuck on learned rigid historical images, thus proposing nothing new and preventing broad analysis of the past and the present. Just as remembering is continually acted out in personal and collective consciousness, forgetting is also acted out, behaved and performed. Certain kinds of commemorative processes, rather than opening up histories, risk solidifying a cultural persistence of failing to acknowledge the reality that history is ever shifting and always viewed from the present. Re-performances and re-enactments failing to adequately acknowledge their position in the present may not engage meaningfully with either the present or the past. Instead, possibly only providing repetitive narrow images of memory without questioning how they are arrived at and certified.

For some artists remaining unstuck from the weight of particular moments in time may involve working through methodologies which hold artworks in the present moment, pre-emptively trying to disrupt overly simplified learned and rehearsed narratives which might be imposed on work and drag it backwards. Engaging with memory at times of commemoration is at its most relevant when connections between how we remember the past and how we feel and behave in the present are openly explored. Questions of memory and history, vital in the here and now, need also to be forward looking.

What are the historic and current challenges for work on memory in academic contexts?

Stef Craps: A major challenge, I would say, is interdisciplinarity: how to arrive at an integrative understanding of memory drawing on various disciplines and areas of expertise? As Astrid Erll points out, over the last three decades, memory has emerged as 'a genuinely transdisciplinary phenomenon whose functioning cannot really be understood through examination from one single perspective'.[9] Memory studies is an area of inquiry that spans the humanities, social sciences, and natural sciences, involving such diverse disciplines as history, sociology, psychology, philosophy, literary studies, media studies, the arts, anthropology, architecture, museology, and neuroscience. Seeing signs of growing convergence, Astrid observes that 'the disciplines of memory studies are steadily moving towards one another, and scholars are increasingly interested in the possibilities offered by interdisciplinary exchange'.[10]

However, some critics remain sceptical of the variegated nature of the field. According to Jeffrey Olick, for example, the 'interdisciplinary integration of memory studies'[11] envisaged by Astrid largely remains at the level of aspiration rather than reality:

> interdisciplinarity is a concept that has never really fulfilled its promise, even in this most 'trans-disciplinary' field. We all write a lot about how we need to take the work of other disciplines seriously, but rarely does this go beyond reading and citation.... Actual cross-disciplinary research, however, has been much rarer than affirmations about its necessity and desirability.... We need to think more about genuine interdisciplinary cooperation, cooperation that is beyond the level of mutual referencing.[12]

A similar concern is expressed by Adam Brown and his colleagues, who question whether scholarly meetings promising interdisciplinary approaches to memory and other such attempts at collaboration across disciplinary lines do not 'more often result in multidisciplinarity, rather than interdisciplinarity, in which scholars are exposed to other disciplines' perspectives, but little is transferred from one academic discipline to the next'.[13] These points are well taken: it seems to me that redeeming the unfulfilled promise of genuine interdisciplinarity in memory research is a challenge that the field does indeed need to address, though this is easier said than done, of course.

Ann Rigney: Going by the number of publications, the frequency of conferences and the burgeoning number of handbooks and readers, the field of memory studies is booming. This has lead to a certain degree of interdisciplinarity with scholars working in different traditions converging on common concepts and theoretical models in order to capture an object of study that cuts across and transcends traditional disciplines. The operative phrase here is 'a certain degree'. Although the journal *Memory Studies* has been very successful in providing a common forum for the different disciplines involved in the field, it is too soon to speak of an integrated interdiscipline of 'memory studies' that would combine the individual, the social, and the cultural dimensions of memory-making into a single field of study. There is certainly a degree of convergence among humanities scholars working on cultural memory and its mediations, on the one hand, and social scientists working on collective memory and its politics, on the other. But taking interdisciplinarity to the next step remains a real challenge. It's a bit like world peace: everyone is for it, but no-one quite knows how to achieve it. The problem is not so much in defining a common point of concern but in finding ways of creating a dialogue that transcends methodological differences and that really seeks to integrate the actor-based perspective of the social sciences with the culture-based perspective of those working in cultural studies. Right now it's more a question of parallel lines that don't often meet. In the future, memory studies might in fact benefit from a narrowing rather than a broadening of the field.

So rather than expand in ever new directions, I would argue for concentrating on developing fruitful forms of collaboration with key partners operating in a more restricted subsection of the potentially bigger field of memory studies. A lot could be gained by bringing together researchers in cultural memory studies, critical heritage studies, the social sciences, and transitional justice around particular issues. Rather than pursue a rather vaguely defined Holy Grail of interdisciplinarity, the idea would be to develop a form of slow scholarship that works on combining forms of knowledge and not just on the pursuit of hot topics. If further extended to collaboration with curators and educationalists, this would also provide a more robust basis upon which to respond to the increasing demands from governmental authorities that academic research be societally relevant, not just in theory but also in practice.

Astrid Erll: There is large and still-untapped potential in 'wide interdisciplinarity'. To give just one example: the neurosciences have greatly refined their insights into the workings of the brain over the past fifteen years. It is now time for a sustained dialogue between the natural sciences and the humanities/social sciences on their respective approaches to memory. Interesting attempts at such a conversation have already been made, for example by Hans J. Markowitsch, Harald Welzer, Suzanne Nalbantian or Thomas J. Anastasio.[14] This may be 'risky' research, but if we seriously understand 'memory' as a 'bio-psycho-socio-cultural' phenomenon, then memory studies by definition *is* a widely interdisciplinary field, and widely transdisciplinary scholarship must constitute its foundational research.

An additional challenge is the further development of memory studies' *international* orientation. Much has been achieved in the past decade. The field of memory studies has progressed from an agglomerate of isolated, nation-specific discourses to a platform of international dialogue and (increasingly) transnational research practice. Admittedly, much of this exchange takes place on English-speaking platforms. Memory studies travels in English translation. It therefore remains important to acknowledge the linguistic variety of speaking and researching about memory. An important task for scholars who want to shape the field of memory studies is to curate translations. There is also the 'uneven geography' of our memory mappings. Only if we keep our eyes and ears open to memory dynamics in seemingly 'remote' places can we really asses and if necessary 'provincialize' our general assumptions about memory.

What are the challenges for memory work in artistic practice?

Paula McFetridge: A challenge that inspires me when looking at commemoration as an artist is the imagining and animation of the moment before an historic turning point: what leads to the outbreak of war or what leads an individual to suggest a ceasefire or what happens in the second before a leader makes a seminal decision? Also, how to give voice to the silent or lesser characters within social events – giving voice to them provides a different lens by which we view the past. Through finding something new to say the past is made relevant to a new audience. In addition, we need to never lose sight of whose commemoration it is – this determines focus, format and ultimately content. Witnessing voices encourages individuals to begin their sharing process. Also, audiences may not be ready to engage with all elements of the narrative in this moment, the artist is responsible for assessing what material it is the best time to animate so it is 'heard' by audiences.

The historic and current challenge continues to be the lack of true artist recruitment and investment when considering commemoration. By this I mean allowing for artistic risk, investment long-term, allowing for provocative commentary and celebrating these artistic interventions as part of central programming. This is only possible by engaging with artists in the early stages of commemoration programme development.

Dominic Thorpe: Regarding art practice and memory, questions of ethics continually raise significant challenges and position the arts at difficult junctions. For example on one hand it is important to question the value of recalling and recounting traumatic experience, not least because deciding to leave certain events and experiences in the past, in so far as may be possible, can be important and necessary for many people. One the other hand telling stories that challenge and illuminate social constructs and behaviours is fundamental to art, therefore it feels important to accept and act on art's role in this regard.

Where human rights abuses have occurred there is often the feeling that it is impossible to have a truly neutral position. This, of course, is far more nuanced than simple images or declarations of guilt or innocence, presence or absence, knowledge or ignorance. It has been my experience as an artist and as an audience member that artistic process can be effective and even vital in identifying positions (known or unknown) in relation to the lives of other people. Important questions arrived at include: What is my position in relation to a particular subject/event and through engagement with art can that position be understood more, changed for the better, to positive not negative effect and in solidarity? Choosing to listen or not has consequences as does the decision to act or not. Not engaging difficult subjects related to historical abuses, echoes of which still persist in everyday behaviour and in the ways current social systems continue to operate, can feel like contributing to the continuation of cultures of silence. If this is the case I wonder at what points could we consider current behaviour in the everyday complicit, however indirect, or otherwise in perpetuation of cultures of silence that lead to traumatic experience?

An important question is; how do those of us who do not have direct experiences of trauma engage such subjects? I have never experienced a crystal clear indication as to how a particular subject matter should be approached and explored, and broadly speaking there is never a consensus dictating whether you should or shouldn't engage with a particular area or subject as an artist. For example I have been both questioned and supported when working with the subject matter of historical child abuse, by people who as children were abused.

I have found engagement and interaction with research and researchers looking at the areas of memory studies, human rights and ethics are necessary to create a broader understanding and theoretical underpinning for questions raised through my practice. In this regard it is important to question how diverse areas and processes of research that cross trajectories at a point of memory studies can inform each other in useful ways.

'Ethical memory' has been defined as a 'form of justice that recognises the political nature of remembering and forgetting'. Is the ideal of ethical memory too utopian?

Dominic Thorpe: For me ethical memory is not about achieving a utopian ideal, it is a recognition that human rights abuses have, do and will happen. It is also a recognition that we must work relentlessly to prevent abuses now and into the future. By situating responsibility for action in the present and not only the past ethical memory has a central role in advocating for human rights. Otherwise what is the point?

Stef Craps: What I'm a little concerned about is a tendency to take 'ethical memory' for granted – to assume that remembering is somehow intrinsically beneficial, and, conversely and consequently, that forgetting in inevitably harmful. There is no valid reason to believe that either is the case; it all depends, I think, on the context you're looking at and the use to which remembering or forgetting is put in that context. It's not hard to think of cases where collective memory, rather than serving the cause of justice, led to or enabled further bloodshed. To give but one example, during the Yugoslav wars of the 1990s Serb leaders justified slaughtering Bosniaks and Kosovars by conjuring up collective memories of the 1453 Fall of Constantinople and the 1389 Battle of Kosovo that fomented and reignited ancient hatreds.

And just as remembering is clearly not always good, so forgetting is not always bad. While it tends to get a bad press, a number of memory scholars have recently tried to rehabilitate forgetting or, at least, called for a more nuanced approach to it, one that would acknowledge its ambivalence. I'm primarily thinking of Paul Connerton and Aleida Assmann,[15] both of whom insist on the need to differentiate between different types or forms of forgetting – some destructive, others constructive. There is also a provocative new book by journalist David Rieff declaring that forgetting is a worthy pursuit.[16] Assmann reminds us, for example, that forgetting was necessary to lay the foundations of a new Europe in the wake of the Second World War, citing a remarkable plea for oblivion made by William Churchill in a speech delivered in Zürich in 1946: 'We must all turn our backs upon the horrors of the past. We must look to the future. We cannot afford to drag forward across the years that are to come the hatreds and revenges, which have sprung from the injuries of the past. If Europe is to be saved from infinite misery, and indeed from final doom, there must be an act of faith in the European family and an act of oblivion against all the crimes and follies of the past.' A similar sentiment can be seen to underlie the South African Truth and Reconciliation Commission, which, in a sense, remembered in order to forget, to impose closure on the apartheid past. As its interim report put it, 'We open wounds only in order to cleanse them, to deal with the past effectively and so to close the door on that dark and horrendous past forever.'[17] The goal, ultimately, was to break the past's hold on the present so as to allow Europe and South Africa, respectively, to begin anew, to make a fresh start. In other words, the distinction between remembering and forgetting doesn't map neatly and unproblematically onto that between good and evil. In reality things are a lot messier and less straightforward; you can't make abstraction of the socio-historical context and commend or condemn either one no matter what.

Ann Rigney: As Luisa Passerini argued in an important article that tends to be overlooked in recent discussions of forgetting, the politics of amnesia have long been recognised.[18] The ancient Greeks had a moratorium on remembering divisive events; the English Civil War was followed by an act of oblivion (which Churchill evoked in his Zürich speech); and the Spanish had their own *pacto de olvido* in the post-Franco years. So there is nothing surprising about forgetting having a political dimension. What is perhaps more noteworthy is the more recent belief that memory is necessarily a good thing; that it is indeed our task to 'make the silences of history speak,' to quote the Romantic historian Jules Michelet, and that anything that is not brought into the open is by definition hidden or repressed.[19] However, as Passerini remarks with respect to the Roma reactions to the Nazi genocide, staying silent can in some circumstances also be read as a sign of strength and not of repression. One of the real achievements of memory studies has been in the development of a set of conceptual tools to describe the dynamics of remembering and forgetting in post-conflict situations or in cases of ongoing contestation and structural inequalities. We now know that neither remembrance nor forgetting works like an on-off switch and that both are complex operations involving degrees of visibility in the public sphere. Studying the dynamics of remembering and forgetting as an integral part of memory has generated insight into different modalities of remembrance, including what Graham Dawson has called 'reparative remembrance.'[20] By this is meant acknowledging past injustice in such a way as to change its affect and, with it, its power to feed into renewed conflict. Reparative remembering, as Dawson argues, is the key to creating a balance between memory and forgetting that does justice to the historical injury caused. I like to think that academic memory studies can provide a vocabulary with which to identify and reflect on different modes of remembrance, thus expanding the range of options available to the public at large; much as artists help to provide images and stories to replace ingrained ones. In that sense both academics and artists are implicated in different ways in the production of collective memory. That being said, it would be foolish to think that academics or artists or any other single group has the power to engineer any particular outcome in what is an extremely complex and multi-sited field.

Paula McFetridge: There is a difference between passively forgetting and actively forgetting – laying to rest cannot be equated to forgiving. If we do not find creative ways of facilitating the sharing of personal and collective trauma if individuals so desire then the hatred, bitterness, anger festers and eventually rises to the surface again and the cycle of violence continues. As an artist, I take my responsibility not to retraumatise very seriously: to ensure this I am acutely aware of the importance of timing when commemorating and questioning the past, as well as putting in place mechanisms for supportive post-show interrogation and discussion, as well as providing support material for long-term subject engagement. Inevitably there is an impact on all participants when unveiling a new 'truth'.

When we speak about memory, particularly collective memory, do we end up focusing on trauma too much in terms of what *needs* to be remembered? What is the downside to making acts of memory synonymous with trauma retrieval?

Stef Craps: Michael Lambek and Paul Antze have noted that 'Increasingly, memory worth talking about – worth remembering – is memory of trauma'.[21] Even though much of my own work has dealt with trauma, I'm wary of this tendency to confine our understanding of memory to trauma, as it comes at the expense of happy memories.

Ann Rigney: In his classic 1882 essay on 'What is a Nation' (whose interest was underscored by Benedict Anderson in *Imagined Communities*),[22] Ernest Renan argued that solidarity is usually based on the memory of shared achievements, but that suffering may connect people even more than joy. Renan was of course writing in the fallout of the Franco-Prussian war a decade earlier, and this may have made him particularly sensitive to the significance of defeats and of suffering at a time when triumphalism was the dominant mode in practices of public commemoration. This is no longer the case. Suffering has dominated public memory culture since at least World War One, as Jay Winter has shown, and has certainly been a dominant theme in memory studies as this emerged in the shadow of the Holocaust.[23] By extension, both collective identity and personal identity have become linked to victimhood and to having a grievance. One comes into an identity and into public memory by being recognised as a victim.

Reflecting the discourse of victimhood, but also feeding into it, memory studies has been largely invested in salvaging, highlighting, and analysing different forms of historical injustice. It has developed a vocabulary to talk about trauma, and investigated modes of reparative remembrance that ensure past suffering is not perpetuated for descendants, with the insult of amnesia added to the original injury. This is all very important, and much has been achieved. But there are also serious downsides that are beginning to come to light. Three in particular come to mind, and they underlie my earlier comment about the need for critical self-reflection in memory studies.

Firstly, the overemphasis on victimhood has drawn attention away from perpetrators and forms of implication as bystanders; in this regard, Michael Rothberg's recent work on 'implicated subjects' promises to provide a badly needed vocabulary with which we can begin to investigate transgenerational and transnational 'implicatedness' in injustice and the particular forms of forgetting this has generated.[24]

And secondly, the dominance of the emphasis on victimhood and the traumatic may in the long term deprive victim groups of imagined agency as 'willful subjects' (to use Sara Ahmed's term), with rights in the present.[25] The cost of having minority identities so firmly linked to historical victimhood may be that their grievances are compartmentalised as an issue in memory and not of the present. In an interesting article on Roma identity politics, Slawomir Kapralski shows how Roma activists began to highlight their role as Porajmos victims in order to gain recognition, but at the cost of depriving themselves of their image as independent-minded and sovereign.[26] Similar points have been made in the context of the historical apologies issued to the indigenous peoples of Australia and Canada: saying sorry, while it opened up expectations on the part of the victim group that things would become different, turned out to change nothing in the present and instead merely transformed structural injustice into a regrettable chapter in history.

Dominic Thorpe: I'd like to add here that making acts of memory synonymous with victim/survivor trauma retrieval does not give broad – or any – consideration to the position of perpetrator and our own proximity to that position. I am interested in how we can engage processes of remembering through art, which disable the kinds of static, narrow and overly sentimental images and narratives of trauma and victimhood which may hinder broader questions of perpetration.

Ann Rigney: Even more fundamentally, the dominance of trauma, suffering, and victimhood in memory studies and memorial practices means that there is an enormous investment in the things that go wrong. Andreas Huyssen warned us more than a decade ago that the huge attention being given in society to memory was a symptom of our failure to imagine a future and ourselves as wilful subjects chasing it.[27] One could add to this general remark that the concentration specifically on traumatic memory has certainly not fed into any confidence in the future, however justified it is by the enormity of the suffering in the modern world. By now we have an excellent set of conceptual tools to describe trauma and analyse how its effects are transferred. Three decades of memory studies and a huge expansion of memorial practices in society have left us very poorly equipped, however, to describe the communication of such things as joy, hope, and aspirations for a better world across generations. This is a major blind spot in the discipline of memory studies which, in its very concentration on trauma, may be limiting the horizon of expectations of the public. This realisation underlay my earlier remarks to the effect that memory studies, in its very commitment to attending to the victims of history, may be helping to sustain a public discourse about memory and identity that is constraining rather than liberating.

Stef Craps: I agree that trauma's domination of the field of memory studies risks displacing memories of how people manage to overcome adversity and successfully fight injustice. However, I think it would be wrong to infer from this that an emphasis on trauma cannot but have politically debilitating effects. Memory-as-trauma studies is not destined to serve as the handmaiden of the status quo, as Wendy Brown and Lauren Berlant have suggested,[28] or as a mere academic alibi for the indulgence of voyeuristic inclinations, as Mark Seltzer would have it.[29] I would argue that it can also help identify and understand situations of exploitation and abuse, and act as an incentive for a sustained and systemic critique of societal conditions. In other words, yes, memory scholars would be well advised to broaden their scope beyond the traumatic, but it's not as if focusing on trauma is politically suspect per se.

Ann Rigney: The answer is not to abandon the study of memory altogether but rather to open up new pathways of research that would help us understand better how memory works to create positive forms of attachment and connectedness. This is not a proposal to return to the celebratory mode of monumental history practiced in the nineteenth century; but to take seriously the potential role of positive affects in the transmission of memory. My own current research is addressing this question by investigating how activism is remembered.

Stef Craps: This is important because, as Carrie Hamilton observes, the privileging of trauma leads to 'the marginalization of activist memories'.[30] Trauma displaces positive legacies of past activisms, memories of mass movements for change such as the student protests of 1968 or the revolutions of 1989. The close association of memory with trauma can be seen as symptomatic of a general 'reluctance to consider the very notion of politics or collective political agency in the present'.[31] Hamilton therefore argues for 'caution in the face of the popularity of trauma' and asks that 'trauma not be allowed to displace other theories and models of memory'.[32] Instead of mourning for what is lost, she writes, memory scholars committed to progressive politics would do well to explore the richness of activist memories, which have been relatively ignored.

Paula McFetridge: Often a traumatic memory can also be a memory of survival / over-coming – it may have been traumatic originally but we lived to tell the tale and bear witness to the past. It can then be celebratory, provide hope. Often reliving a past reduces the trauma. With *Belfast by Moonlight* (staged in St George's Church to commemorate the 100th anniversary of the foundation of Belfast) Carlo Gébler gave voice to six women from different periods over the 100-year period.[33] Produced by Kabosh, their spirits return on the night of a full moon to bear witness to each other's private and public histories; each have died in tragic circumstances but it is essentially about survival. It's about living to tell the tale and acting as inspiration for others.

Can you say what 'moving memory' means to your work, or how you would situate your work in the context of 'moving memory'?

Stef Craps: As it happens, I have just edited a new book on this topic with Lucy Bond and Pieter Vermeulen.[34] The point of departure for the collection is our observation that what unites much of the most exciting research going on in the field of memory studies today is a tendency to regard memory not as fixed but as fluid, not as static but as dynamic, not as bound but as unbound. Memory is increasingly being studied as something that does not stay put but circulates, migrates, travels. The book explores what we consider to be the four most important dimensions of the mobility of memory: its transcultural, transgenerational, transmedial, and transdisciplinary drift.

Whereas early work in memory studies focused on the ways in which memories are located in certain sites or objects, and shared within particular communities, constituting or reinforcing group identity, in recent years the transcultural or transnational circulation of memories has moved to the centre of attention, as critics have highlighted the ways that phenomena such as migration and the rise of mass cultural technologies allowing for global dissemination challenge the idea that memories adhere to a static location in place or time.

At the same time, there has been a marked increase of interest in how memory travels between different media, and specifically in the role of evolving digital media in the production, preservation, and transfer of memories. As the Holocaust begins to pass out of living memory, the question of how memories of survivors of historical traumas are transmitted to, and inherited by, members of later generations has become another area of intense inquiry. Furthermore, memory studies appears to be moving towards greater interdisciplinarity, or, at least, enhanced awareness of the necessity or desirability of cross-fertilization between memory research in the humanities, social sciences, and natural sciences.

Rather than treating the four dimensions of memory's 'unboundedness' in isolation, the book brings these different aspects together to allow readers to trace resonances between the diverse dynamics of memory, and to offer them insight into the ways certain forms of mobility inflect others. The volume explores, for instance, how the transgenerational transmission of cultural memories is shaped by different media; how, when memories of violence take the shape not only of punctual traumas but increasingly also of ecological devastation, ecocriticism and ecology emerge as privileged interlocutors in the study of memory across cultural and national contexts; how the tools developed in the field of digital humanities allow new forms of archive to be recognized as media of memory; and how the diasporic spread of communities has affected the travel and translation of transgenerational memories. In so doing, *Memory Unbound* shows how considering different dimensions of mobility across cultures, generations, media, and disciplines is indispensable for the study of the dynamics of memory.

My own work in memory studies, though, has been primarily concerned with transcultural memory. In my monograph *Postcolonial Witnessing: Trauma Out of Bounds*[35] and in various journal articles and book chapters, I examine how, why, and to what effect the memory of the Holocaust is evoked in literary texts that connect the Nazi genocide of the European Jews with other exceptionally destructive, criminal, and catastrophic histories, such as slavery, colonialism, and other genocides. I tend to dwell on the risks involved in remembering across cultural and national boundaries, the reason being that many proponents of what Astrid Erll calls the 'transcultural turn'[36] in memory studies minimize them or ignore them altogether. Much work in transcultural memory studies articulates a very hopeful vision: it is characterized by a strong belief in the emancipatory potential, the cathartic or healing effects of remembering across cultural and national borders. Personally, I think a healthy dose of scepticism is called for. After all, very often Holocaust comparisons, for example, are used in ways that do not lead to greater transcultural understanding and the establishment of a universal human rights culture. I do think the notion that transcultural or transnational remembrance can have beneficial effects—in principle if certainly not always in practice—is worth considering, but not uncritically.

Ann Rigney: 'Moving memory' as such is a not concept that I work with and in a sense I find it tautological. Of course memory moves; it does so by definition. As I've been arguing for quite a long time now, memory is continuously 'on the move' in the fundamental sense that it is dependent on reiteration and recursivity, and on renewed acts of recollection; it is a dynamic and not static phenomenon. I wrote once that memory is like a swimmer: it has to keep moving in order to stay afloat. Without new acts of recall a narrative becomes inert and hence ceases to exist as memory; without contestation too, memory reverts to inert indifference. So at this point in time, it seems to me important, not just to celebrate flows and movements, but to examine in more detail how narratives and models of remembrance travel and when they don't; and to consider the direction in which they travel and the blockages and points of resistance they meet along the way. Too often claims to go beyond methodological nationalism have led to a celebration of a seemingly borderless or 'unbounded' world. We need to work with a more complicated topography in order to understand better the asymmetries in the 'free movement' of practices and narratives. Anna Tsing has aptly referred to the 'frictions' that characterise our world where information flows unevenly – not just because not everyone has access to first world media, but also because local communities continue to creatively resist such hegemony.[37] Differences and dissensus are as vital to the future of memory, conceived in dynamic terms, as is agreement.

In an attempt to capture some of this complexity, I recently edited a collection of essays with Chiara De Cesari called *Transnational Memory: Circulation, Articulation, Scales*.[38] The section on circulation deals with the flow of narratives and models across national and cultural borders. With the idea of 'articulation,' however, we wanted to emphasize the continuing importance of borders: the points of articulation, of connection, where differences meet, hybridize, or refuse to engage; or where there are points of resistance to hegemonic practices being imposed from outside. Finally, with the idea of 'scales', we underline the importance of multiscalar analysis in memory studies. Moving beyond methodological nationalism is not just a matter of jumping to the larger scale of the macro-regional, the global or the planetary, but involves rethinking the traditional hierarchy of scales that privileges the big over the small, the global over the local and the intimate, and examines the interrelations between these. Multiscalar analysis allows among other things for a rethinking of the role of the arts as carriers of memory that circulate across the world (arguably more freely than disciplined forms of knowledge) and yet at the point of arrival affect people in the intimate realm of pleasure and emotions. In this way, as I have argued with relation to Europe, the arts may become a conduit for creating new imagined communities that operate over large distances while mobilising individual subjects. We need more multiscalar analysis to come up with models of community, memory, and identity that are better fitted to the lived realities of today's entangled world.

Astrid Erll: The term 'moving memories' is an operative metaphor. First, as Stef and Ann have explained, it can describe 'memory unbound' or 'memory on the move', or what I call 'travelling memory'.[39] Second, it hints at the affective and emotional side of memory. It asks about how representations of 'our' past and that of 'other people' affect us, thus referring to memory that is capable of moving audiences. Both aspects of the metaphor are connected. Moving memories make memories move. Affect and emotions carry images and narratives about the past from person to person and across different kinds of socio-cultural boundaries. As much as I like this fertile metaphor, I would not overemphasize the role of emotions to the exclusion of other dynamics of travelling memory. Images and narratives about the past can also move because of sheer curiosity, economic interests, or military-strategic reasons. The concept of 'moving memory' (in its double sense) is not a key to all doors of the memory process, but is clearly a product of our field's current emphasis on ethics, empathy, and solidarity in memory culture.

Paula McFettridge: Memory is fluid and changes continually, it is context specific: informed by location, distance from the original event, distance from the central protagonist, what sparks the remembering, who is with you when you remember. Theatre and performance work seems to me to be particularly suitable for discussions of moving memory, given the emotional provocation possible in an artistic commemoration through its 'live-ness'. Also the calibre of engagement and animation of informed discussion varies performance-location to performance-location, audience to audience, and this flexibility means the memories within theatre (both onstage and in the audience) are constantly 'moving'. Kabosh's *Those you Pass on the Street* has been performed to over forty-eight different communities in three years locally, nationally and internationally; the performances range from single-identity closed performances to cross-community performances hosted by local organisations to presentations in theatres.[40] Each performance is followed by a facilitated discussion where issues about dealing with the past can be aired. There are individuals who have experienced the play in recent months who were not ready to engage with the play when it premiered in 2014; they are now ready to participate in conflict resolution narratives as their distance from the conflict has increased and their personal contexts have shifted in the past three years. Consequently their memory of conflict has shifted sufficiently for them to begin to have conversations about painful memories.

Dominic Thorpe: Moving memory brings to mind a feeling that memory may evolve or be placed, but never truly settles. Moving memory for me relates to a need for constantly probing and renewing our living connections. Deep down we forget nothing. Every sense, movement, gesture, sound, touch, vision, smell, feeling and thought. This well of experiences is the raw material of art. Artworks are not simply consumed by us as audiences. They don't just confirm what we think we know or only give us information about what we are not yet aware of. The most effective artworks help us find and address what we do know but have not yet admitted to ourselves, what we have buried, what we have failed to acknowledge openly or what we have trouble articulating. They align with and trigger our memories and imaginations, helping us find and negotiate new questions and positions which are not oversimplified or polarised, but are complex and potentially very difficult.

For me, experiencing particularly affecting or moving artworks can result in the internalising of other people's stories on such a deep level, lasting connections are created with my own life experiences. In this way artworks can put us in the picture even as audience. They can illuminate our close proximity to each other and position us in relation to our society and our histories in ways that can be deeply personal, undeniable and potentially transformative in a manner that everyday life can very often resist.

Feminist and queer theory, as well as critical race studies, postcolonial studies and subfields including subaltern studies, have focused centrally on the relationship between memory and privilege, arguing that minoritarian subjects are regularly violently denied the right to individual and collective memory, and therefore have to form counter-memories, counter-archives and counter modes of expression through the creation of subcultures. Do you think that the insights of these fields and their recuperation/retrieval of

minority memories have made any impact on mainstream or hegemonic discourses of memory?

Stef Craps: It has taken quite a while for memory studies to wake up to the postcolonial critique and to start addressing issues of colonialism and its legacies. As Michael Rothberg has pointed out, the founding texts of the field, by eminent scholars such as Maurice Halbwachs, Pierre Nora, and Jan and Aleida Assmann, exhibit certain limitations restricting the ability or inclination of early memory studies to engage with colonial or postcolonial realities.[41] For example, Halbwachs's organicism, his tendency to conceive of the various groups in which collective memory is located as homogeneous and closed entities, makes his work less obviously useful for understanding processes of colonization, globalization, and migration, which by their very nature dislocate such communities. Nora's influential *Lieux de mémoire* project, for its part, is marked by colonial amnesia: it minimizes France's imperial history to the point of making it a *non-lieu de mémoire*. And the Assmanns' seminal work on cultural memory has tended to stress the role of institutionalized canons in the formation and transmission of collective memories at the expense of alternative archives and non-canonical memory traditions. Early work in memory studies was thus shaped by an imperial mindset, which, I'm afraid, still persists today, though there is at least a growing awareness of this as a problem.

I myself have spent a good deal of my career so far critiquing the Eurocentric tendencies of the related field of trauma studies, which is something of a subfield of memory studies, even if it has a rather different history. Here too, though, experiences of non-Western or minority groups have tended to be marginalized or ignored, despite the omnipresence of violence and suffering in the world. As is apparent from the work of Cathy Caruth, Shoshana Felman and Dori Laub, Geoffrey Hartman, and Dominick LaCapra, trauma studies as a field of cultural scholarship developed out of an engagement with Holocaust testimony, literature, and history. Moreover, a flurry of trauma-theoretical publications also followed in the wake of the terrorist attacks of 9/11. If trauma studies is to stay relevant in the globalized world of the twenty-first century, though, it will have to go beyond its focus on key Western trauma sites and wean itself off its dependence on supposedly universal models of trauma and recovery that are rooted in the history of Western modernity. It seems to me that this process is well underway now: pluralization and diversification are among the most pronounced trends in recent trauma scholarship, though much work remains to be done.

Ann Rigney: As Stef's work testifies, more needs to be done, particularly in expanding knowledge of traditions of commemoration in non-Western settings. Moreover, as I indicated earlier, there is a certain tension between the notion of minoritarian memories and subjects, and the idea of social justice in the present. It would help if we could develop stronger models to conceptualise the dynamics of contestation so that 'minority' becomes not just a byword for 'ghetto' but a fundamental challenge to dominant narratives about both the past and the present. Again, dissensus and agonism rather than recognition should be key words.

Astrid Erll: The challenge for minoritarian memories in Europe today lies in the dynamics of recognition and participation. It is important that minority groups not only articulate their past experience, but that they also actively take their stories into the heart of society and its memory cultures. Put simply and using the metaphor of a museum: minoritarian memories should not remain in the special exhibition (as a showcase on difference), but become an integral part of the permanent exhibition (where difference is seen as a *constitutive* part of society). At the moment, European memory cultures seem particularly prone to the problem of providing apparent recognition without granting real participation. For Nancy Fraser, 'the notion of *parity of participation*' constitutes the 'normative core' of the discussion about recognition and redistribution.[42] If all members of society are meant to participate 'on par with others in social life',[43] then memories must not only be shared, but be *shared on par*.

In the midst of an ongoing European and global migration crisis, what is the relationship between migration and memory, both in this political moment, and in the circumstances leading up to it?

Ann Rigney: Unfortunately, memory has been a cornerstone in the building of fortress Europe. It has been linked to migration in the form of a defensive bulwark: Europe has its own national and regional traditions; you don't share in those traditions, so keep out. A more constructive and humane approach is ethically demanded. There is an urgent need both to lay down an archive of migrant experiences for future remembrance as an integral part of European life and to scour the annals of European history for cases that resonate multidirectionally with present-day dilemmas: the turning away of ships carrying Jewish refugees from various ports across Europe for example. Indeed, if Europeans care as much about Holocaust remembrance as its official status within the European Union would suggest, then isn't this our chance to 'make good' on the past by not repeating the same mistakes? Here again, we see the importance of refusing to 'pastify' memory. Let us consider memory instead as unfinished business from the past and the present as an opportunity to act differently.

Paula McFetridge: This is why arts activists aim to challenge the keeper of the memory (the source material) as well as impacting on those who were never a part of it. The artist frames the narrative to maximise engagement with today's new audiences. The objective is to offset collective amnesia about the past. In 2009 Kabosh premiered a play in the Belfast Jewish synagogue. Entitled *This is what we Sang*, and written by Gavin Kostick, the play was inspired by an oral archive conducted by Jo Egan over a 12-month period.[44] This involved interviewing forty-five members of the aging Jewish community – some still residing in Belfast and some who had left since the start of the conflict in 1969. The interviews were transcribed and returned to the participants so the voice of this diminishing community is now archived. Through staging the play Kabosh ensured audiences looked at both the Belfast Blitz and the conflict through a different lens, as well as encouraging audiences to consider the contribution made by the Jewish community to the evolution of Belfast. Through engaging with the story of a sizable migrant story we hoped attitudes to current migrants would be reassessed. In addition the Belfast Jewish community were empowered by other communities bearing witness to their narratives.

Stef Craps: I've been struck by the coincidence of the migration crisis with the centenary of the First World War and by the abundance of historical echoes, as well as by what I can only describe as our collective inability to hear them. Piet Chielens, the director of the In Flanders Fields museum in Ieper, has expressed his consternation over the fact that while commemorating a traumatic war that took place here in Flanders one hundred years ago, we are humiliating refugees fleeing war in the present.[45] In particular, he was shocked by statements made by leading politicians from his home province of West Flanders, which saw some of the worst fighting of the war, who are on record saying things like, 'Don't give food to refugees,' or, 'We should stop them from setting up camp here at all costs.' They speak lofty words about peace and honouring the victims at a ceremony to commemorate the First World War one day, only to fulminate against the victims of war and persecution who are knocking on our door the next.

Similarly, the *New York Times* published an article in the summer of 2015 about how Europeans, despite facing one of the continent's worst humanitarian crises since the Second World War, seem blind to images that recall that blackest time in their history.[46] These images – of migrants locked into trains, police putting numbers on people's arms, babies handed over barbed wire, soldiers herding crowds of bedraggled men, women, and children – evoke memories of the Holocaust, yet Europeans by and large seem oblivious to these historical parallels. Remarkably, the countries that are most resistant to immigration and diversity, such as Hungary, Poland, Slovakia, and the Czech Republic, are among those that suffered the most during the Second World War and produced the most refugees in its aftermath. As a Human Rights Watch official quoted in the article puts it, 'It is hard to understand how people lose their sense of history so quickly. We all say we have learned the lessons of history, but to be turning away these desperate people who are fleeing a horrific situation suggests that we haven't learned the lessons at all.'

We are astoundingly good, it seems, at ignoring the discrepancy between the words spoken at commemorative ceremonies about lessons learnt from history and our actions in the present, which are often completely at odds with those lessons. Historical commemorations become hollow rituals when there is such a glaring contrast between the ways in which as a society we remember the past and act in the present, when our actions obviously contradict the timeless values we profess to hold dear in those ceremonies. I'm not exactly sure what to make of this historical disconnect, this collective form of cognitive dissonance, which may not be an entirely new phenomenon but which has become very hard to ignore in the current climate. Do we need more memory, better memory, more accurate memory to combat moral complacency and self-congratulation, or do commemorative practices inevitably promote and foster such attitudes? And are we as memory scholars, who like to think of ourselves as progressive, complicit in the widespread reduction of historical remembrance to mere virtue signalling?

Paula McFetridge: To shake the public out of its complacency and its apparent inability to make the connection between historical migration and the current political situation it is imperative artists continue to explore new ways of humanising immigrants and emigrants; giving them a voice, sharing their journeys and present situation, making connections, challenging social systems that prevent integration and equality of rights. The key question for the artist is how to do this and not simply speak to those engaged with the migration narrative and how not to ensure the audience aren't complacent voyeurs – what information do they require to be activists and champions for change. Also within this area of theatre for social change we need to consider how the experiences are sourced and collated. And if the archiving of stories is for animation now or in the future – we must be sensitive to the importance of timing. Kabosh is currently working with Belfast playwright Rosemary Jenkinson on a new commission *Lives in Translation* resulting from a series of interviews conducted with female Somalian refugees (scheduled to premiere September 2017).

Dominic Thorpe: Selective solidarity can seem to draw on particular inherited concepts and senses of national identity to facilitate a placing of the shared experience of migration in this moment as secondary, unconnected or even irrelevant. Each year in Ireland around the time of St Patrick's Day (March 17th) Irish politicians make calls to US politicians for recognition and positive action in relation to the plight of Irish illegal emigrants in America, the so called 'undocumented Irish'. This call for compassion contrasts with the treatment of 'undocumented' in Ireland or the treatment of those who come to seek asylum in Ireland and are forced to live in the widely criticised Direct Provision asylum system, a system branded 'a form of institutionalised poverty' by the special rapporteur on children Geoffrey Shannon.[47] Lentin refers to Ireland as having become a 'diaspora state', leading to a 2004 referendum where Irish citizens voted to deny the right of citizenship to children born in Ireland to non-national parents.[48] The referendum did not include children born outside Ireland who are entitled to Irish citizenship if they have at least one Irish grandparent. Such a prioritising of bloodline over geography indicates the complexity of relationship between migration and memory in Ireland, a place with a history of poverty, discrimination, and mass emigration.

I remember hearing an interview on an Irish talk radio programme around nine years ago where the host was speaking on the phone with an Irish man who had emigrated to America to seek employment a number years previously and was now living and working there illegally. The man was lamenting the cruel reality that he could not return temporarily to Ireland for his father's funeral. Because of his illegal status he would not be allowed re-entry to America, despite having built a life there. At the time the conversation was happening there was an economic boom in Ireland and the number of people coming to Ireland looking for work and seeking asylum had increased. The radio host mentioned this in passing to which the man suggested too many foreigners were being allowed into Ireland. At this point instead of trying in any way to explore the complexity of the often simultaneous contrasting positions taken when discussing lived realities of migration, the radio presenter momentarily stumbled over the conversation before quickly bringing the focus back to the man's plight.

My response at that time to was to hire approximately eighty advertising spaces on three national radio stations over one week, during which were played audio recordings of a number of segments of interviews with two people, both from war torn countries, who had recently come to live in Ireland overlaid with recordings of traditional Irish emigration songs.[49] I have never experienced questions of migration and memory sitting well together. That they most often need to be forced and the spaces in which they are articulated and drawn out need to be created, recreated, and forced when necessary, is telling.

Astrid Erll: I would like, finally, to consider some of the positive aspects in the handling of the current refugee crisis and discuss how these may be connected with memory. In 2015, when almost one million refugees, mainly from Syria and Afghanistan, came to Germany, the 'welcome culture' emerged not only as a political slogan, but indeed found a broad social basis. At the same time, other parts of society voiced xenophobic, specifically anti-Muslim, sentiments, and Germany saw the rise of political populism. Despite this, the welcoming attitude of a large part of German society is a social fact and, it seems to me, was at least partly the result of an effective memory culture. It was shaped – premediated – by cultural memories about the millions who became exiles and refugees during the Nazi era. At the same time, prospective memory appears to be at work here. Since the 1990s, Germany has (as has Europe at large) developed a highly reflexive memory culture. People have become attuned to thinking in terms of remembering and being remembered. Many Germans are clearly aware that the current refugee crisis is a 'historical moment' that will shape the nation and Europe, and they are sensitive to the question of how this moment may be remembered in the future. There is an acute awareness of what Axel Honneth calls the 'recognitional structure of collective memory',[50] which connects past, present and future generations – albeit no longer in homogeneous ethnic or national frameworks, but in structures that interlink members of today's society with future generations in thoroughly transnational and transcultural formations. If 'a group must be able to expect from its prospectively recognized descendants that they will reciprocally recognitionally approve the currently valid self-understanding'[51], then actions today must be conceived of as potential objects of memory of tomorrow's 'new Germans'[52] (Münkler and Münkler) – or, by extension, tomorrow's 'new Europeans'.

NOTES

1. Maurice Halbwachs, *Les cadres sociaux de la mémoire* (Paris: Albin Michel, 1994 [1925]). See also Jeffrey K. Olick, Vered Vinitzky-Seroussi, and Daniel Levy, eds., *The Collective Memory Reader* (Oxford: Oxford University Press, 2011).

2. Elisabeth F. Loftus and Katherine Ketcham, *The Myth of Repressed Memory: False Memories and Allegations of Sexual Abuse* (New York: St. Martin's Press, 1994); Jan Assmann, *Das kulturelle Gedächtnis: Schrift, Erinnerung und politische Identität in frühen Hochkulturen* (Munich: Beck, 1992); Jeffrey K. Olick, *The Politics of Regret: On Collective Memory and Historical Responsibility* (London: Routledge, 2007).

3. Dirk A. Moses, 'Genocide and the Terror of History', *Parallax* 17.4 (2011), 90–108; Michael Rothberg, *Multidirectional Memory: Remembering the Holocaust in the Age of Decolonization* (Stanford, CA: Stanford University Press, 2009).

4. Paul Ricoeur, 'Memory – History – Forgetting', in *Meaning and Representation in History*, ed. by Jörn Rüsen (Oxford: Berghahn Books, 2006), 9–19.

5. See Joep Leerssen and Ann Rigney, eds., *Commemorating Writers in Nineteenth-Century Europe: Nation-Building and Centenary Fever* (Basingstoke: Palgrave Macmillan, 2014).

6. Written by Laurence McKeown, directed by Paula McFetridge, produced by Kabosh, performed by James Doran and Vincent Higgins; premiered 21 October 2016 Girdwood Cultural Hub.

7. Yael Zerubavel, *Recovered Roots: Collective Memory and the Making of Israeli National Tradition* (Chicago: Chicago University Press, 1995).

8. See, for example, the 2009 Report of the Commission to Inquire into Child Abuse (www.childabusecommission.ie).

9. Astrid Erll, *Memory in Culture*, trans. by Sara B. Young (Basingstoke: Palgrave Macmillan, 2011), p.38.

10. Erll, *Memory in Culture*, p.38.

11. Erll, *Memory in Culture*, p.175.

12. Jeffrey K. Olick, ' "Collective Memory": A Memoir and Prospect', *Memory Studies* 1.1 (2008), pp.23–24.

13. Adam D. Brown et al., 'Introduction: Is an Interdisciplinary Field of Memory Studies Possible?', *International Journal of Politics, Culture, and Society* 22 (2009), p.118.

14. Hans J. Markowitsch and Harald Welzer, *The Development of Autobiographical Memory* (Hove: Psychology Press, 2010 [2005]); *The Memory Process: Neuroscientific and Humanistic Perspectives*, ed. by Suzanne Nalbantian, Paul M. Matthews, and James L. McClelland (Cambridge, MA: MIT Press, 2011); *Individual and Collective Memory Consolidation: Analogous Processes on Different Levels*, ed. by Thomas J. Anastasio et al. (Cambridge, MA: MIT Press, 2012).

15. Paul Connerton, 'Seven Types of Forgetting', *Memory Studies* 1.1 (2008), 59–71; Aleida Assmann, 'Forms of Forgetting', public lecture held at Castrum Peregrini in Amsterdam on 1 October 2014 on being awarded the 2014 Dr. A. H. Heineken Prize for History, *CastrumPeregrini.org*, 30 October 2014, < http://castrumperegrini.org/2014/10/30/forms-of-forgetting/ >, accessed 7 June 2016.

16. David Rieff, *In Praise of Forgetting: Historical Memory and Its Ironies* (New Haven, CT: Yale University Press, 2016).

17. Truth and Reconciliation Commission of South Africa, *Truth and Reconciliation Commission of South Africa Interim Report* (Cape Town: Truth and Reconciliation Commission, 1996).

18. Luisa Passerini, 'Memories between Silence and Oblivion', in *Memory, History, Nation: Contested Pasts*, ed. by Katharine Hodgkin and Susannah Radstone (London: Routledge, 2003), pp.238–54.

19. *Jules Michelet, Journal* I (1828–1848), ed. by Paul Viallaneix, (Paris: Gallimard, 1959), pp.377–378.

20. Graham Dawson, *Making Peace with the Past? Memory, Trauma and the Irish Troubles* (Manchester: Manchester University Press, 2007).

21. Michael Lambek and Paul Antze, 'Introduction: Forecasting Memory', in *Tense Past: Cultural Essays in Trauma and Memory*, ed. by Paul Antze and Michael Lambek (London: Routledge, 1996), p.xii.

22. Ernest Renan, 'Qu'est-ce qu'une nation?' [1882], *Oeuvres Complètes d'Ernest Renan*, ed. by Henriette Psichari (Paris: Calmann-Lévy, 1947–61), vol 1, 886–907; Benedict Anderson, *Imagined Communities: Reflections on the Origins and Spread of Nationalism* (London: Verso, 1991 [1983]), 187–206.

23. Jay M. Winter, *Sites of Memory, Sites of Mourning: The Great War in European Cultural History* (Cambridge: Cambridge University Press, 1995).

24. Michael Rothberg. 'Multidirectional Memory and the Implicated Subject: On Sebald and Kentridge', in *Performing Memory in Art and Popular Culture*, ed. by Liedeke Plate, and Anneke Smelik (New York: Routledge, 2013), 39–58.

25. Sara Ahmed, *Willful Subjects* (Durham, NC: Duke University Press, 2014).

26. Slawomir Kapralskim 'Memory, Identity, and Roma Transnational Nationalism', in *Transnational Memory. Circulation, Articulation, Scales*, ed. by Chiara De Cesari and Ann Rigney (Berlin: De Gruyter, 2014), pp.195–218.

27. Andreas Huyssen, 'Present Pasts: Media, Politics, Amnesia', *Public Culture* 12.1 (2000), 21–38.

28. Wendy Brown, *States of Injury: Power and Freedom in Late Modernity* (Princeton, NJ: Princeton University Press, 1995); Lauren Berlant, 'The Subject of True Feeling: Pain, Privacy, and Politics', in *Traumatizing Theory: The Cultural Politics of Affect in and beyond Psychoanalysis*, ed. by Karyn Ball (New York: Other Press, 2007), 305–47.

29. Mark Seltzer, 'Wound Culture: Trauma in the Pathological Public Sphere', *October* 80 (Spring 1997), 3–26.

30. Carrie Hamilton, 'Activist Memories: The Politics of Trauma and the Pleasures of Politics', in *The Future of Memory*, ed. by Richard Crownshaw, Jane Kilby, and Antony Rowland (New York: Berghahn, 2010), p.266.

31. Kristin Ross, qtd. in Hamilton, p.269.

32. Hamilton, p.275, p.276.

33. *Belfast by Moonlight* written by Carlo Gébler with original music by Neil Martin, directed by Paula McFetridge, produced by Kabosh, performed by Bernadette Brown, Maria Connolly, Roisin Gallagher, Laura Hughes, Carol Moore, and Kerri Quinn. Premiered in St George's Church, Belfast, November 2013.

34. Lucy Bond, Stef Craps, and Pieter Vermeulen, eds., *Memory Unbound: Tracing the Dynamics of Memory Studies* (New York: Berghahn, 2017).

35. Stef Craps, *Postcolonial Witnessing: Trauma Out of Bounds* (Basingstoke: Palgrave Macmillan, 2013).

36. Astrid Erll, 'Travelling Memory', *Parallax* 17.4 (2011), 4–18: (p.9).

37. Anna L. Tsing, *Friction: An Ethnography of Global Connection* (Princeton, NJ: Princeton University Press, 2005).

38. Chiara De Cesari and Ann Rigney, eds. *Transnational Memory: Circulation, Articulation, Scales* (Berlin: De Gruyter, 2014).

39. Astrid Erll, 'Travelling Memory', 4–18; Ann Rigney, *The Afterlives of Walter Scott: Memory on the Move* (Oxford: Oxford University Press, 2012); Bond, Craps, and Vermeulen (2017).

40. *Those you Pass in the Street* by Laurence McKeown, directed by Paula McFetridge, produced by Kabosh, original cast: Vincent Higgins, Laura Hughes, Paul Kennedy, and Carol Moore; premiered February 2014 in Skainos Centre, Belfast.

41. Michael Rothberg, 'Remembering Back: Cultural Memory, Colonial Legacies, and Postcolonial Studies', in *The Oxford Handbook of Postcolonial Studies*, ed. by Graham Huggan (Oxford: Oxford University Press, 2012), 359–79.

42. Nancy Fraser, 'Social Justice in the Age of Identity Politics: Redistribution, Recognition, and Participation', in Nancy Fraser and Axel Honneth, *Redistribution or Recognition? A Political-Philosophical Exchange* (New York: Verso, 2003), 7–109, (p.36).

43. Fraser, p.38.

44. *This is What we Sang* by Gavin Kostick with original music by Neil Martin, directed by Paula McFetridge, produced by Kabosh; original cast: Alan Burke, Jo Donnelly, Laura Hughes, Paul Kennedy, and Lalor Roddy; premiered in the Belfast synagogue October 2009.

45. Piet Chielens, 'Merkel heeft meer ruggengraat dan de rest samen', interview with Marijke Libert, *Knack.be*, 9 March 2016, < http://www.knack.be/nieuws/wereld/merkel-heeft-meer-ruggengraat-dan-de-rest-samen/article-longread-676133.html> (accessed 7 June 2016).

46. Rick Lyman, 'Treatment of Migrants Evokes Memories of Europe's Darkest Hour', *NYTimes.com*, 4 September 2015 < http://www.nytimes.com/2015/09/05/world/treatment-of-migrants-evokes-memories-of-europes-darkest-hour.html> (accessed 7 June 2016).

47. Geoffrey Shannon, Fifth Report of the Special Rapporteur on Child Protection: A Report Submitted to the Oireachtas (2011).

48. Ronit Lentin, 'Illegal in Ireland, Irish Illegals: Diaspora Nation as Racial State', *Irish Political Studies* 22.4 (December 2007).

49. *Signatures* Project (with Brian Maguire and Brian O'Connor). Commissioned by Dun Laoghaire Rathdown County Council 2008.

50. Axel Honneth, 'The Recognitional Structure of Collective Memory', in *Memory: A History*, ed. by Dmitri Nikulin (Oxford: Oxford University Press, 2015), 316–24.

51. Honneth, p.324.

52. Herfried Münkler and Marina Münkler, *Die Neuen Deutschen: Ein Land vor seiner Zukunft* (Berlin: Rowohlt, 2016).

List of Books Reviewed

Oona Frawley (editor), *Memory Ireland, Volume 1: History and Modernity*. New York: Syracuse University Press, 2011. 264 pages. $34.95 USD

Oona Frawley (editor), *Memory Ireland Volume 2: Diaspora and Memory Practices*. Syracuse, New York: Syracuse University Press, 2012. 287 pages. $39.95 USD

Oona Frawley (editor), *Memory Ireland, Volume 3: The Famine and the Troubles*. Syracuse: Syracuse University Press, 2014. 375 pages. $44.95 USD

Oona Frawley and Katherine O'Callaghan (editors), *Memory Ireland Volume 4: James Joyce and Cultural Memory*. Syracuse, NY: Syracuse University Press, 2014. xi+234 pages. $44.95 USD

Fintan Walsh, *Queer Performance and Contemporary Ireland: Dissent and Disorientation*. Basingstoke: Palgrave Macmillan, 2016. 189 pages. £58.00 GBP

Niall Carson, *Rebel by Vocation: Seán O'Faoláin and the generation of The Bell*. Manchester: Manchester University Press, 2016. vii + 178 pages. £75.00 GBP

Irish University Review 47.1 (2017): 197
DOI: 10.3366/iur.2017.0264
© Edinburgh University Press
www.euppublishing.com/iur

Book Reviews

Oona Frawley (editor), *Memory Ireland, Volume 1: History and Modernity*. New York: Syracuse University Press, 2011. 264 pages. $34.95 USD.

The idea of cultural memory poses many challenges for scholars and researchers. As this valuable collection of essays demonstrates, the relationships between group and individual memory can be difficult to unravel and understand, reflected and refracted as they are through multiple processes of transmission, through social, political and cultural frames, and through the intricacies of the individual mind. The *Memory Ireland* series, edited by Oona Frawley, combines robust framing chapters that map the theoretical terrain for readers with essays that explore the performance and action of memory in varied contexts, ranging from Edmund Campion's *Two Bokes of the Histories of Ireland* (c. 1571) to an online Irish-language hoax in the aftermath of the 9/11 attacks on the Twin Towers in New York.

Memory Ireland, Volume 1 opens with chapters by Oona Frawley and Barbara A. Misztal that trace recent academic discourses around and between the ideas of history and memory, gauging the 'truth value' accorded to these different categories of engagement with the past. Misztal's essay centres on the idea of evidence. 'As history becomes one among many types of narratives and memory is appreciated for its authenticity and truthfulness', she writes, 'the boundary line between memory and history is becoming fluid' (16). That boundary line is significant precisely because it complicates, extends, or contracts what can, and what has, been taken as evidence within truth claims about the past. In her essay on theories of memory in an Irish postcolonial context, Frawley explores the points of intersection between cognitive science, narrative theory, and postcolonial studies that can inform methodological approaches to 'reading' memory in Irish culture. This emphasis on method is particularly valuable in navigating the different sources or forms of 'memory evidence' presented by the contributing authors throughout the volume. Memory often provides a necessary corrective to the silences within institutional or official histories, particularly in its emphasis on witness and bodily experience, as demonstrated in David Cregan's essay on queer

Irish University Review 47.1 (2017): 198–215
© Edinburgh University Press
www.euppublishing.com/iur

memory in Ireland. However, as Frawley, Malcolm Sen, and others throughout the volume reiterate, memory is inexact, a valuable but malleable and problematic form of evidence that cannot be ignored, but that must be treated carefully in order to retain its integrity and position within discourses of history, and particularly when historical events are under consideration in legal decisions and processes. This quality of memory requires those who engage in its theorization to be especially attentive to source, and to the validity of claims being made for, and about, groups of people in the present and in the past.

The relationship between memory and the body is a central theme throughout the book, both in relation to memories of bodily experiences otherwise unrecorded, but also in the intimate relationship of memory to the body, and to the cognitive and neurological functioning of the brain. Anne Dolan's exploration of the relationship between dead bodies, buried and unburied, and the memories of the Irish Civil War, further emphasizes the visceral, physical action of memory in society. Indeed, Dolan's inclusion of the evidence of memory – accounts provided by those who witnessed the leaking coffins of executed Republican soldiers at Beggar's Bush Barracks – reflects the difficulty and necessity of accessing and embedding such material within broader historical narratives. The extent to which such evidence can become part of public and official processes of remembering within Ireland's 'Decade of Centenaries' remains to be seen. The relationship between personal and public, or official, memory is explored by several of the contributing authors, including Holly Maples' essay on the centenary of the Abbey Theatre. Guy Beiner's exploration of the social memory of the Irish Rebellion of 1798 is particularly valuable in its consideration of the position of memory cultures within public space, to the multiple locations of remembering, to issues such as class and religion in shaping memory practices, and in his attention to parallel 'memory' events, such as Queen Victoria's Diamond Jubilee. Mary E. Daly's fascinating essay on De Valera as 'obsessive historian', absorbed with shaping future memories of the past, traces the close relationship between the intensely personal memory of an individual, and their potential to impact public or national memory. The responses of institutions to the evidence of memory are also examined. In her essay on representations of the experience of women within the Irish Magdalene Laundry system, Emilie Pine refers to Bertie Ahern's 1999 apology to the children abused while in State care. The phenomenon of the state apology for historic wrongdoing reflects the need for compensation and apportions blame. It is based on the presence of those who remain wronged, and who continually suffer due to their memory. If those specific bodies are no longer present, they are represented by others, or by monuments or actions that ensure that their grievances do not become subsumed into historiographical accounts that work to establish, as Linda Connolly has argued, 'the context of the times', implying a society based on assent and consent.[1] The presence of memory necessitates the apology and the compensation, meaning that an event remains current as an issue of political significance. The presence of memory, individual or collective, direct or constructed, acts to personalize and politicize our understanding of the past.

The majority of the essays in this volume focus on those monuments or actions that represent and transmit memory. Material objects and artistic representations are considered as points through which the operation of memory in society can be traced, reflections of the operation of memory between people through time. While P.J. Mathews' essay focuses on the individual perspective of Synge as manifest in his writing, many of the contributions focus on the social meaning of sites, or objects, of memory. Máirín Ní Cheallaigh considers the position of archaeological field monuments and their relationship to collective memories of place, particularly as they were threatened by destruction due to increasingly intensive farming practices during the nineteenth century. Mary Helen Thuente, who draws on a wide range of textual sources, images, and instruments to illuminate her reading, outlines the iconic image of the harp as a palimpsest of cultural memory. The representation of memory through dramatic narrative, is considered by Pine, whose essay provides a valuable consideration of the risks of narrative strategies in incorporating memory into 'mainstream' practices, and the need to ensure that 'misrepresentations' do not lead to distortions within popular history, and by extension, popular memory. Lorraine Ryan's essay engages with the idea of multiculturalization and cultural memory, and the need to reconsider the boundaries imposed around 'our' cultural memory. This essay, in its references to the Celtic Tiger era, inadvertently commemorates its own cultural moment. While the evidence base within this essay relies on newspaper reports and Irish artworks, a broader range of sources, representing the perspectives of the 'new Irish' would have been welcome. Alan Titley provides the final essay, but it sits somewhat awkwardly within the volume. While his subject and theme are certainly worthy of inclusion, Titley makes many broad claims and sweeping statements about Irish cultural life, based on assumptions about what 'Cyril Citizen' or 'Alison Anybody' may or may not know, rather than drawing on evidence or sources to substantiate his argument.

In her introduction to the volume, Frawley notes that memory studies is both daunting and exciting in its potential to 'link the neuroscientist's work to that of a literary critic' (xiii). The multiple approaches and methods employed by the contributors of this volume demonstrate the potential for humanities research to inform and enrich a wide range of disciplines engaged in researching aspects of human and social behaviour. Irish memory studies, therefore, in its careful and nuanced exploration of the past, may have a central role to play in the future of Irish STEAM research.

NIAMH NIC GABHANN
University of Limerick
DOI: 10.3366/iur.2017.0265

NOTE

1. http://linda-connolly.blogspot.ie/2015/03/the-debate-about-1916-commemoration-is.html (accessed 3 November 2016).

Oona Frawley (editor), *Memory Ireland Volume 2: Diaspora and Memory Practices*. Syracuse, New York: Syracuse University Press, 2012. 287 pages. $39.95 USD.

Oona Frawley's edited collection *Memory Ireland Volume 2: Diaspora and Memory Practices* addresses, in two discreet sections, the role of memory in Irish diasporic communities and the various ways that memory is enacted in the performance of Irish cultural identity. The volume showcases the interdisciplinarity of memory studies, with contributions from scholars in literature (ranging in focus from Joyce to genre fiction), history, cultural studies, music and visual arts, as well as two personal essays by prominent Irish writers.

The first section, 'Memory and the Irish Diaspora', discusses the wide range of memory practices deployed by Irish immigrants to negotiate cultural identity in new national contexts. Many of the chapters in this section focus on literary engagements with memory. Aidan Arrowsmith addresses the variety of uses for nostalgia within Irish diasporic writing, ranging from a desire for "authenticity" whose notions of cultural purity are rooted in a regressive, Romantic nationalism; to a more nuanced appreciation of memory's mediation through narrative, using nostalgia's 'acknowledgement of absence' to facilitate a more productive and future-oriented dialogue between past and present. Chad Habel, drawing on concepts developed by Deleuze and Guattari, argues that Irish-Australian fiction features a shift from an 'arborescent' model of cultural identity which prioritises ancestral claims to Irish culture and identity, to a 'rhizomatic' model which complicates the idea of inherited identity through its emphasis on the web of 'lateral connections' within communities and across time. Katrin Urschel suggests that Irish-Canadian authors, in their explorations of Irish spaces, utilise two theoretical concepts of space: a 'settler' perspective which emphasises exploration and the creation of new memories, and Bakhtin's chronotope which imagines places as temporal layers and 'excavates' collective memories through historical traces. Maureen Reddy, acknowledging that few contemporary Irish fiction writers have addressed the topic of race, suggests that those who do use the figure of the American immigrant, the new national context enabling a consciousness of 'whiteness' as part of Irish cultural heritage.

Other chapters in this section focus on cultural and historical memory practices. James P. Byrne suggests that nineteenth-century Irish-American immigrants nostalgically reimagined their cultural heritage to counter damaging Irish stereotypes and become 'effective citizen' of their new country. Spurgeon Thompson and Maggie Williams both write about physical mementos: Thompson defines kitsch as an 'ambiguous signifier', which both distances and connects one to the missing homeland, while Williams explores how souvenirs construct and communicate Irish cultural identity. Tanja Bueltmann documents various St. Patrick's Day celebrations in late nineteenth century New Zealand, arguing that such celebrations were not usually politicised but were inclusive and celebratory, perhaps reflecting the fact that most of these immigrants relocated by choice. Nuala Ní Dhomhnaill, in a personal essay, recounts her childhood memories as an Irish immigrant in England, reflecting on the ways that this experience has shaped her personally, politically, and aesthetically.

The volume's second section, 'Memory Practices', is united in a focus on what Frawley identifies as 'ways of cultural remembering that result from and are shaped by particular cultural forms' (129). While this section bears little immediate connection to the previous, it shares a conceptual interest in the ways that marginalised communities – such as Travellers, immigrants *to* Ireland, and Gaelic speakers – use memory to establish and challenge cultural identities. Joep Leerssen, drawing on the idea of metempsychosis developed in Joyce's *Ulysses* as a loose social bond constructed through individual memories, argues that Ireland's Celtic Revival constitutes a cultural metempsychosis, whereby Gaelic traditions are resurrected and internalised to create a collective identity in an English-speaking Ireland. Gail Baylis explores the way that photography, as a mediated representation of reality, assumes meaning based on cultural needs, tracing the example of a famous eviction photograph originally encoded as an indictment of English imperialism in the destruction of Irish home life, and later used in a Celtic Tiger newspaper as a rejection of nostalgia. Katie Brown and Steve Coleman each discuss music as a memory practice. Brown argues that music, especially after the decline of the Irish language, becomes both a metaphor and a language for the communication of nationalist sentiments, while Coleman suggests that traditional Irish music, especially the Irish-language lyric, narrates a 'nonsynchronous' cultural memory, particularly through the way it encourages multiple meanings and interpretations. Michael OhAodha argues that, while Travellers are often written out of Irish historical narratives, stereotypically constructed as 'others' and 'helpless victims', the memory practices within this community, including autobiography and storytelling, preserve a very different history.

Of course, cultural memory is not only, or even primarily, performed through textual representations. Beginning with the nationalist identity politics at work in the establishment of the Gaelic Athletic Association, Sara Brady argues that the Gaelic games offer a means of performing Irish identity, from Irish-American immigrants who used the games as a means of resisting assimilation, to recent immigrants to Ireland who become part of their communities through sport. Hasia Diner and Rhona Richman Kenneally both discuss food as a cultural memory practice. Diner suggests that the Irish are historically unusual in that food is not a significant component of their cultural identity; given Ireland's experience of Famine, she argues, food became disassociated from performances of identity and pleasure. Kenneally challenges Diner's claims through analysing the ways that Irish cookbooks of the twentieth century have engaged with the 'traditional Irish cottage' as a cultural icon, negotiating both national identity and women's roles within the nation. Finally, Paul Muldoon discusses how alcohol has shaped both personal and cultural memory within Ireland; as a taboo subject, it is 'spoken in code or sideways' (249), a discursive practice he traces through Stevenson's *Treasure Ireland*.

With its impressive range of focus and depth of analysis, Frawley's *Memory Ireland Volume 2* proves itself an invaluable resource to the field of Irish memory studies, while also offering theoretical contributions to memory and cultural studies more broadly. Most significantly, this volume productively expands the parameters of Irish memory studies; as Frawley puts it, 'Irish cultural memory... is itself diasporic, dispersed' (11), across global distances as well as across a wide range of memory practices, from memorial construction to recreational sport.

BRANDI BYRD
University College Dublin
DOI: 10.3366/iur.2017.0266

Oona Frawley (editor), *Memory Ireland, Volume 3: The Famine and the Troubles*. Syracuse: Syracuse University Press, 2014. 375 pages. $44.95 USD.

Memory Studies is a flourishing area of academic enquiry within contemporary scholarship and, as Oona Frawley notes, 'two periods [have] influenced our sense of memory in an Irish cultural context' to a seminal degree: the Irish Famine, which first introduced Memory Studies in an Irish context, and the Troubles (3). As 'moments that can be identified as particularly important in the cultural memory of a group' (1), Frawley suggests these periods can be understood as 'memory cruxes', which 'center around perceived historical spaces that pose questions and offer conflicting, oppositional, and sometimes intensely problematic answers about the way that a culture considers its past' (2). Both periods are indelibly marked by 'trauma' and Frawley's introduction offers an astute and necessary unpacking of the move – which so often passes without comment – between the individual and the collective in recent work in Trauma and Memory Studies. In probing at what it means to be part 'of the trauma of a culture' (8), Frawley also gestures towards how trauma can be a key force in the production of 'cultural memory', as nebulous and slippery as that term might be.

'Trauma' is far from a neutral term and the relationship between Memory Studies and Trauma Studies should not necessarily be taken as an essential one. Indeed, the most perceptive scholarship within Memory Studies cautions a critical awareness and healthy scepticism towards, what Emilie Pine has labelled, 'the tendency of Irish culture to refashion the past so that it is read exclusively under the sign of trauma'.[2] This collection follows this discerning lead, with Joseph Valente's contribution seeking to help 'clarify the potential, the limitations, the dangers, and above all the ideological stakes and motives of this recent addition [of Trauma Studies] to the arsenal of nationalist historiography and cultural analysis' (174). The collection is distinguished by a sophisticated and nuanced approach to Trauma and Memory Studies. Enabled by Pierre Nora's concept of *lieux de mémoir*, or sites of memory, the essays cover a broad swath of disciplinary ground, including the dynamics between memory and literature, photography, sculpture, museums, historical buildings, art and film.

The essays tend to collect, loosely, around two main areas within Memory Studies, namely, the haunting, affective power of (traumatic) memory and patterns and processes of commemoration (which is not to suggest that there is no degree of overlap between the two, of course). David Lloyd, following Avery Gordon's assertion that the ghost signals loss but also, potentially, 'simultaneously represent a future possibility, a hope',[3] reads the spectres of the Famine gesturing towards 'the memory of another mode of living' (23). Emily Mark-Fitzgerald's contribution, on 'Photography and the Visual Legacy of the Famine', argues that the Famine's spectrality is often figured as absence in visual art, explicating how 'the Famine continues to elude placement within a fixed frame and lay bare the tensions attending encounters with the Famine's fragmentary and volatile material traces' (137). In their insightful chapters on the afterlives of the Troubles, Stefanie Lehner and Gerald Dawe explore how the spectral affects of trauma and violence shape – or perhaps, more accurately, disfigure – literary narratives of memory. Where Dawe, developing an idea from Joseph Brodsky,[4] elucidates the peculiar power of poetry to capture and 'retain' things that cannot be expressed otherwise, Lehner illuminates the 'innovative narrative techniques [used] to encode the traumatic experiences of the Troubles' (291) in Seamus Deane's *Reading in the Dark* (1996) and Anna Burns' *No Bones* (2001). Fionna Barber's chapter is particularly attuned to the complexities of memory, trauma and representation in the North; she writes, 'art practice in Northern Ireland works to problematize the process of representation itself, to make us as viewers aware that, like the act of remembering, the making of visual images is a process that is highly selective and partial' (238).

Commemorative processes and cultural heritage are becoming central to the enquiries of Memory Studies, demonstrated in this collection through contributions from Margaret Kelleher and Richard Kearney, who trace how the Famine has been commemorated through sculpture and various monuments across the North Atlantic diaspora. Niamh Ann Kelly's fascinating chapter highlights the difficulties of remembering individuals within the architectures of the state and the mass death that took place in workhouses during the Famine. The collection is sensitive to the radical differences involved in commemorating the Famine and the Troubles, a period of history within living memory; remembrance and commemoration in the North has involved active practices of sharing stories and testimonies. However, as Graham Dawson highlights in his chapter on Bloody Sunday, most critical analysis within Irish Memory Studies has focused on the collective, following Maurice Halbwach's work (196).[5] Given that we still have access to recollections from individuals who lived through the period, Dawson advocates that we engage with these individual memory-narratives, which 'may enable greater understanding of the effects of violent conflict upon the subjectivities of those affected and further insight into the human dimensions of peacemaking in culture' (197).

Kris Brown's assertion that 'aspects of commemoration and memorialization can become new zones of political and cultural skirmishing in a divided society' reminds us just how vital and relevant Memory Studies is to contemporary Irish cultural analysis (311). This collection, then, is a rigorous and nuanced addition to literature in the field. As definitive moments in Irish history, aligning these events makes sense: although it is a shame that none of the contributions seek to actively analyse the two 'memory cruxes' in tandem; one wonders, perhaps, whether Joseph Lennon's intriguing chapter on the Famine and Terence MacSwiney's hunger strike might have been even richer for stretching into the later hunger strikes of the Troubles. However, this does not diminish the achievements of this compelling collection, which makes a significant contribution to our understanding of the Irish past and present.

ALISON GARDEN
University College Dublin
DOI: 10.3366/iur.2017.0267

NOTES

2. Emilie Pine, *The Politics of Irish Memory: Performing Remembrance in Contemporary Irish Culture*, (London: Palgrave Macmillan, 2011). 7.

3. Avery Gordon, *Ghostly Matters: Haunting and the Sociological Imagination*, (Minneapolis: University of Minnesota Press. 1997), 64.

4. Joseph Brodsky, 'The Keening Muse'. In *Less Than* One, (New York: Farrar, Strauss, Giroux. 1986). 52.

5. Maurice Halbwachs, *On Collective Memory* (New York: Harper and Row, 1980).

Oona Frawley and Katherine O'Callaghan (editors), *Memory Ireland Volume 4: James Joyce and Cultural Memory*. Syracuse, NY: Syracuse University Press, 2014. xi+234 pages. $44.95 USD.

James Joyce's works have been a touchstone for both historically-minded readers and professional historians for at least the past fifty years, and for good reason. As Oona Frawley notes in her introduction, 'What is extraordinary is that . . . Joyce's texts and the characters within them come to themselves [*sic*] reflect on and deliver analyses of history' (1). Therefore, the fourth and final instalment in the *Memory Ireland* project focuses exclusively on Joyce as 'a case study' because he is recognised as an 'exemplary author to consider in relation to how it is that history is remembered and recycled, as how the individual-as-actor produces, participates in, and impacts that history as it unfolds in the present' (2). In this way, cultural memory studies productively take up Joyce's works at the intersection of literary representation and historical documentation, and the volume amply demonstrates the valuable insights that can be gleaned from such an approach.

Vincent Cheng and Ellen Carol Jones's essays consolidate for a non-Joycean audience the output of years of research and consideration in their established work in the field, while other essays in the volume open up exciting new vistas of possibilities to be pursued. Skilfully merging both of these strands, Anne Fogarty's essay presents a skilful rereading of Joyce's most famous short story, 'The Dead', that probes the interstices of individual, private as well as social, collective memories. She illuminates a long critical tradition that has sought to stabilise and contain the fluid narrative of Gabriel and Gretta Conroy and the rest of the company in attendance at the Morkan sisters' dinner and then persuasively posits an alternative reading that maintains the open and unresolved status of personal, familial, and national memories and identities that the story frames so carefully. Similarly, Declan Kiberd's 'Old Testament and New' is a stimulating and thought-provoking case study in cultural, historical, and intertextual traditions. In a fresh and exemplary way, the essay explores how Joyce wove together Judaic, Greek, and Christian traditions to create his modernist Irish masterpiece.

Abby Bender provides an interesting and instructive essay on 'Joyce and Jewish Memory', but it is clearly a step too far to claim that 'the story of the Israelites escaping Egypt and journeying through the wilderness nevertheless remains at the core of *Ulysses* and its meditation on the birth of the Irish nation' (62). Likewise, Tracey Schwarze's informative overview of the turbulent life and trials of Roger Casement presents a series of tenuous connections and forced readings to underscore the significance of a rather slight mention of the reformer and revolutionary in the barroom scene in the 'Cyclops' episode of *Ulysses*.

In two standout essays at the centre of the book, Katherine O'Callaghan and Len Platt turn our attention to the relatively new and rich field of cultural memory studies of *Finnegans Wake*. Platt's essay begins with a solid descriptive analysis of the intersection of cultural memory and Joyce studies. Methodically deploying Pierre Nora's fundamental work in the field, he then goes on to examine both the representation of the historical record and various historiographical models in one of the darkest and most complex chapters in *Finnegans Wake* (Book III, chapter 3). He concludes that 'Like Nora (and Vico), Joyce sees national definition, whether shaped by the state or its citizens, in terms of a selective appropriation of tradition' (122). In what is proving to be fruitful new critical terrain,

O'Callaghan interjects ecocritical concerns in her survey of 'the absent presence of ancient forests' (95) that reverberates throughout Joyce's works from 'The Dead' to 'Cyclops' and from one beginning to the other in *Finnegans Wake*. She persuasively shows that while Joyce may have relied on and parodied established nationalist tropes about the deforestation of Ireland in his earlier works, he reclaims both the historical reality and the symbolic tradition of this calamity by intertwining the remnants of Ireland's lost trees as bog oaks with the productive, future-oriented activity of writing that is a well-spring of *Finnegans Wake*.

In his engaging and timely study of two events that happened just five days apart in June 2004, Jason King in 'Commemorating *Ulysses*, the Bloomsday Centenary, and the Irish Citizenship Referendum' probes the dichotomous ways in which Joyce's real and make-believe legacies have been misappropriated in Ireland. Under a flashy veneer of global consumerism, the Centenary celebrations promoted Joyce as an icon of Irish cosmopolitan national inclusiveness, while at the same time the rescission of citizenship rights to Irish-born children of immigrants made manifest the fact that 'the definition of Irish nationality had not expanded but constricted' since Bloom's encounter with his compatriots in Barney Kiernan's pub one hundred years before (173). More specifically, King argues that the image of Joyce, *Ulysses*, and multicultural Ireland that the organisers of the government-sponsored Bloomsday centenary tried to present to the nation and the world was 'at odds with the actual life experiences of those immigrant theatre practitioners who had been called upon to perform it [the 'Parable of the Plums' street performance]' (175). King ends on a historically realistic note by asking that we should 'reimagine Leopold Bloom as an exemplary member of the Irish host society and role model for the dominant culture rather than defining him exclusively as a minority subject in a colonial setting' (182). In his essay, Luke Gibbons reverses the lens on much critical work on Joyce and Irish nationalism by arguing that 'little has been written on the equally complex responses of Irish nationalists to Joyce' (188). In a granular, archivally-informed and anecdotal montage, he focuses on Joyce's friendship with the glass maker and seemingly virtuoso *Ulysses* reader, Thomas Pugh, a veteran on 1916 Rising and 'the first to follow in the footsteps of Bloom and Stephen Dedalus, compiling the earliest photographic record of key locations in *Ulysses*' (190).

By bringing together these multi-faceted strands of cultural memory as represented in James Joyce's works, this volume is an important contribution to Joyce and Irish studies. But I do have a final small quibble: while the 1992 Penguin trade edition unobtrusively serves as the standard reference for the quotations from *A Portrait of the Artist as a Young Man*, it is not at all clear to me why the volume references either the rare (and now quite valuable) 1916 first edition of *Dubliners* or for that matter the superb 1936 limited deluxe first English edition of *Ulysses*, neither of which readers of this work will be fortunate enough to be able to consult on their shelves.

LUCA CRISPI
University College Dublin
DOI: 10.3366/iur.2017.0268

Fintan Walsh, *Queer Performance and Contemporary Ireland: Dissent and Disorientation*. Basingstoke: Palgrave Macmillan, 2016. 189 pages. £58.00 GBP.

Fintan Walsh states in the opening lines of this book that he 'attempts to understand how queer performance ... articulates experiences of oppression, exclusion and displacement, while imagining and cultivating more accommodating, inclusive and sustaining modes of interpersonal intimacy, social support, public participation and cultural belonging' (1). An ambitious statement that is certainly lived up to throughout, this book is essential reading for not only those with an interest in Irish theatre, but for anyone concerned with the transformative potential of queer performance. Walsh employs the second wave feminist mantra of 'the personal is political' throughout to showcase the power of queer performance to affect political and social change. The arguments presented in this book are as challenging and thought provoking as the individual performances examined. It is a highly interdisciplinary work that offers deeply persuasive arguments for the vital importance of queer performance in Ireland.

Walsh concisely explains his interpretation of the term 'queer' as 'a capacious index for a range of non-normative sexualities, bodies, desires and subject positions typically housed within the LGBTQ umbrella, I also deploy the term to track thoughts, feelings and actions that unsettle subjects from identity categories, and the social order that would otherwise fix them' (2). The book is a queer text in itself as it invites the reader to challenge the very ways in which we interact with and support queer performance in Ireland.

All of the performances analysed throughout the book specifically relate to living with the aftermath of the Celtic Tigers years of 1997–2007 in Ireland. Walsh argues that 'queer performance has been instrumental in exploring the interconnection between gender and sexuality and issues of migration, religion, place, age, economics and class, ethnicity and national identity – all of which were affected by the boom years and their aftermath' (3). While focusing on contemporary performances, Walsh manages to simultaneously map out a well-rounded history of queer performance in Ireland and this book serves as an excellent insight into Irish queer performance both North and South of the border. He highlights the monumentally transitionary period that Ireland is currently undergoing as a result of the global economic downturn of the early twenty-first century, and comments on the ability of queer theatre and performance to make sense of such change. In relation to the Celtic Tiger years, Walsh states that 'Irish theatre was far from apolitical or apathetic during the time period in question. But in order to observe this work, I suggest we should not only look for the big 'state of the nation' play, but also attend to the wide range of performance forms represented in this book, which may appear marginal and even minor to some' (13).

The book is divided into seven main chapters that each look at a different kind of performance with several examples supplied of each. The individual chapters provide a general introduction to Queer Performance and Contemporary Ireland, Activism, Drag and Solo Performance, Reparative Therapies and Political Performers, Transforming Shame and Testimonial Performance, Intergenerational Moves and Documentary Theatre, Site-Specific Roots and Routes, and Vertiginous Loss, Love and Belonging on the National Stage. The book perfectly marries performance analysis with the theoretical framework, employing the ideas of theorists such as Butler, Dolan, Martin, and Deleuze, and applying them in innovative and contemplative ways. It takes a fresh approach to performance analysis in not only looking at strictly theatrical performance, but also examining the performance of self and of a public persona in his critique of the retired Northern Irish politician Iris Robinson. Walsh deconstructs Robinson's public expressions of homophobia and contextualizes her public moralizing and private infidelities within a country deeply rooted in sectarianism and religious fundamentalism. He uses his definition of the term 'queer' to queer Iris Robinson's performance of self as he 'centralize[s] the Robinsons' media enactments of heterosexual heteronormativity, which in their hyperbolic moralizing, inadvertently queer themselves' (47). Such an interpretation of the Robinsons offers the reader an original approach to a critique of homophobic rhetoric in the public sphere.

The book begins with an analysis of prolific Irish drag performer Panti Bliss, also known as Rory O'Neill, and Bliss's 'Noble Call' speech on the main stage of the Abbey Theatre, on 1 February 2014; and it ends with a study of two shows directed by Wayne Jordan, namely the April 2012 musical *Alice in Funderland* and the April 2014 production of Shakespeare's *Twelfth Night*, both of which also took place on the main stage of the Abbey. Walsh uses these examples to highlight the importance of showcasing queer performance on prolific stages to increase their audience reach and impact, and speaks of 'THISISPOPBABY's ambition to make room for a new generation at the national theatre, led by a queer sensibility' (122). While there is a heavy emphasis on the work of the Dublin-based theatre company, THISISPOPBABY, set up in 2007 by Jennifer Jennings and Phillip McMahon, throughout the book, Walsh rightly argues that this company has been particularly focused on the work of queer artists and queer performance since its inception, and that it 'has been at the forefront of making and curating theatre and performance in contemporary Ireland' (121). He uses the work of THISISPOPBABY to comment on the success of staging queer Irish performance in the largest houses in Ireland in the past number of years, and the need to continue to stage queer work in this way.

The book has a heavily feminist ethos as Walsh reflects on the need for staging a plethora of queer voices, and not just those of middle-class white homosexual men. He critiques the often narrow focus of LGBTQ voices visible in the public eye, stating that 'It remains true of Irish society, as it does elsewhere, that within the LGBTQ umbrella, young, white, middle-class, able bodied gay men dominate and are more warmly embraced than lesbians, transgender people, people of colour – the list, unfortunately, goes on. The status of migrants, travellers and the policing of women's bodies across Ireland continue to reveal and enact deep-seated prejudices' (144–5). In order to counteract this limiting tendency, Walsh includes the work of gay men, lesbian women, drag performers, and transgender artists who come from differing backgrounds, experiences, ages, and generations. The result of such a carefully curated performance list grants the reader a well-balanced guide to queer performance in Ireland. Walsh analyses theatre shows such as Amy Conroy's *I (Heart) Alice (Heart) I* (2012), Una McKevitt's *The Big Deal* (2011), Veronica Dyas's *In My Bed* (2011), Mark O'Halloran's *Trade* (2011), Philip McMahon's *Danny and Chantelle (Still Here)* (2006), Neil Watkins' *The Year of Magical Wanking* (2011), and Panti Bliss's trilogy *In These Shoes* (2007), *All Dolled Up* (2007), and *A Woman in Progress* (2009). As Walsh declares, 'each chapter represents a distinct performance form or context, and an examination of the case study's queer themes, concerns or aesthetics' (17). In examining such shows, Walsh eloquently covers issues such as gender identity, the expression of sexualities, sex work, violence, feelings of shame, addiction, the desire for a sense of 'home', political tensions, the need to 'fit in', and disillusionment with contemporary governance. The performances included incorporate many forms of theatre, such as documentary theatre, ensemble performance, devised work, one-person performance, and theatrical activism. Walsh also examines more non-traditional forms of performance, from Iris Robinson's homophobic comments on the success of the Alternative Miss Ireland pageant (1987, 1996–2012). While all of the performances covered may not initially appear compatible, Walsh effectively ties them together as he guides the reader through an exploration of queer Irish history.

This comprehensive text is a completely necessary read and is an excellent addition to the field of Irish theatre and performance studies. Walsh provides an unparalleled insight into queer performance in Ireland, and the book as a whole is well written, cleverly edited, and highly informative for the academic and the casual reader.

CAROLE QUIGLEY
Trinity College Dublin
DOI: 10.3366/iur.2017.0269

Niall Carson, *Rebel by Vocation: Seán O'Faoláin and the generation of The Bell*. Manchester: Manchester University Press, 2016. vii + 178 pages. £75.00 GBP.

There has been an upsurge in critical reappraisals of Seán O'Faoláin's diverse writings in recent years, with incisive monographs by Paul Delaney and Kelly Matthews, a number of new articles appearing in journals and as chapters in edited collections, and a 2013 memoir by O'Faoláin's daughter, Julia O'Faoláin. Not since an anniversary edition of *The Irish Review* in 2000 has so much attention been given to this important figure in Irish literary history. The focus on O'Faoláin is accompanied by another welcome development in Irish Studies, with the emergence of new work on Irish culture in the mid-twentieth century. Such work includes Bryce Evans' comparative economic and social history of the Second World War, as well as a selection of essays on Irish literature and wartime Europe, edited by Dorothea Depner and Guy Woodward.

Arguably, the main record of cultural debate in Ireland around this time was *The Bell* (1940–1954), the periodical co-founded and edited by O'Faoláin and Peadar O'Donnell. It is perhaps not surprising, therefore, that Niall Carson's monograph, in a similar vein to Matthews' earlier study, focuses the majority of its attention on that 'little magazine'. Through its emphasis on O'Faoláin's political and literary contributions to *The Bell*, *Rebel by Vocation* adds context and nuance to a writer whose work engaged with many major national and international events over the course of the twentieth century. As Carson points out 'the existence of *The Bell* owed its vitality to the ambiguity of these difficult times leading up to, and including the Second World War, as it acted as a running social commentary to the period' (61). In his first book, Carson has created a highly engaging and informative keyhole glance into Ireland during the period of the Second World War.

The book opens with a quotation from Frank O'Connor upon his return to Ireland in 1948, and diagnoses O'Connor's mood of melancholic disillusionment as indicative of the general attitude of writers in the years after the deaths of W.B. Yeats and James Joyce. Much of what is said here is already in the public domain regarding the disillusionment of this generation of writers and their desire, especially evident in the pages of *The Bell*, to create a lasting cultural bulwark against what they perceived to be middle-class anti-intellectualism and lazy Catholic appeals to a false sense of modesty in post-independence Ireland.

Carson rightly remarks that these writers have often been critically misunderstood, sandwiched between two forms of modernism and overshadowed within Irish Studies by such towering figures as Yeats, Joyce, and Samuel Beckett. As such, Carson calls for O'Faoláin and his contemporaries to be considered within an international framework. Some analysis of intermodernism and middlebrow cultures in the UK and USA would have been helpful here – especially since Carson defines O'Faoláin and his generation as 'more public and less elitist' (7).

As it stands, Carson is content with merely outlining the literary and sociological frameworks that writers in *The Bell* drew upon. Thus, the tantalising reference to 'Mass Observation' is not adequately explored. For example, Carson asserts that O'Faoláin's belief that the social structure in Ireland was too thin to support the type of state-of-the-nation novels that were being produced in Britain in the late 1930s led him to construct *The Bell* along Mass Observation movement lines. Carson also remarks, not unreasonably, that 'within these dominant strands – Mass Observation, fears of a 'thinly composed' culture, and intellectual self-doubt exacerbated by neutrality – . . . *The Bell* should be considered' (134). But the lack of any contrasting examination of the motives of Tom Harrisson, Charles Madge, and Humphrey Jennings in setting up Mass Observation in the UK weakens this argument. Indeed, despite Carson's claims in the introduction, the lack of international contextualisation hampers the detailed and scholarly analyses that are advanced.

This monograph is about O'Faoláin and his work, and is viewed through the prism of O'Faoláin's most lasting legacy, *The Bell*. The 'generation' that the title alludes to is treated in an auxiliary way, with Frank O'Connor and Peadar O'Donnell receiving more detailed investigation than writers such as Róisín Walsh or Anthony Cronin. Rather than offering a sustained examination of this 'generation's' literary work or worth, Carson supplies biographical details of writers associated with *The Bell*, particularly in relation to the scandalous affairs of Geoffrey Taylor Phibbs. In a rather strange oversight, Phibbs's subsequent connections with British and American literary culture are glossed over. As the poetry editor of both *The Bell* (1941–45) and *Time and Tide* (1954–56), a comparative assessment of poet selection or editorial practice would surely have been illuminating. The assessment of O'Donnell as an interesting, if flawed, figure in Irish cultural, political, and literary life, by contrast, adds depth and context to the intellectual and political debates that raged within the pages of *The Bell*.

Rebel by Vocation brings to life the petty spats and squabbles of literary Dublin in the 1940s (or as O'Faoláin dismissively termed it, the 'Wamps' – writers, actors, musicians, painters, sculptors – boozing club), with examples such as the debate surrounding Louis Lynch D'Alton's Abbey play, *The Money Doesn't Matter*, disagreements between Flann O'Brien and O'Faoláin, and Patrick Kavanagh's criticism of O'Connor's writing style. Yet Carson's admiration for O'Faoláin's intellectual abilities sometimes impedes his mainly cool and steady assessment. For example, Carson calls O'Faoláin's reply to Kavanagh a 'controlled and sharp analysis', yet also notes that in the same article O'Faoláin quickly 'escalated to personal invective' (101). The meticulous use of archival material allows Carson to penetrate to the roots of the bad tempered disagreement between O'Faoláin and Austin Clarke; a quarrel that lasted for the whole of their careers, and that curtailed Clarke's access to *The Bell*. Carson judges that these 'pathetic squabbles' were the result of a 'sense of isolation and frustration' that faced the intelligentsia in neutral Ireland (114). It would be interesting to find out if all 'little magazines' were so congested with personal animosities, or whether Ireland, because of its size and relative newness to the literary marketplace at home, was a special case in point.

Rebel by Vocation excels at complicating the picture of O'Faoláin as an early revisionist historian, and shows some of the contradictions inherent in his work. Whilst not debunking the oft-referenced centrality of *The Bell*, and of O'Faoláin in particular, in the fight against the hegemony of the Irish Catholic Church and censorship, Carson adds insight to the picture by showing that O'Faoláin did not object to either, he merely disagreed with the degree of power that particular institutions wielded. As a 'consummate builder of his own legacy', the contradictions and equivocations in O'Faoláin's body of work are interpreted as mainly stemming from the writer's desire to develop 'narratives of self-progression' (124). Carson also does well to demystify the claim that *The Bell* was a 'bastion of conservative realism,' referencing two experimental metafictional horror stories printed in the magazine in the 1950s, by John Hewitt and by Myles Na gCopaleen, as valid examples to undermine this assumption (149).

Carson's identification of Elizabeth Bowen, O'Faoláin, and *The Bell*'s double bind in trying to create a specifically Irish aesthetic whilst also fostering an international perspective, is illuminating for any national or regional study's examination of 'the age-old see-saw between internationalism and exceptionality' (44). Perhaps, as Carson suggests, the sheer diversity of articles, stories, editorials, and poetry within *The Bell* nurtured a type of literature that was rooted in the particular whilst gesturing toward the cosmopolitan: 'a magazine that was Irish, but unselfconsciously so' (157). The catholic approach to the material that *The Bell* espoused is reflected in the structure of this monograph, jumping as it does from consideration of short stories, to polemic editorials, to political articles, to literary squabbles. By focusing almost exclusively on the years of *The Bell* in an effort to elucidate the complexity of O'Faoláin, Carson touches upon, but never satisfactorily analyses, the subversive doubleness within O'Faoláin's work. That said, *Rebel by Vocation* is a well-researched and lively book that adds depth to our knowledge of mid-twentieth century Irish literary and political culture.

MUIREANN LEECH
DOI: 10.3366/iur.2017.0270

List of Books Received

Cardin, Bertrand, *Colum McCann's Intertexts: Books Talk to One Another.* Cork: Cork University Press, 2016. 246 pages. €39.00 EUR, hardback.

Clifton, Harry, *Ireland and its Elsewheres: Writings from the Ireland Chair of Poetry.* Dublin: UCD Press, 2015. 50 pages. €20.00 EUR, hardback.

Frazier, Adrian, *The Adulterous Muse: Maud Gonne, Lucien Millevoye and W.B. Yeats.* Dublin: The Lilliput, 2016. 320 pages. €20.00 EUR, paperback.

Gladwin, Derek, *Contentious Terrains: Boglands, Ireland, Postcolonial Gothic.* Cork: Cork University Press, 2016. 312 pages. €39.00 EUR, hardback.

Hassett, Joseph M., *The Ulysses Trials: Beauty and Truth Meet the Law.* Dublin: The Lilliput Press, 2016. 240 pages. €25.00 EUR, hardback.

Haughton, Miriam and Mária Kurdi (editors), *Radical Contemporary Theatre Practices by Women in Ireland.* Dublin: Carysfort Press, 2015. 276 pages. €25.00 EUR, paperback.

Kelly, James and Susan Hegarty (editors), *Schools and Schooling, 1650–2000: New Perspectives on the History of Education.* Dublin: Four Courts Press, 2017. 208 pages. €45.00 EUR, hardback.

Jamison, Anne, *E.Œ. Somerville and Martin Ross: Female Authorship and Literary Collaboration.* Cork: Cork University Press, 2016. 256 pages. €39.00 EUR, hardback.

Kiberd, Declan and P.J. Mathews (editors), *Handbook of the Irish Revival: An Anthology of Irish Cultural and Political Writings, 1891–1922.* Notre Dame: University of Notre Dame Press, 2015. 506 pages. $25.00 USD, paperback.

Kochis, Matthew J. and Heather L. Lusty (editors), *Modernists at Odds: Reconsidering Joyce and Lawrence.* Gainesville: University Press of Florida, 2015. 272 pages. $74.95 USD, hardback.

Irish University Review 47.1 (2017): 216–217
DOI: 10.3366/iur.2017.0271
© Edinburgh University Press
www.euppublishing.com/iur

McNulty, Eugene and Róisín Ní Ghairbhí (editors), *Patrick Pearse and The Theatre*. Dublin: Four Courts Press, 2017. 204 pages. €45.00 EUR, hardback.

Mannion, Elizabeth (editor), *The Contemporary Irish Detective Novel*. Basingstoke: Palgrave Macmillan, 2016. 168 pages. £55.00 GBP, paperback.

O'Brien, Eugene (editor), *'The Soul Exceeds its Circumstances': The Later Poetry of Seamus Heaney*. Notre Dame: University of Notre Dame Press, 2016. 418 pages. $50.00 USD, hardback.

O'Gorman, Siobhán and Charlotte McIvor (editors), *Devised Performance in Irish Theatre: Histories and Contemporary Practice*. Dublin: Carysfort Press, 2015. 200 pages. €25.00 EUR, paperback.

O'Malley, Cormac K.H. (editor), *Modern Ireland and Revolution: Ernie O'Malley in Context*. Sallins: Irish Academic Press, 2016. 292 pages. €29.99 EUR, hardback.

Ó Murchú, Liam P. (editor), *Rosa Anglica: Reassessments*. Dublin: Irish Texts Society, 2016. 218 pages. No price given.

O'Toole, Tina, Gillian McIntosh and Muireann O'Cinnéide (editors), *Women Writing War: Ireland 1880–1922*. Dublin: UCD Press, 2016. 170 pages. €30.00 EUR, paperback.

Pilz, Anna and Whitney Standlee (editors), *Irish Women's Writing 1878–1922: Advancing the Cause of Liberty*. Manchester: Manchester University Press, 2016. 280 pages. £70.00 GBP, hardback.

Rankin Russell, Richard, *Seamus Heaney: An Introduction*. Edinburgh: Edinburgh University Press, 2016. 312 pages. £19.99 GBP, paperback.

Roche, Anthony, *The Irish Dramatic Revival 1899–1939*. London: Bloomsbury, 2015. 272 pages. £21.99 GBP, paperback.

Ruprecht Fadem, Maureen E., *The Literature of Northern Ireland: Spectral Borderlands*. Basingstoke: Palgrave Macmillan, 2015. 232 pages. £58.00 GBP, hardback.

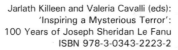

imagining
i re land

Edited by Eamon Maher

The concepts of Ireland and 'Irishness' are in constant flux as we reappraise the notion of cultural and national specificity in a world assailed from all angles by the forces of globalisation and uniformity. *Reimagining Ireland* is a scholarly book series which interrogates Ireland's past and present and suggests possibilities for the future by looking at Ireland's literature, culture and history and subjecting them to the most up-to-date critical appraisals associated with sociology, literary theory, historiography, political science and theology.

Recent Titles:

Marguerite Corporaal, Christopher Cusack
and Ruud van den Beuken (eds):
Irish Studies and the Dynamics of Memory:
Transitions and Transformations
ISBN 978-3-0343-2236-2

Anne Karhio:
'Slight Return':
Paul Muldoon's Poetics of Place
ISBN 978-3-0343-1986-7

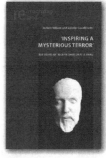

Jarlath Killeen and Valeria Cavalli (eds):
'Inspiring a Mysterious Terror':
100 Years of Joseph Sheridan Le Fanu
ISBN 978-3-0343-2223-2

For more information see www.peterlang.com